The "Still Point"

This book was manufactured with the assistance of a grant from the Ford Foundation.

The "Still Point"

Theme and Variations in the Writings of T. S. Eliot, Coleridge, Yeats, Henry James, Virginia Woolf, and D. H. Lawrence

By

ETHEL F. CORNWELL

RUTGERS UNIVERSITY PRESS

NEW BRUNSWICK   NEW JERSEY

Permission to quote has been kindly granted by the following publishers:

Grove Press—D. H. Lawrence: *Lady Chatterley's Lover*, 1959.

Harcourt, Brace & World, Inc.—T. S. Eliot: From *After Strange Gods: A Primer of Modern Heresy*, 1934; "Ash Wednesday" in *Collected Poems of T. S. Eliot, 1909-1935*, copyright, 1936, by Harcourt, Brace & World, Inc. and reprinted with their permission; "Burnt Norton" in *Four Quartets*, copyright, 1943, by T. S. Eliot. Reprinted by permission of Harcourt, Brace & World, Inc.; *The Cocktail Party*, 1950; "The Dry Salvages" in *Four Quartets*, copyright, 1943, by T. S. Eliot. Reprinted by permission of Harcourt, Brace & World, Inc.; "East Coker" in *Four Quartets*, copyright, 1943, by T. S. Eliot. Reprinted by permission of Harcourt, Brace & World, Inc.; *The Family Reunion*, copyright, 1939, by T. S. Eliot. Reprinted by permission of Harcourt, Brace & World, Inc.; *The Idea of a Christian Society*, 1940; "Little Gidding" in *Four Quartets*, copyright, 1943, by T. S. Eliot. Reprinted by permission of Harcourt, Brace & World, Inc.; *Murder in the Cathedral*, copyright, 1935, by Harcourt, Brace & World, Inc. and reprinted with their permission; *Notes Towards the Definition of Culture*, 1949; *Selected Essays*, 1950; "A Song for Simeon" in *Collected Poems of T. S. Eliot, 1909-1935*, copyright, 1936, by Harcourt, Brace & World, Inc. and reprinted with their permission; "The Waste Land" in *Collected Poems of T. S. Eliot, 1909-1935*, copyright, 1936, by Harcourt, Brace & World, Inc. and reprinted with their permission.

E. M. Forster: *Virginia Woolf*, 1942.

Virginia Woolf: *Between the Acts*, 1941; *The Captain's Deathbed and Other Essays*, ed. Leonard Woolf, 1950; *The Common Reader, First and Second Series*, 1948; *Death of the Moth and Other Essays*, ed. Leonard Woolf, 1942; *Granite and Rainbow*, ed. Leonard Woolf, 1958; *A Haunted House and Other Short Stories*, ed. Leonard Woolf, 1944; *Mrs. Dalloway*, 1925; *The Moment and Other Essays*, ed. Leonard Woolf, 1948; *Orlando*, 1928; *A Room of One's Own*, 1929; *To the Lighthouse*, copyright, 1927, by Harcourt, Brace & World, Inc., renewed, 1955, by Leonard Woolf; *The Voyage Out*, 1920; *The Waves*, 1931; *A Writer's Diary, Being Extracts from the Diary of Virginia Woolf*, ed. Leonard Woolf, 1954; *The Years*, 1937.

Rupert Hart-Davis, Ltd.—Henry James: *The Tragic Muse*, 1948.

W. B. Yeats: *The Letters of W. B. Yeats*, ed. Alan Wade, 1954.

Alfred A. Knopf, Inc.—D. H. Lawrence: *Assorted Articles*, 1930, reprinted in *The Later D. H. Lawrence*, ed. William York Tindall, copyright, 1952, by Alfred A. Knopf, Inc.; *The Man Who Died*, 1931; *The Plumed Serpent*, 1951.

The Macmillan Company—Richard Ellmann: *Yeats: The Man and the Masks*, 1948.

Joseph Hone: *W. B. Yeats: 1865-1939*, 1943.

Henry James: *French Poets and Novelists*, 1904.

Stephen Gwynn, ed.: *Scattering Branches: Tributes to the Memory of W. B. Yeats*, 1940.

Virginia Moore: *The Unicorn: William Butler Yeats' Search for Reality*, 1954.

John H. Muirhead: *Coleridge as Philosopher*, 1930.

Elizabeth Stevenson: *The Crooked Corridor: A Study of Henry James*, 1949.

W. B. Yeats: *Autobiographies: Reveries of a Childhood and Youth and The Trembling of the Veil*, 1927; *The Autobiography of W. B. Yeats, Consisting of Reveries of a Childhood and Youth, with The Trembling of the Veil, and Dramatis Personae*, 1938; *Collected Plays*, 1934; *Collected Poems*, 1946; *The Collected Poems of W. B. Yeats*, 1957; *The Cutting of an Agate*, 1912; *Early Poems and Stories*, 1925; *Ideas of Good and Evil*, 1903; *Per Amica Silentia Lunae*, 1918; *Plays and Controversies*, 1923; *A Vision*, 1937; *Wheels and Butterflies*, 1935.

Oxford University Press—Henry James: *The Art of Fiction and Other Essays*, ed. Morris Roberts, 1948; *The Notebooks of Henry James*, ed. F. O. Matthiessen and Kenneth Murdock, 1947.

W. B. Yeats: *Letters on Poetry from W. B. Yeats to Dorothy Wellesley*, ed. Dorothy Wellesley, 1940.

Charles Scribner's Sons—Elizabeth A. Drew: *T. S. Eliot: The Design of His Poetry*, 1949.

Henry James: *The Art of the Novel: Critical Prefaces*, ed. R. P. Blackmur, 1937; *The Golden Bowl*, 1904; *The Letters of Henry James*, selected and ed. Percy Lubbock, 1920; *Notes of a Son and Brother*, 1914; *Notes on Novelists, with Some Other Notes*, 1914.

Laurence Pollinger, Ltd., and the estate of the late Frieda Lawrence—D. H. Lawrence: *Psychoanalysis and the Unconscious*, William Heinemann, Ltd., 1931.

The Viking Press, Inc.—D. H. Lawrence: *Apocalypse*, 1932; *The Letters of D. H. Lawrence*, ed. Aldous Huxley, 1932; *Phoenix: The Posthumous Papers of D. H. Lawrence*, ed. Edward McDonald, 1936; *Psychoanalysis and the Unconscious*, copyright 1921 by Thomas Seltzer, Inc., 1949 by Frieda Lawrence, reprinted by permission of The Viking Press, Inc.; *The Rainbow*, copyright 1915 by D. H. Lawrence, 1943 by Frieda Lawrence, reprinted by permission of The Viking Press; *Sons and Lovers*, reprinted by permission of The Viking Press, Inc., all rights reserved; *Women in Love*, copyright 1920, 1922, by D. H. Lawrence, 1948 by Frieda Lawrence, reprinted by permission of The Viking Press, Inc.

For
My Father

Acknowledgments

The following work was developed from a dissertation written for Tulane University in partial fulfilment of the requirements for a doctoral degree. I wish to thank the librarians of Hofstra and Adelphi colleges, of the East Meadow Public Library, East Meadow, New York, and of the University of Toledo and Bowling Green State University for their assistance in obtaining material for the revision. And though the bibliography indicates my general debts, I should like to express additional thanks to Elizabeth Drew, whose Bread Loaf lectures in modern poetry opened a new door for me, and to Richard Harter Fogle, without whose critical assistance and continuing encouragement this particular book would not have been written.

Footnote references are to editions first listed in the bibliography, and, unless otherwise indicated, refer to works by the particular author under discussion at the time. Multiple page listings refer to passages in the order quoted.

ETHEL F. CORNWELL

Toledo, Ohio
March 1962

Contents

The "Still Point"

Introduction

Ever since the dawn of consciousness, when man first became aware of the distinction between the *self* and the *not-self*, he has been subject to the concomitant desires for individuation and for union; the desire to preserve and develop his individual identity, and the desire to merge himself with something greater than and outside himself, to escape the burden of selfhood by identifying himself with some power that would duplicate or return him to the undifferentiated state from which his awakened consciousness wrenched him.[1] The question of choice, balance, or alternation between these conflicting needs has been the basic problem in man's relationship with his fellow men, his universe, his god. And ultimately, he has but three choices: to preserve his individuality by withholding himself, being careful, as James put it, not to "melt too much into the universe," but to be "as solid and dense and fixed as you can"; or to merge himself completely, seeking the absolute release from self in a kind of Nirvana; or to attempt some combination of the two that will satisfy one need without denying the other, as, for example, Eliot's dance within the dance.

The problem has been variously put. Lawrence has at different times defined the basic conflict as that of the desire for creation and the desire for dissolution; the desire for life and the desire for death; "the love that makes me join and fuse toward a universal oneness" and "the hate that makes me detach myself."[2] But however one phrases it, the problem of the inner versus the outer, the self versus the not-self, the need for individuation versus the need for union, is one that has troubled many ages, none more so than the present one. The "progress in self-consciousness" that Maritain found in painting, and Eliot in poetry and criticism, [3] is a characteristic feature in the development of the modern mind and one that has increased man's self-awareness and sense of isolation at the very time when, for other reasons, his conventional faith recedes. Herein lies the crux of the modern situation, for in Western civilization until the advent of Darwin, Christian dogma supplied both an explanation for the Fall, the "separation from God," and a generally accepted formula for the recovery of the lost Eden and the reconciliation of man's two opposing desires, offering a supernatural union which promised to preserve one's essential self not only in this life but in the next, where one was to retain his individuality with all the responsibilities and discomforts of selfhood miraculously removed.

The blow that modern science dealt to conventional religion, to man's concept of a purposive universe and his place in it, and the consequent regression from an early-Victorian optimism to a twentieth-century despair, is one from which we have not yet recovered. As Mr. Spender puts it, the modern writer is faced "by the experience of an all-pervading Present, which is a world without belief." [4] Among those protesting most loudly against the modern condition is the author of *The Waste Land*—a title which has become a byword for both the spiritual sterility of today's world and the attitude of protest against it. Mr. Eliot's attempts to find an answer to and an escape from the modern Waste Land resulted in his "still point" concept as it is presented in *Four Quartets*. Here, in its final form, the "still point" becomes the source of all energy, pattern, and movement, the spiritual center where all opposites are reconciled, the complete vision perceived, complete reality experienced, and complete being attained. One may experience temporary union with the still point in moments of acute mental and emotional awareness, such as the moment of ecstasy. Ultimate, final union with the still point, however, may be obtained only by a lifetime of conscious effort, a Christian way of life, for union with the still point is equivalent to union with God.

The ideas that Mr. Eliot has incorporated in his still point concept are not new—the concept of union with an outside spiritual center has been a commonplace among Christian and Buddhist writers for centuries, and the reconciliation of opposites was a pet theme of Heraclitus; what is important is his persistent effort to rephrase them in twentieth-century terms to meet twentieth-century needs. For in its final form the still point represents a complex of ideas which in themselves reflect certain viewpoints and thematic preoccupations characteristic of our age. It is my purpose, therefore, to use Eliot's concept as a frame of reference for a closer look at the thought patterns of certain nineteenth- and twentieth-century writers—generally considered representative of their age—who have recognized the approaching or existing Waste Land and sought an answer, an escape, in forms that bear definite similarities to Eliot's; accordingly, my emphasis will be upon the idea rather than the image, upon the metaphysical rather than the metaphorical or mechanical aspects involved.

The still point is Eliot's concept; one cannot expect to find exact parallels. What one does find in the writers under discussion—Coleridge, Yeats, James, Lawrence, and Virginia Woolf—is the attempt to define and to unify themselves with a similar center, or to achieve the kind of values and the state of being which the still point embodies. For it seems that when conventional religious beliefs have been threatened, conventional concepts of Deity invalidated or destroyed, the writer who is religiously or philosophically inclined will seek an abstract ideal or center which can serve as a re-definition of, or a spiritual substitute for, a conventional God.

In a world without belief the thinking man may be expected to question the nature of reality, and of his own personal identity; and in a self-conscious age, one may look for emphasis not only upon the present self but upon the present moment. One may also expect that any salvation offered the isolated soul will involve wholeness of being or vision, or both; and this by the reconciliation of such opposites as the past and the present, the self and the other, mind and matter, the conscious and the unconscious. For such are the needs of the modern, whose mind, as Virginia Woolf put it,

> is full of monstrous, hybrid, unmanageable emotions. That the age of the earth is 3,000,000,000 years; that human life lasts but a second; that the capacity of the human mind is nevertheless boundless; that life is infinitely beautiful yet repulsive; that one's fellow creatures are adorable but disgusting; that science and religion have between them destroyed belief; that all bonds of union seem broken, yet some control must exist—it is in this atmosphere of doubt and conflict that writers have now to create. . . .[5]

As finally presented, Eliot's still point involves four characteristic features: the concept of certain absolutes—such as complete reality, complete being, the complete vision—all of which involve a reconciliation of opposites; the concept of an abstract, spiritual center outside oneself, from which emanates all movement, pattern, and meaning, and with which one must identify himself to maintain his spiritual development and achieve such absolutes as "real" being, the whole vision; emphasis upon the timeless moment—of ecstasy, of reality, of illumination—a moment of acute mental and emotional awareness, independent of time past or time future, that enables one to experience temporary union with the still point (the moment itself being a kind of still point, a "time of tension," such as the pause between two waves of the sea, but not to be confused with what Eliot terms *the* still point, the outside center ⁶); emphasis upon a conscious way of life, a definite set of requirements as the only means of attaining permanent union with the center and final realization of the absolutes one seeks. In each of the writers to be examined one finds some of the features characteristic of Eliot's concept— and many of the ideas and attitudes that led to its development.

For an early indication of the approaching "Waste Land" and the first manifestation of the still point concept, one must go back to Coleridge and the ecstatic moment. Though one also finds the ecstatic moment in Wordsworth,⁷ Coleridge's distinction between science and poetry, his psychological approach to criticism, and his emphasis upon organic unity make him the father of modern criticism and a more kindred spirit to the modern writers than his fellow Romantics. He offers a closer parallel to the thought patterns under discussion, indeed foreshadows many of the ideas characteristic of the later writers. He anticipated Eliot's use of the imagination to amalgamate "disparate experience," fuse thought and feeling, the perceiver and the perceived; and, like Eliot, sought the Divine through a recognition of the One in the Many, the eternal in the temporal.⁸ His emphasis upon intuition and revelation is echoed in the writings of Eliot, Yeats, Mrs. Woolf, and Lawrence—as is his insistence upon the "law of polarity" and the reconciliation of opposites; and his doctrine of organic unity is emphatically re-voiced by D. H. Lawrence.

Coleridge's recognition of the threat that reason and science offered to conventional Christianity, and his persistent efforts to interpret orthodox Christianity in terms acceptable to an increasingly scientific world, not only laid the foundation of modern "broad church" doctrine but also indicate the first stage in the disintegration of orthodox beliefs which led to our twentieth-century Waste Land. He foresaw the approaching Waste Land, and, as D. H. Lawrence was to do after him, attacked the mechanistic philosophy of his day as one that robbed man of his god, and life of its wonder and mystery, leaving no place for revelation. Little wonder that he rejected the Cartesian system, for Coleridge considered all truth "a species of revelation," the greatest of which comes to one in moments of joy, an ecstatic joy which, by activating the imagination, enables one to perceive the natural world and its organic unity as a symbol of the spiritual world, and to identify himself with the "Supreme Reality" (in and behind nature) which is God. As in Eliot's case, union with the Coleridgean center is equivalent to union with God.

Of the six writers included in this study, Coleridge and Eliot alone maintain an orthodox Christian concept of God. [9] James and Virginia Woolf substitute an abstract ideal; Lawrence and Yeats invent private religions. Yeats, like Eliot, believed that somewhere along the line in the past few centuries, the whole man had been lost. The elaborate system that Yeats constructed was his attempt to recover the whole man and trace the soul's development through its various stages (or lives, for he believed in reincarnation) until it reaches its still point, the "phaseless sphere," where opposites are reconciled, one achieves "Unity of Being," and experiences "ultimate reality."

Yeats was obsessed with the conflict between subjectivity and objectivity, the self and the not-self, which he conceived in terms of an alternating dominance symbolized by two gyres, one waxing as the other wanes. Writing to Ethel Manin (October 20, 1938) toward the end of his life, Yeats said, "To me all things are made of the conflict of two states of consciousness, beings or persons which die each other's life, live each other's death. That is true of life and death themselves. Two cones (or whirls), the apex of each in the other's base." [10]

In this world, Yeats felt, no one is complete. "The acts and nature of a Spirit during any one life are a section or abstraction of reality and are unhappy because incomplete. They are a gyre or part of a gyre, whereas reality is a sphere." [11] Only when one reaches the phaseless sphere does he achieve wholeness and experience complete reality.

> There all the barrel-hoops are knit
> There all the serpent-tails are bit
> There all the gyres converge in one,
> There all the planets drop in the sun. [12]

The goals are similar, but what Eliot attempts to achieve in terms of Christian dogma, Yeats attempts by means of the occult.

Henry James, who did not believe in any power transcending the mind and spirit of man, turned to art and aesthetic ideals to supply what he could not find in a chaotic and meaningless world, and in the development of his craft, introduced a technique and a viewpoint that have become characteristic of modern fiction, leading toward what is now called the "stream of consciousness" and emphasizing the inner life and experience—for his particular goal was a fully developed consciousness capable of serving an aesthetic ideal. Acquiring full consciousness and maintaining the aesthetic ideal necessitate a deliberate way of life. One must apply the aesthetic ideal to conduct and life; one must be willing to acknowledge ugliness as well as beauty, evil as well as good—the ugliness and evil to be compensated for by the *beauty* of full unconsciousness, in itself an aesthetic ideal. One must have a mind open to impressions; he must develop his understanding and his perception to "the pitch of passion," that he may extend the borders of consciousness. And this is to be achieved by a "process of vision"—the vision which one acquires in separate moments of experience, moments of acute mental and emotional awareness that lead one toward full consciousness wherein full personal reality is achieved.

In all of this, James reflects the general temper of his age perhaps more than he would have liked to admit, at times coming perilously close to the "faint, pale, embarrassed, exquisite Pater," whom he condemned.[13] For it was Pater who sought in art the "perfect identification of matter and form," insisting that "in its consummate moments, the end is not distinct from the means, the form from the matter, the subject from the expression." And it was Pater who proclaimed the aesthetic sensibility as the one yielding the most in the way of a quickened consciousness. "Great passions may give us this quickened sense of life. . . . Only be sure that it is passion—that it does yield you this fruit of a quickened, multiplied consciousness. Of this wisdom, the poetic passion, the desire of beauty, the love of art for art's sake, has most; for art comes to you professing frankly to give nothing but the highest quality to your moments as they pass, and simply for those moments' sake." [14]

In Pater there is always the suggestion that the chief value of the aesthetic sensibility is its extension of consciousness, whereas in James, the emphasis is reversed and the "practice of consciousness" serves an aesthetic purpose.

Viewing her age as one of doubt and conflict, when "the mind is full of monstrous, hybrid, unmanageable emotions," Virginia Woolf felt that "the fine fabric of a lyric is no more fitted to contain this point of view than a rose leaf to envelop the rugged immensity of a rock." She questioned whether poetry is capable of expressing what today's poets would force it to; and she questioned as well the loss of dramatic power that modern novelists sacrifice to a minutiae of psychological detail. The modern condition calls for a form different from either prose or poetry, but uniting the best of both. The future novel, Virginia Woolf prophesied, "will be written in prose, but in prose which has many of the characteristics of poetry." It will be more dramatic, "stand further back from life," and give "the outline rather than the detail" of the relations of man to nature, to fate, and to his dreams. It will "spring at the heart of its subject as the poet does"; but it will also have the freedom and the flexibility of prose, and its ability to present the contrast and complexity of life.[15]

The above, written for the *New York Herald Tribune* in 1927, explains the particular form that Virginia Woolf adopted a few years later in *The Waves*, as well as her concern for form itself; for each of her novels is an experiment in form and a fresh attempt to present the contrast and complexity of life and the "myriad impressions" that the mind receives.

James's preoccupation with form is derived from his aesthetic ideal; Mrs. Woolf's, from her concern for "reality." Nevertheless, Virginia Woolf's moment of reality provides a link between James's moment of experience and Eliot's moment of ecstasy, and it is perhaps because she benefited from the ripening of ideas and techniques that James and his generation were just beginning to develop, that her moments are more clearly isolated, more metaphysically advanced, and therefore closer to Eliot's ecstatic moment. Where James seeks full, personal consciousness, Mrs. Woolf seeks an absolute, impersonal "reality," which, like Eliot's still point, includes and reconciles the opposing forces or truths that confront one in everyday living. But reality can be grasped or understood only by revelation and intuition, by the flashes of vision that one receives in moments of acute mental and emotional awareness; these are one's moments of reality. The lesser ones offer minor revelations. The greater ones signify one's momentary union with impersonal, total reality; then, as in Eliot's moment of union with the still point, one perceives the whole vision. The difficulty is that life continually interrupts the moment and dissolves one's vision, so that it must be perpetually remade. One must, therefore, have "silence and solitude" to experience the moment of reality, of illumination. And one must have courage: to seek the truth and to live by one's vision. Thus and only thus may one live in contact with that total reality "besides which nothing matters."

D. H. Lawrence, our final subject, is a twentieth-century Romantic who has much in common with Coleridge. He seeks to expand emotional consciousness as James seeks to expand mental consciousness, and offers what I consider the most direct contrast to Eliot's concept that one can find in modern literature.

One effect of the "progress in self-consciousness" that Eliot noted in poetry and criticism was the persistent attempt to analyze the process of artistic creation; this of course led inevitably to some recognition of the unconscious, which, as Morse Peckham has pointed out, appears in Coleridge, Wordsworth, and Carlyle, goes back to Hartley, Kant, Leibniz, and is implied in Locke, but "appears only in full force with the appearance of dynamic organicism," a characteristic feature of Romantic thought, particularly Coleridge's. Moreover, the unconscious appears as "a postulate to the creative imagination," though, spatially, the Romantics placed it outside and above, whereas we conceive of the unconscious as inside and underneath.[16] What Mr. Baker calls "the dark side" of Coleridge's theory of imagination, "that is, the part played by the unconscious," became Lawrence's main preoccupation.[17]

Lawrence felt that modern civilization had reached a dead end; he believed that by the pursuit of a false individualism and the elevation of mind over body, man had become a half-being cut off from the past, from his fellow men, and from the cosmos.

It is useless to think that we can get along without a conception of what man is, and without a belief in ourselves, and without the morality to support this belief. The only point is that our conception, our belief, and our morality, though valid for the time being, is valid only for the time being.[18]

As an answer to the problem, Lawrence offered a "religion" which would enable man to develop his entire being and renew his lost connections. Lawrence recognized "the passionate struggle into conscious being" [19] as a necessary part of one's development as an individual, but felt that it was too often maintained at the expense of one's dark, unconscious being. His objective is the achievement of one's soul, one's "fullness of being," one's "totality of consciousness"; and this is to be accomplished by a perfection of the sexual relationship, by the rebirth and renewal that one undergoes during a complete, physical union, when, for a moment, he reaches the center of reality and is united with "the dark almighty of the beginning," the "Unknown Mover," the "unfathomable life-mystery" that lies at the center of the universe. In that moment, opposites are reconciled, one achieves complete being, merges with impersonal reality, and "arrives in the absolute." That is the timeless moment offering the "new knowledge of Eternity in the flux of Time" which Ursula sought. Eliot and Lawrence seek similar goals, but from opposite directions; for Eliot's is essentially an intellectual approach, Lawrence's, a physical one.

In the treatment of Lawrence, I have confined the discussion to certain key novels and nonfictional works. I did not feel that there was anything to be gained by discussing his poetry, for reasons with which Lawrence himself would have agreed:

> The whole is greater than the part. And therefore, I who am a man alive, am greater than my soul, or spirit, or body, or mind, or consciousness, or anything else that is merely a part of me. I am a man, and alive. I am a man alive, and as long as I can, I intend to go on being man alive.

For this reason I am a novelist. And being a novelist, I consider myself superior to the saint, the scientist, the philosopher, and the poet, who are all great masters of different bits of man alive, but never get the whole hog.[20]

Since it is impossible in a book of this kind to get the whole hog, I have kept to those works most likely to reveal the whole skeleton. No attempt has been made at a comprehensive coverage of any author's works; I have tried instead to present those which best illustrate basic themes, my general practice being to examine the author's nonfictional writings for direct statements regarding basic purposes and beliefs, then to examine key works for the conscious or unconscious application of the writer's ideas. As Eliot said of his own critical output, "It is a by-product of my private poetry-workshop; or a prolongation of the thinking that went into the formation of my own verse." [21]

D. H. Lawrence said much the same thing, insisting that his novels were written first and that his nonfiction represented a later, conscious extension of themes and insights that emerged unconsciously in his fiction. Whether first or last, it is the bald statement that best confirms the thematic preoccupations of major concern here, those which cluster about the still point concept. For each of the writers manifests one or more of the features characteristic of Eliot's still point; each recognizes "the destructive element," and each attempts in his own way some answer to the problems posed by a world without order, a world without meaning, a world without belief.

Notes

[1] Throughout, I shall use "the conscious" to refer to that part of the mind which is aware of its own activity, at the time of its activity, and therefore subject to the control of the reasoning faculty; and "consciousness," as the state or condition of such awareness. Wherever the individual authors use the term in a different sense, I shall try to indicate that difference.

[2] *Phoenix: The Posthumous Papers of D. H. Lawrence*, ed. Edward McDonald, pp. 678, 680, 694.

3 See T. S. Eliot, *The Use of Poetry and the Use of Criticism*, p. 1 13.

4 Stephen Spender, *The Destructive Element: A Study of Modern Writers and Beliefs*, p. 14.

5 "The Narrow Bridge of Art," *Granite and Rainbow*, ed. Leonard Woolf, p. 12.

6 Henry James and Virginia Woolf present a similar difficulty in that they distinguish between greater and lesser moments of illumination, of reality; but in their case the distinction is a matter of degree, whereas with Eliot it is a matter of kind. Eliot's metaphor was originally used to indicate the intersection of time and eternity, but grew to mean much more than that, eventually becoming the metaphysical symbol for an outside spiritual center, union with which is equivalent to union with God. It is the outside center that I am primarily concerned with, and this I shall designate as *the* still point (following the Eliot chapter which develops this distinction), in contradistinction to the timeless moment that occurs in one's life as *a* still point, and occasionally lifts one to *the* still point.

7 Feeling his own creative power "like one of Nature's," the Romantic poet experiences a union of the two in certain moments of ecstatic joy during which he melts into, or merges with, the landscape in a complete union of subject and object, perceiver and perceived. It is the "feeling intellect" responding to the "never-failing principle of joy" he finds in Nature that leads Wordsworth to the ecstatic moment,

> . . . that serene and blessed mood,
> In which the affections gently lead us on, —
> Until, the breath of this corporeal frame
> And even the motion of our human blood
> Almost suspended, we are laid asleep
> In body, and become a living soul:
> While with an eye made quiet by the power
> Of harmony, and the deep power of joy,
> We see into the life of things.

And again, this is the state of Wordsworth's "growing Youth" in *The Excursion*,

> . . . when, from the naked top
> Of some bold headland, he beheld the sun
> Rise up, and bathe the world in light! He looked—
> Ocean and earth, the solid frame of earth
> And ocean's liquid mass, in gladness lay
> Beneath him:—Far and wide the clouds were touched,
> And in their silent faces could he read
> Unutterable love. Sound needed none,
> Nor any voice of joy; his spirit drank
> The spectacle: sensation, soul, and form,

All melted into him; they swallowed up
His animal being; in them did he live,
And by them did he live; they were his life.
In such access of mind, in such high hour
Of visitation from the living God,
Thought was not; in enjoyment it expired.
No thanks he breathed, he proffered no request;
Rapt into still communion that transcends
The imperfect offices of prayer and praise . . .

(See *The Prelude*, Bk. 13, l. 312; Bk. 14, l. 168; Bk. 2, l. 450. *Tintern Abbey* ll. 41-49; and *The Excursion*, Bk. 1, ll. 198-216. See also "The Recovery of Joy: Wordsworth's Poetry," Ch. 7 in Henry Van Dyke's *Companionable Books*.)

[8] Ignoring chronology in Coleridge's case, I have worked from the better known to the lesser known; thus Coleridge is examined in terms of Eliot's ideas, for Eliot leaves few doubts regarding his basic themes and beliefs, whereas Coleridge, who left a great many, is still the subject of widely varying claims and contentions.

[9] Eliot is a Unitarian turned Anglican; and Coleridge, who temporarily espoused Unitarianism, abandoned it for a defense of the Trinity that brought him ever closer to the Anglican position.

[10] *The Letters of W. B. Yeats*, ed. Allan Wade, pp. 917-918.

[11] See the "Seven Propositions," quoted by Virginia Moore, *The Unicorn*, pp. 378-379, which Yeats composed after the revision of *A Vision*, but never published.

[12] "There," *The Collected Poems of W. B. Yeats*, p. 284.

[13] Letter to Edmund Gosse, December 13, 1894, *The Letters of Henry James*, ed. Percy Lubbock, I, 222.

[14] *The Renaissance*, Modern Library ed., pp. 114; 198-199.

[15] "The Narrow Bridge of Art," passim.

[16] See Morse Peckham, "Toward a Theory of Romanticism," *PMLA*, LXVI (March, 1951), 10-13.

[17] James V. Baker, *The Sacred River: Coleridge's Theory of the Imagination*, p. 7.

[18] "Education of the People," *Phoenix*, p. 615.

[19] Foreword to *Women in Love*, Modern Library, ed., p. x.

[20] *Phoenix*, p. 535.

[21] T. S. Eliot, *On Poetry and Poets*, p. 117.

1

Eliot's Concept of the "Still Point"

> The World is trying the experiment of attempting to form
> a civilized but non-Christian mentality. The experiment
> will fail; but we must be very patient in awaiting its
> collapse; meanwhile redeeming the time: so that the
> Faith may be preserved alive through the dark ages be-
> fore us; to renew and rebuild civilization, and save the
> World from suicide.[1]

This quotation, taken from "Thoughts after Lambeth,"
throws significant light upon Eliot's aim and work; for having
protested the modern "Waste Land," Eliot set about "redeem-
ing the time," attempting, through poetry, to present Christian ideas in a form acceptable to the would-be "civilized but
non-Christian mentality." This attempt culminates in Eliot's
"still point" as it appears in *Four Quartets*. Its development is
a gradual, and perhaps an unconscious one; for the final concept involves most, if not all, of Eliot's major ideas. One
finds Eliot's statements about tradition, order, wholeness,
opposites, reality, and language reiterated in both his prose
and poetry, repeated and extended until all are integrated in
Four Quartets and its central image.

As a complex of ideas, the still point can best be understood by tracing the various lines of thought that lead to its final development; to begin with, Eliot's concept of tradition, which

> . . . involves, in the first place, the historical sense, which we may call nearly indispensable to any one who would continue to be a poet beyond his twenty-fifth year; and the historical sense involves a perception, not only of the pastness of the past, but of its presence; the historical sense compels a man to write not merely with his own generation in his bones, but with a feeling that the whole of the literature of Europe from Homer and within it the whole of the literature of his own country has a simultaneous existence and composes a simultaneous order. This historical sense, which is a sense of the time-less as well as of the temporal and of the timeless and of the temporal together, is what makes a writer traditional. And it is at the same time what makes a writer most acutely conscious of his place in time, of his own con-temporaneity.
>
> No poet, no artist of any art, has his complete meaning alone. His significance, his appreciation is the apprecia-tion of his relation to the dead poets and artists.

After Strange Gods, which develops the implications of "Tradition and the Individual Talent," presents tradition as a movement which, though it advances, yet maintains con-tact with its source in the past. Later, in Part V of "Little Gidding," Eliot reaffirms the importance of tradition in yet another way, remarking that

> . . . A people without history
> Is not redeemed from time, for history is a pattern
> Of timeless moments. . . .

These statements concerning tradition, together with his statements concerning order, do much to explain Eliot's choice of form, as well as the content of his poetry. His references to mythology, anthropology, and his rewoven lines from past literature become understandable when one sees them as an attempt to impose order, to affirm the unity of past and present, and to show our complex modern life as both similar and dissimilar to the past. In his compression of past, present, and future into a single moment, a single phrase, Eliot evinces his historical sense and his desire for integration. It is his historical sense that leads him, as an artist, to deny the effectiveness of free verse except when it appears within and offers a contrast to a more formal pattern; it is his historical sense that leads him, as a man, to adopt a traditional religion and to condemn the Renaissance as a "depraved May," a false spring leading away from, not toward, values that can be preserved only within a unified religious tradition. For Eliot, the attempt to live a self-sufficient existence without tradition and without faith can produce only lost souls, like those of *Murder in the Cathedral*, who face "emptiness, absence, separation from God," and will become "united forever, nothing with nothing"; or produce "decent godless people," like those of *The Rock*, who "toil for six days [and], on the seventh . . . must motor. . . ." [2]

One is not an individual apart, existing in a separate moment cut away from time past or time to come, but is of necessity a part of all time, all tradition; the attempt to deny one's past, the failure to recognize one's place in the pattern—either as an artist or an individual—is, for Eliot, a form of self-destruction.

> Where is the Life we have lost in living?
> Where is the wisdom we have lost in knowledge?
> Where is the knowledge we have lost in information?
> The cycles of Heaven in twenty centuries
> Bring us farther from GOD and nearer to the Dust.

Lacking faith and tradition, man walks backward, away from God toward nothingness. This is the self-destruction that Eliot sees in the world in which he lives and writes. But from a mere recognition of the modern "Waste Land," Eliot's poetry progresses toward a conception of the way out as a way back, which is at the same time a way forward.

Although *Four Quartets*, which contain Eliot's most mature statements about the way forward, did not appear until 1943, he wrote an article in 1923 which, in retrospect, points clearly toward the poetical and philosophical development that was to culminate in the later work. What he had to say about order and myth in his discussion of Joyce's *Ulysses* not only indicates his conviction that literature must give order to the chaos of modern life but also hints at the form he himself was later to adopt in an effort to achieve that purpose. To Eliot, Joyce's use of myth was equivalent to a scientific discovery offering a method which all writers must thereafter pursue if they wished to come to grips with their contemporary world.

> It is simply a way of controlling, of ordering, of giving a shape and a significance to the immense panorama of futility and anarchy which is contemporary history. It is a method already adumbrated by Mr. Yeats, and of the need for which I believe Mr. Yeats to have been the first contemporary to be conscious.[3]

What Eliot implies is that the simple narrative method is suitable only when the material or the world one is dealing with has an inherent order of its own; when that order is lacking, as Eliot firmly believes it is today, a more artificial, more contrived method of arrangement, such as Joyce's use of myth, must be employed. Herein, of course, lies an explanation of Eliot's choice of form.

This insistence upon the necessity of order in life and art is to be found throughout Eliot's writings. *For Lancelot Andrewes*, subtitled "essays on style and order," contains an essay on Machiavelli, whom Eliot defends for two reasons: Machiavelli's recognition of the established church as being of great-

est value to the State; and his recognition of the fact that,
"Liberty is good; but more important is order; and the maintenance of order justifies every means." Again, in *The Idea of a
Christian Society*, Eliot condemns the piecemeal efforts of
politicians with the statement that "unless we can find a pattern into which all problems of life can have their place, we
are only likely to go on complicating chaos." [4]

Nowhere, however, is Eliot's concern for pattern and order
more clearly demonstrated than in the *Four Quartets*. Most
obvious, of course, is the precise arrangement of the poems
and their parts. Each quartet is divided into five sections
containing (I) statement and counterstatement; (II) a lyrical
beginning and colloquial elaboration; (III) some concept of
movement and of detachment from self; (IV) a lyric treating
of death and rebirth; (V) a conversational passage leading
into another lyric wherein the themes are restated. Each
quartet treats the same question, from a different approach;
and the whole is restated and unified in the last poem, "Little
Gidding."

The content of the quartets is equally concerned with the
necessity of pattern and order. In "Burnt Norton" the boarhound and the boar, the hunter and the hunted, are "reconciled among the stars," and that reconciliation is possible
only because of the formal pattern which contains them. Or
to put it another way, as Eliot does in the final section of
"Burnt Norton" in his passage on art:

> . . . Words, after speech, reach
> Into the silence. Only by the form, the pattern,
> Can words or music reach
> The stillness, as a Chinese jar still
> Moves perpetually in its stillness.
> Not the stillness of the violin, while the note lasts,
> Not that only, but the co-existence,
> Or say that the end precedes the beginning,

Only by means of the pattern can words, music, or the Chinese jar express movement; the pattern is movement. Only by means of the pattern can words or music become timeless and enduring; for the pattern is timeless; as an absolute, it existed before the word or the note was written, and will continue to exist after the word is uttered and the note is played. Only by the pattern can the individual life or the work of art have movement and meaning. It is the pattern that grants timelessness to art, the pattern that leads the individual to the still point; for the pattern is "the dance," and "the dance" originates at the still point:

> . . . Except for the point, the still point,
> There would be no dance, and there is only the dance.[5]

Closely allied to Eliot's ideas about order and pattern are his ideas about wholeness and unity. He admires the Metaphysicals because they were capable of "forming new wholes" and of expressing felt thoughts which unify intellect and emotion:

> Tennyson and Browning are poets, and they think; but they do not feel their thoughts as immediately as the odour of a rose. A thought to Donne was an experience; it modified his sensibility. When a poet's mind is perfectly equipped for its work, it is constantly amalgamating disparate experience; the ordinary man's experience is chaotic, irregular, fragmentary. The latter falls in love, or reads Spinoza, and these two experiences have nothing to do with each other, or with the noise of the typewriter or the smell of cooking; in the mind of the poet these experiences are always forming new wholes.[6]

Eliot believes that all life is one; thus he takes exception to Arnold's remark that it is an advantage for a poet to deal with a beautiful world:

We mean all sorts of things, I know, by Beauty. But the essential advantage for a poet is not to have a beautiful world with which to deal: it is to be able to see beneath both beauty and ugliness; to see the boredom, and the horror, and the glory.[7]

Eliot will not separate beauty and ugliness, birth and death, time present and time past, or time past and time future; for him, the pairs of seeming opposites are but two sides of the same card.

In *The Family Reunion* Amy comments:

> You none of you understand how old you are
> And death will come to you as a mild surprise,
> A momentary shudder in a vacant room.
> Only Agatha seems to discover some meaning in death
> Which I cannot find.[8]

The essential oneness of life and death is the meaning that Agatha discovers but Amy cannot find. A similar recognition of this oneness lies behind Harry's indifference to death and his comments about time. He warns his family that they are incapable of understanding him because they "isolate the single event," and when the doctor broaches the subject of past and future, Harry demands:

> Oh, is there any difference!
> How can we be concerned with the past
> And not with the future? or with the future
> And not with the past? . . .

This is also what Eliot is talking about in "East Coker" when he says, "In my beginning is my end," and, "In my end is my beginning"; and in Part I of "Burnt Norton" when he says:

> Time present and time past
> Are both perhaps present in time future,
> And time future contained in time past.

Because all is one, the modern man's attempt at an individualistic separation from tradition, from God, and from society as a whole can only result in an existence that is meaningless and un-Christian. Eliot would have his fellow men develop first of all a Christian community; that is, "one in which there is a unified religious-social code of behavior." [9] Equally important is the need to "re-establish a vital connexion between the individual and the race"; [10] it is a duty of the artist in particular to recognize this need and to answer it as best he can. But the basic problem is a lack of wholeness in the individual and the need for a way toward integration and fulfillment. Eliot condemns Arnold because he does not offer an adequate concept of the whole man; conversely, he applauds Pascal for his successful efforts to "find peace through a satisfaction of the whole being." [11]

Eliot is one of those "who can only find peace through a satisfaction of the whole being." His writings are a search for that kind of peace, the same search which, in *The Family Reunion*, leads Harry to his final salvation.

In the beginning, Harry is incapable of finding salvation because his vision is fragmentary. Agatha says to him:

> There are certain points I do not yet understand:
> They will be clear later. I am also convinced
> That you only hold a fragment of the explanation.
> It is only because of what you do not understand
> That you feel the need to declare what you do.
> There is more to understand: hold fast to that
> As the way to freedom. [12]

What Harry has been declaring is that on a steamer crossing the Atlantic he pushed his wife overboard. What he has to learn is that the external fact is irrelevant; it is the internal fact, the internal truth that matters. The important thing is not to discover whether he actually pushed her or afterwards imagined that he had because he recognized an unconscious wish to, but to discover the meaning of that wish and the atonement he must make. Once Harry finally perceives the truth, the whole vision, he realizes that:

> The things I thought were real are shadows, and the real
> Are what I thought were private shadows. . . .

Significantly, Harry has to come home in order to find himself and to reach an end that is a new beginning. It is not until after he returns that Harry can actually *see* and come to terms with the Fates who have been pursuing him as "private shadows." First of all, he has to recover his past, confront his childhood self and discover its meaning—a fact that only Agatha has understanding enough to recognize:

> The man who returns will have to meet
> The boy who left. Round by the stables,
> In the coach-house, in the orchard,
> In the plantation, down the corridor
> That led to the nursery, round the corner
> Of the new wing, he will have to face him—
> And it will not be a very *jolly* corner.
> When the loop in time comes—and it does not come for everybody—
> The hidden is revealed, and the spectres show themselves.

There is a noticeable parallel between Harry's effort to recapture his past and Eliot's effort, in *Four Quartets*, to recapture the moment in the rose-garden. "We had the experience but missed the meaning." One may approach the meaning by restoring the experience, or restore the experience by approaching the meaning. The *Four Quartets* is an attempt to do the latter, to understand and thus recapture the ecstatic moment experienced in the garden; and the ecstatic moment is one way of reaching the still point, one way of seeing the whole vision.

In everyday life, achieving the whole vision requires that one become aware of "the world around the corner," which most men ignore,

> Reflecting a pocket-torch of observation
> Upon each other's opacity
> Neglecting all the admonitions
> From the world around the corner
> The wind's talk in the dry holly-tree
> The inclination of the moon
> The attraction of the dark passage
> The paw under the door.

Much is implied by "the world around the corner." I believe that Eliot wishes to suggest what I spoke of earlier as the other side of the card, all of the unseen world which the seen world implies: the death which life implies, and the rebirth of which death is a foreshadowing; the past that lies concealed in the present, and the future that the present implies; the world of the possible, contained in the actual, and the world of the spirit, which the physical implies.

The "wind's talk" in the holly-tree and the "inclination of the moon" are on a par with the "winter lightning" and the "waterfall" to which Eliot refers in *Four Quartets;* on a par with the children in the apple-tree that Eliot describes in one of the "Landscapes," and returns to in "Burnt Norton"; "the woodthrush singing through the fog," which Marina's father hears; and the thrush that leads one, in "Burnt Norton," to a "world around the corner"—the rose-garden where the ecstatic moment is experienced. All are, in a sense, "Intimations of Immortality." In one instance, as incarnations of the life force in the same way that Christ is the Incarnation of the Word, they are hints of "the world around the corner," where the meaning of life is to be found; and in the other, they actually lead one to the experiencing of an ecstatic moment, and thus toward the still point. The concrete manifestation of the life force (the "winter lightning," the "waterfall") is one of the many "hints followed by guesses" that Eliot speaks of in "The Dry Salvages"—as is the imagined experience ("the wild thyme unseen"), and the ecstatic moment itself ("the distraction fit, lost in a shaft of sunlight").

Basically what Eliot says is that all life is one; what he urges is that man recognize the inherent oneness of things and strive for an art, a society, an individual existence which is a reflection of and in harmony with that oneness.[13] To achieve the last, more than wholeness of vision is required. To find oneself and become an integrated personality, one must progress from an awareness of "the world around the corner" toward an identification with some center greater than and outside oneself. *Four Quartets* is the culmination of Eliot's attempt to define that center and the way, or ways, toward it:

> We must be still and still moving
> Into another intensity
> For a further union, a deeper communion [14]

The "further union" Eliot speaks of in "East Coker" is a spiritual one involving the complete identification and self-surrender that is described in "The Dry Salvages" by the "music heard so deeply/ That it is not heard at all, but you are the music/ While the music lasts." Looking back, one can see this concept of union developing in Eliot's earlier writings. In the 1919 essay on "Tradition and the Individual Talent," Eliot expresses it in his demand for the impersonality of the artist and in his definition of the "process of depersonalization":

> What happens is a continual surrender of himself as he is at the moment to something which is more valuable. The progress of an artist is a continual self-sacrifice, a continual extinction of personality.[15]

"The Hollow Men" and "Ash-Wednesday" express the same concept with regard to love. In the former, the "Multifoliate rose" (a reference to Dante's symbol of Eternal Love) signifies earthly love, the single rose, which has been transformed into a love that is all-encompassing and divine. In "Ash-Wednesday," Part II, the same idea is indicated:

> The single Rose
> Is now the Garden
> Where all loves end

The garden where worldly love ends is the garden where a comprehension of, and an approach to, Divine Love begin. The basic union is the same, whether it is a question of the artist and his work or the individual and the Divine. The part must be expanded to include the whole; the personal transcended by the impersonal; and the self surrendered to a "something which is more valuable."

In an article dealing with Eliot's archetypal imagery in relation to Jung's theories of psychological wholeness and the "individuation process," Genevieve Foster suggests a parallel which is further developed by Elizabeth Drew in *T. S. Eliot: The Design of His Poetry*. The purpose of the latter is to explore a "parallel in symbolic content between the progression of dream symbols described by Jung as arising during what he calls 'the integration of the personality' (and which he relates to the history of myth), and some of those appearing in Eliot's poetry during the course of its development." [16] When one considers Eliot's earlier statements about myth, and his own use of myth, the comparison between his symbols and those which mark the Jungian stages of integration assumes a more than casual significance. In a discussion of "Ash-Wednesday" Miss Drew writes:

> the scattering of the bones is the symbol of the dissolution of the old ego as the center of being, while the Rose and the Garden become the new center. "Belladonna, the

Lady of the Rocks/ The Lady of Situations," has been transformed into this gracious reconciling figure through whom the poet reaches his revelation, and to whom, therefore, the bones address their song.

Both Miss Drew and Miss Foster agree that "Ash-Wednesday" is the poem that marks the real beginning of the ego's shift from self toward a new center of being. This shift is the first step toward the "further union" that Eliot urges in "East Coker."

As I suggested earlier, Eliot's still point is the gradual outgrowth of certain lines of thought which converge in *Four Quartets*. Yet remaining for consideration are the reconciliation of opposites, Eliot's concept of reality, and the relationship of these ideas.

Four Quartets describes the still point as the point at which all opposites are reconciled; but this reconciliation is, for Eliot, a matter of balance or tension. On the human plane, it becomes a question of moral tension, of the balance that must be maintained between the temporal and the spiritual. Moreover, as Eliot points out in *The Idea of a Christian Society*, he believes that "the only possibility of control and balance is a religious control and balance." The temporal and the spiritual can be harmonized, but they can never be identified:

> There would always remain a dual allegiance, to the State and to the Church, to one's countrymen and to one's fellow-Christians everywhere, and the latter would always have the primacy. There would always be a tension and this tension is essential to the idea of a Christian society, and is a distinguishing mark between a Christian and a Pagan society.[17]

Moral tension is essential for society and the individual; it is requisite for spiritual growth. In the last section of "Ash-Wednesday" Eliot describes temporal existence as merely

"The dreamcrossed twilight between birth and dying," in contrast to the dawn of spiritual existence, which becomes "the time of tension between dying and birth."

Eliot's most direct poetical statement, however, occurs in Part III of "Little Gidding":

There are three conditions which often look alike
Yet differ completely, flourish in the same hedgerow:
Attachment to self and to things and to persons, detachment
From self and from things and from persons; and, growing
    between them, indifference
Which resembles the others as death resembles life,
Being between two lives—unflowering between
The live and the dead nettle. . . .

Attachment is one kind of movement or life; and detachment, another. The moral struggle involved in the shift from attachment to detachment is equivalent to "the time of tension between dying and birth"; it precedes the shift and is therefore "alive" as a kind of restrained motion, or pregnant stillness. Mere indifference, on the other hand, is death—not the kind of death that is a beginning, but the kind of death that is "unflowering," a complete void, a spiritual nothingness. Eliot makes a definite distinction between the void and the pregnant stillness. The former is illustrated in "The Hollow Men" by "the Shadow" which falls between "the idea/ And the reality," "the motion/ And the act," "the conception/ And the creation." The latter is illustrated in "Little Gidding" by "the stillness/ Between two waves of the sea." The lull between the waves is a "time of tension," and tension itself produces a kind of still point between two movements or two forces.

Eliot's ideas of reality are best revealed, I think, in his symbolic use of "the eyes" and "light." Traditionally thought of as windows of the soul, "the eyes" in "The Hollow Men" become the central image of the poem and suggest

Beatrice's eyes, which woke Dante to spiritual vision in the "Purgatorio." [18] There are no eyes in the "cactus land" of "the hollow men," "death's dream kingdom," which is death in life. It is in "death's twilight kingdom," or purgatory, that the eyes appear. There, death is not an "unflowering" void, but a "time of tension," the twilight before a spiritual rebirth:

> There, the eyes are
> Sunlight on a broken column

The difficulty is that "the hollow men" do not wish to be awakened, to be reborn; they cannot face "the eyes" or the "sunlight" because they cannot bear the intense reality of spiritual vision. For them the eyes become "Eyes I dare not meet in dreams." They are content to be scarecrows, hollow men acted upon but not acting; consequently, they are doomed souls who will remain empty, incomplete, and visionless:

> Sightless, unless
> The eyes reappear
> As the perpetual star
> Multifoliate rose
> Of death's twilight kingdom

In *The Family Reunion*, Harry's first reactions are very similar to those of "the hollow men." He reproaches his mother because the curtains are not drawn when he arrives:

How can you sit in this blaze of light for all the world to look at?
If you knew how you looked, when I saw you through the window!
Do you like to be stared at by eyes through a window? [19]

He is constantly under the impression that the eyes of the Eumenides are watching him, and he cannot endure the eyes

or the light because both symbolize a reality he has not yet
learned to face.

Eliot returns again and again to the notion that reality is
too intense for human beings to bear except in moments, and
to the use of light to symbolize both the intensity of reality
and the vision which reveals it. The moment of beauty expressed in "La Figlia Che Piange" by the girl in the garden
with "Her hair over her arms and her arms full of flowers" is
similarly represented in Part I of *The Waste Land:*

"You gave me hyacinths first a year ago;
"They called me the hyacinth girl."
—Yet when we came back, late, from the Hyacinth garden,
Your arms full, and your hair wet, I could not
Speak, and my eyes failed, I was neither
Living nor dead, and I knew nothing,
Looking into the heart of light, the silence.

Here, physical or natural beauty produces an ecstatic moment
of timeless reality, just as the imaged experience does in the
rose-garden scene of "Burnt Norton," Part I, where the trans-
forming powers and the intense reality of the vision are indicated by the empty pool which suddenly became filled "with
water out of sunlight," and the surface which "glittered out
of heart of light."

Murder in the Cathedral contains a further development of
the light imagery and the concept of reality that one finds in
Four Quartets. The foreknowledge of impending evil and the
certainty that this evil is part of a Divine Destiny which man
can do nothing to avert are revelations which come to the
Chorus of Women "in a shaft of sunlight":

Some malady is coming upon us. We wait, we wait,
And the saints and martyrs wait, for those who shall be
    martyrs and saints.
Destiny waits in the hand of God, shaping the still unshapen:
I have seen these things in a shaft of sunlight.[20]

Later, in Part II, when the Chorus is agonizing over its increased forebodings not only of Becket's death but also of a spiritual void to come, Becket urges them to be at peace and assures them of two things: that the moment of agony they experience now will be transformed into a moment of ecstasy when the whole vision of God's purpose is finally revealed to them; and that in the meantime, because "Human kind cannot bear very much reality," the revelations they have just received and the present pain they suffer will slip from them, become less and less real, until remembered only as a dream.

Peace, and be at peace with your thoughts and visions.
These things had to come to you and you to accept them.
This is your share of the eternal burden,
The perpetual glory. This is one moment,
But know that another
Shall pierce you with a sudden painful joy
When the figure of God's purpose is made complete.
You shall forget these things, toiling in the household,
You shall remember them, droning by the fire,
When age and forgetfulness sweeten memory
Only like a dream that has often been told
And often been changed in the telling. They will seem unreal.
Human kind cannot bear very much reality.

As the above suggests, "Burnt Norton" not only unifies both the ideas and the imagery employed in Eliot's earlier treatments of reality but also repeats some of the exact phraseology. The association of the eye image with reality recurs in the rose-garden passage of Part I, where the "unseen eyebeam" is used to signify the reality of the imaged experience:

> And the unseen eyebeam crossed, for the roses
> Had the look of flowers that are looked at.

The ecstatic moment in the rose-garden is equivalent to that which Becket describes as piercing one with "a sudden painful joy" when the whole vision appears; and the moment, as well as the illumination it offers, is recalled at the close of Part V by the lines which begin "Sudden *in a shaft of sunlight* . . ." (italics mine)—the exact phrase the Chorus of Women used in referring to their moment of revelation. The implication that reality is revealed only in moments or flashes is an idea that Eliot's earlier works have already suggested, and the notion that its intensity is too great to be borne *except* in moments is restated, Part I, in Becket's own words:

> Go, go, go, said the bird: *human kind*
> *Cannot bear very much reality.* (italics mine)

Traditionally used in religious symbolism, and associated by Eliot with a reality too intense for human kind to bear, the light image develops a further significance in "Burnt Norton." It becomes, in fact, the linking symbol between the moment of ecstasy, of reality, of illumination, and the still point, or center, which one reaches in such a moment.

Eliot's earlier use of the light image in *The Waste Land*—particularly in the phrase, "the heart of light, the silence"—suggests a kind of center that foreshadows the still point of the *Four Quartets* and the identification of light with that still point. It is not until "Burnt Norton," however, that the relationship of the two is made explicit. Following Eliot's paradoxical definition of the still point in Part II is a passage which expands that definition and connects the light image with the still point:

The inner freedom from the practical desire,
The release from action and suffering, release from the inner
And the outer compulsion, yet surrounded
By a grace of sense, a white light still and moving,

The "white light still and moving" not only symbolizes the reality, the whole vision, and the ecstatic peace one finds at the still point, but also suggests, through traditional connotations that Eliot deliberately invokes, the Holy Ghost.

The identification of light with the still point is reaffirmed in the lines of Part IV that treat of the kingfisher's death:

. . . After the kingfisher's wing
Has answered light to light, and is silent, the light is still
At the still point of the turning world.

After the kingfisher's spirit has been absorbed into the infinite and his bodily form stilled, the light is "still" at the center of the world. "Still," here, is a play on words indicating both "yet" and "unmoving." The latter use of "still" involves a paradox that links the light image with the reconciling tension I discussed earlier, and clarifies the relationship that both light and tension bear to Eliot's concept of reality. The "white light" identified with the still point is both "still" and "moving." Like the still point, it is defined through paradox, as indeed it would have to be; for paradox itself is a kind of reconciling tension between two opposites, and Eliot's "tension," as I have already suggested, produces a kind of still point. To make the circle complete, both the light image and the still point involve reality, which Eliot defines elsewhere in *terms* of tension. Just as light becomes the linking symbol between the moment of reality and the still point, so tension becomes the linking idea between the concept of reality and that of the still point.

Although it did not appear until 1949, six years after the *Four Quartets*, *Notes Towards the Definition of Culture* expands some of the earlier ideas that were integrated in the still point and therefore helps clarify that concept. In *The Idea of a Christian Society*, Eliot had advanced the theory that a moral tension between the temporal and the spiritual is essential to the maintenance of a Christian society. In *Notes Towards a Definition of Culture*, this idea of tension includes all of the frictions produced by an advanced civilization and the increase of specialized functions:

while the individuals of a tribe, or of a group of islands or villages, may have separate functions—of which the most peculiar are those of the king and the witch-doctor—it is only at a much further stage that religion, science, politics and art become abstractly conceived apart from each other. And just as the functions of individuals become hereditary, and hereditary function hardens into class or caste distinction, and class distinction leads to conflict, so do religion, politics, science and art reach a point at which there is conscious struggle between them for autonomy or dominance. This friction is, at some stages and in some situations, highly creative. . . .[21]

In the same discussion, Eliot goes on to say that tension is essential to any society, both between and within its various branches, and that, within limits, organic unity depends upon a tension or friction between the parts, without which unity would become mere petrifaction.

The theory of unity and diversity which Eliot has asserted in regard to political and social structure, he repeats in regard to religious structure, with the addition that a struggle or tension between conflicting ideas is as essential to the promotion of truth as a tension between parts is to the maintenance of unity:

As in the relation between the social classes, and as in the relation of the several regions of a country to each other and to the central power, it would seem that a constant struggle between the centripetal and the centrifugal forces is desirable. For without the struggle no *balance* can be maintained; and if either force won the result would be deplorable [that is, petrifaction on the one hand; and complete disintegration on the other]. . . . Christendom should be one: the form of organization and the locus of powers in that unity are questions upon which we cannot pronounce. But within that unity there should be an endless conflict between ideas—for it is only by the *struggle* against constantly appearing false ideas that the truth is enlarged and clarified, and in the conflict with heresy that orthodoxy is developed to meet the needs of the times; an endless effort also on the part of each region to shape its Christianity to suit itself, an effort which should neither be wholly suppressed nor left wholly unchecked. (italics mine)

For future reference, I should like to point out Eliot's use of the word "balance" in connection with the words "struggle" and "tension." For it is struggle that produces the balanced tension Eliot equates with reconciliation. Moreover, it is from a state of tension that truth and reality emerge. "Struggle" is a tension not yet balanced, but it is a step *toward* reality.

> It is in fact in moments of moral and spiritual struggle depending upon spiritual sanctions, rather than in those "bewildering moments" in which we are all very much alike, that men and women come nearest to being real.[22]

Only by a complete integration of the personality can the individual fully realize himself as a spiritual being, and become "real." Integration and reality, however, are absolutes that are completely realized only at the still point; therefore, as Eliot sees it, the individual is never completely real except during those moments when he is unified with the still point. Outside of such moments, the best he can do is to approach a real existence; and he does so by spiritual struggles toward a balanced tension he cannot perfectly achieve, because that, too, is an absolute which is fully realized only at the still point.[23]

So far, I have been primarily concerned with the ideas involved in the still point concept. These are more or less concentrated in three key symbols, however: the rose-garden, the wheel, and the point. Before going any further, I should like to consider two articles which trace the development of these symbols and the themes involved: Leonard Unger's "T. S. Eliot's Rose Garden: A Persistent Theme" and Louis L. Martz's "The Wheel and the Point: Aspects of Imagery and Theme in Eliot's Later Poetry." [24]

Unger traces the rose-garden theme, or the moment of ecstasy, through "Burnt Norton" (with some slight mention of "East Coker" and "The Dry Salvages," which had just appeared at the time of his article), and interprets that moment of ecstasy in terms of a childhood sexual experience which, from "Ash-Wednesday" on, leads beyond the experience itself toward God. To justify his claim that the ecstasy is a sexual-religious one, Mr. Unger points, quite rightly I think, to Eliot's interest in and interpretation of the childhood experience that Dante records in the *Vita Nuova*, and from which springs Dante's use of Beatrice as a spiritual symbol:

> The attitude of Dante to the fundamental experience of the *Vita Nuova* can only be understood by accustoming ourselves to find meanings in *final causes* rather than in origins. It is not, I believe, meant as a description of what he *consciously* felt on his meeting with Beatrice, but rather as a description of what that meant on mature reflection upon it. The final cause is the attraction towards God. [25]

In considering Eliot's use of the rose-garden theme prior to "Burnt Norton," Unger places his greatest emphasis upon *The Family Reunion;* since the play contains a significant use of the wheel and the moment, as well as the rose-garden, I should like to make a few additions to Mr. Unger's observations.

First of all I would call attention to Agatha's description, in Part II, Scene II, of a moment of agonized, burning intensity she had experienced in the past:

There are hours when there seems to be no past or future,
Only a present moment of pointed light
When you want to burn. When you stretch out your hand
To the flames. They only come once,
Thank God, that kind. Perhaps there is another kind,
I believe, across a whole Thibet of broken stones
That lie, fang up, a lifetime's march. I have believed this.[26]

The distinction that Agatha makes between the two moments is an important one. The first is a moment of reality too agonizing and too intense to be borne; the second, implying a final peace and joy, is the product of "a lifetime's march." This is a distinction similar to the one that Becket makes between the moment of agony the Chorus of Women have experienced and the moment of joy they will experience when the whole vision is revealed.

As Mr. Unger points out, it is Agatha who opens the door to the rose-garden for Harry and thus enables him to find himself and begin his long journey toward rebirth. She leads the way by describing her own experience when she looked into the rose-garden, and heard "tiny voices."

And then a black raven flew over.
And then I was only my own feet walking
Away, down a concrete corridor
In a dead air. Only feet walking
And sharp heels scraping. Over and under
Echo and noise of feet.
I was only the feet, and the eye
Seeing the feet: the unwinking eye
Fixing the movement. Over and under.

Significantly, when Harry comes to an imaginary meeting with Agatha in the imaginary garden (their moment of recognition as spiritual son and mother), the wheel stops. The wheel, as it is used in *The Family Reunion*, symbolizes the re-

volving chain of external events, the pattern of time, pattern
of suffering, pattern of fate, to which man is bound in his
temporal existence. In Part I, Scene I, referring to the night
when he accidentally, or deliberately, pushed his wife overboard, Harry says:

> . . . One thinks to escape
> By violence, but one is still alone
> In an over-crowded desert, jostled by ghosts.
> It was only reversing the senseless direction
> For a momentary rest on the burning wheel
> That cloudless night in the mid-Atlantic
> When I pushed her over.

Disposing of his wife had afforded Harry only momentary
respite, only a momentary pause as the wheel reversed direction. Now, however, during the imaginary meeting in the
garden, the wheel stops completely—thus signifying a timeless moment, a moment of reality, a moment of truth: a still
point in the lives of Agatha and Harry. Harry says:

> The chain breaks,
> The wheel stops, and the noise of machinery,
> And the desert is cleared, under the judicial sun
> Of the final eye, and the awful evacuation
> Cleanses.
> I was not there, you were not there, only our phantasms
> And what did not happen is as true as what did happen,
> O my dear, and you walked through the little door
> And I ran to meet you in the rose-garden.

In his study of the wheel and the point, Mr. Martz links
Unger's rose-garden interpretation to the still point, which he
considers the dominant symbol of Eliot's poetry since *The
Waste Land* and which he interprets as a "still point of peace."
The discussion is centered upon *Murder in the Cathedral*, as it
relates to the *Four Quartets*, and upon Becket's "still point of

peace," which is finally realized in the latter's death. The turning wheel is interpreted as the pattern of suffering and action which Becket describes; and the axis, as the "still point of peace."

Although I am in general agreement with Mr. Martz's thesis, there are a few points I should like to make. First, in regard to the Becket speech in Part I which Martz quotes as his point of departure:

Peace. And let them be, in their exaltation.
They [the Chorus of Women] speak better than they know,
    and beyond your understanding.
They know and do not know, what it is to act or suffer.
They know and do not know, that acting is suffering
And suffering is action. Neither does the actor suffer
Nor the patient act. But both are fixed
In an eternal action, an eternal patience
To which all must consent that it may be willed
And which all must suffer that they may will it,
That the pattern may subsist, for the pattern is the action
And the suffering, that the wheel may turn and still
Be forever still.[27]

The wheel is both the "pattern of time" and the "pattern of fate," which man can neither "turn" himself, nor escape from:

. . . Only
The fool, fixed in his folly, may think
He can turn the wheel on which he turns.

But man must consent to its turning, "that the pattern may subsist"; that the individual life, in other words, may have direction and meaning. The pattern is suffering and action, or discipline—which is the counterpart of action; and the necessity of such suffering and action in the development of one's spiritual being (the only form of existence which has meaning) is one of Eliot's dominant themes.

In *The Family Reunion*, Harry discovers that to find salvation and obtain release from private suffering, one must reach
beyond his personal agonies and experience universal suffering:

> We must try to penetrate the other private worlds
> Of make-believe and fear. To rest in our own suffering
> Is evasion of suffering. We must learn to suffer more. [28]

Again, *The Idea of a Christian Society* asserts that a society
must become Christian if it would continue to survive, and
"That prospect involves, at least, discipline, inconvenience
and discomfort: but here as hereafter the alternative to hell is
purgatory." [29] In "Ash-Wednesday," as well as in *Murder in
the Cathedral*, suffering and self-discipline are offered as the
way to God; and in *Four Quartets*, as a way to the still point.

I agree therefore with Mr. Martz's statement that the wheel
symbolizes the pattern of action and suffering; I also agree that
the axis is the still point; but I cannot agree that the still
point is peace—an interpretation which seems to me to be only
a part-truth. In reference to the latter, I should like to com-
ment on the passages from the two "Coriolan" poems which
Martz cites to substantiate his thesis; the first is from "Tri-
umphal March," and the second is from "Difficulties of a
Statesman":

> O hidden under the dove's wing, hidden in the turtle's breast,
> Under the palmtree at noon, under the running water
> At the still point of the turning world. O hidden.

> * * *

> O hidden under the . . . Hidden under the . . . [sic]
> Where the dove's foot rested and locked for a moment,
> A still moment, repose of noon . . .

What is hidden is the meaning of life, the whole vision,
which is to be found only at the still point, although there
are intimations of it "under the dove's wing," "under the

running water"; and revelations of it in a "still moment" of peace, a "repose of noon." This still moment is a pregnant stillness, and as such, a kind of still point, but not *the* still point. To define the latter in terms of peace, alone, seems an oversimplification; for the still point is not peace, although it offers peace—a problem I shall return to in "East Coker." Moreover, there are moments other than peaceful ones which produce the pregnant stillness that is *a* still point in the life of an individual. There are, for example, the moments of agony which Agatha and the Chorus of Women experience, and which both Agatha and Becket distinguish from "another kind"—this being the ecstatic moment which, Becket says, "shall pierce you with a sudden painful joy/ When the figure of God's purpose is made complete."

The still point concept as it finally appears in *Four Quartets* is so complex that definition is all but impossible, and can be attempted only in the paradoxical terms that Eliot himself employs. One would be fairly safe in asserting that this concept integrates all of Eliot's major beliefs and is the culmination of his thinking, both as man and as poet. I have tried to suggest its gradual emergence by tracing some of the major ideas and symbols involved. That the concept has lain in the back of his mind from the beginning, waiting for development and expression, is indicated by a 1916 essay in which he attempts to distinguish the soul from the "finite center" of F. H. Bradley's *Truth and Reality;* significantly, Eliot defines that center in terms which he later employs to define his own concept of the still point:

> The soul only differs from the finite center in being considered as something not identical with its states. The finite center so far as I can pretend to understand it *is* immediate experience. It is not in time, though we are more or less forced to think of it under temporal conditions. "It comes to itself as all the world and not as one

among others. And it has properly no duration through which it lasts. It can contain a lapse and a before and after, but these are subordinate." The finite center in a sense contains its own past and future.[30]

The still point of *Four Quartets* is presented first in "Burnt Norton" as attainable in an isolated moment, "with no before and after," and presented finally in "Little Gidding" as attainable by a certain way of life. It is the center outside oneself that one feels he has reached in a moment of reality, a moment of intense spiritual awareness and of "sudden illumination." It is "The point of intersection of the timeless/ With time," the point at which the whole vision appears and all opposites are reconciled. And as the source of all movement, pattern, and meaning, it is, like Dante's "unmoved mover," definable only by paradox:

At the still point of the turning world. Neither flesh nor
    fleshless;
Neither from nor towards; at the still point, there the dance
    is,
But neither arrest nor movement. And do not call it fixity,
Where past and future are gathered. Neither movement from
    nor towards,
Neither ascent nor decline. Except for the point, the still
    point,
There would be no dance, and there is only the dance.
I can only say, *there* we have been: but I cannot say where.
And I cannot say, how long, for that is to place it in time.[31]

For the individual, reaching the still point is equivalent to achieving wholeness of being, the complete integration of personality that allows one to perceive the whole vision and to develop one's spiritual self to the utmost:

The inner freedom from the practical desire,
The release from action and suffering, release from the inner

And the outer compulsion, yet surrounded
By a grace of sense, a white light still and moving,
Erhebung without motion, concentration
Without elimination, both a new world
And the old made explicit, understood
In the completion of its partial ecstasy,
The resolution of its partial horror.

In her comparison of Eliot's imagery to the Jungian symbols representing various stages of personality integration, Miss Drew makes an interesting parallel between Eliot's still point and Jung's "mandala" image, which she explains as follows:

> In the mandala pattern, the circle suggests the imagined wholeness of being, and the center the point at which the resolution of opposites occurs which makes such a sense of wholeness possible. For Jung sees the pattern of "reality" in the Heraclitean terms of a dynamic system in which a central energy perpetuates itself by opposing forces which, though apparently antitheses, are found to be phases of one cyclical process. As Heraclitus says: "The unlike is joined together and from differences result most beautiful harmony, and all things take place by strife." [32]

The similarity between the Jungian or the Heraclitean "reality" and the concepts of oneness and reconciliation involved in Eliot's definition of "reality" immediately becomes apparent. It is Eliot's concept of oneness that allows him to see beauty and ugliness, birth and death, the way up and the way down, merely as different phases of the same thing, and to unite these opposites at the still point, where complete "reality" is found. And it is Eliot's concept of reconciliation as "tension" that makes this union possible, and explains his paradoxical definition of the still point as an unmoved mover which contains both stillness and movement, though it is neither. As an absolute, tension becomes, for Eliot, a kind of synonym for Divine Energy. It is the force that perpetuates itself by an opposition producing both harmony and movement; it is the force that reconciles the boarhound and the boar, holds them in the pattern and thus creates "the dance." This, I think, explains why Eliot always sees the still point in terms of tension, and tension in terms of the pregnant stillness which is a kind of still point.

Throughout his poetry, Eliot consistently treats reality in terms of opposites and a third mediating force or center, from which emanate such revelations of truth and visions of reality as occur. It is interesting to notice the process of abstraction that Eliot's third quantity undergoes. In *The Waste Land* the center or reconciling force is personified by Tiresias, who is "throbbing between two lives" and has "foresuffered all." In him the two sexes meet, and all opposites are reconciled. It is he who unifies the poem and transmits the vision it offers. *The Family Reunion* is a mid-point in Eliot's transition from the personified mediator to the final abstraction. Agatha is a kind of mediator between the old Harry and the new one; it is she who leads him to the rose-garden and the moment of illumination that makes the new Harry possible. Mary performs a similar function when she offers an insight into his nature which Harry immediately recognizes as true:

Even if, as you say, Wishwood is a cheat,
Your family a delusion—than [sic] it's *all* a delusion,
Everything you feel—I don't mean what you think,
But what you feel. You attach yourself to loathing
As others do to loving: an infatuation
That's wrong, a good that's misdirected. You deceive yourself
Like the man convinced that he is paralysed
Or like the man who believes that he is blind
While he still sees the sunlight. I know that this is true.[33]

It is not only Mary who sees herself as a medium, revealing truths she did not know she knew; Harry also sees her as such.

Moreover, when Mary's revelation strikes him, Harry imagines her voice (the revelation) as coming from "the silence/ Between two storms"—from a still point similar to the one that is a source of vision in the last passage of "Little Gidding." Harry says:

> . . . you seem
> Like someone who comes from a very long distance,
> Or the distant waterfall in the forest,
> Inaccessible, half-heard.
> And I hear your voice as in the silence
> Between two storms, one hears the moderate usual noises
> In the grass and leaves, of life persisting,
> Which ordinarily pass unnoticed.

In *Four Quartets* the personified mediator is done away with and the final abstraction is reached in the still point, the center at which opposites are reconciled and the whole vision offered. In "Little Gidding," Part V, this center is suggested by "the stillness/ Between two waves of the sea," from which come the this-world voices offering an other-world vision to those who have the ears to hear and the eyes to perceive:

> The voice of the hidden waterfall
> And the children in the apple-tree
> Not known, because not looked for
> But heard, half-heard, in the stillness
> Between two waves of the sea.

As I suggested earlier, "Burnt Norton," the first *Quartet*, is concerned with the still point as it is reached in the single, isolated moment of intense feeling or spiritual awareness. It is just such a moment that is represented by the experience in the rose-garden—an experience that the poet strives to interpret, in order that he may re-live it. He is impelled to do so for the same reason that Harry is impelled to recapture his past: to complete "the loop in time" so that the hidden may be revealed and the whole vision perceived.

Appropriately, it is a bird which urges the poet to revisit the garden in search of "other echoes":

> Quick, said the bird, find them, find them,
> Round the corner. Through the first gate,
> Into our first world, shall we follow
> The deception of the thrush? Into our first world.[34]

As an incarnation of the life force, the bird is one of the many "hints" pointing to "the world around the corner" that Harry sought. "Our first world" is intended to represent, I think, the world of childhood, which is also a world of fancy, a dream world; and the "deception" of the thrush not only suggests that the experience is an imagined one but also suggests the elusive quality of the vision itself, which man may at times perceive, but cannot sustain.

> Dry the pool, dry concrete, brown edged,
> And the pool was filled with water out of sunlight,
> And the lotus rose, quietly, quietly,
> The surface glittered out of heart of light,
> And they were behind us, reflected in the pool.
> Then a cloud passed, and the pool was empty.

In one moment of intense awareness, the drained pool is suddenly transformed, "filled with water out of sunlight," and the still point is reached, the moment of reality experienced, the whole vision perceived—in much the same fashion that one experiences sudden illumination in a dream. But the moment passes; the illumination recedes; for time will not stand still, nor can man long bear the intensity, the hard, bright glitter of reality:

> Go, said the bird, for the leaves were full of children,
> Hidden excitedly, containing laughter.
> Go, go, go, said the bird: human kind
> Cannot bear very much reality.

Although the moment in the rose-garden and all like moments which enable us to reach the still point are in themselves timeless, they can be remembered only when placed in a time reference:

> To be conscious is not to be in time
> But only in time can the moment in the rose-garden,
> The moment in the arbour where the rain beat,
> The moment in the draughty church at smokefall
> Be remembered; involved with past and future.

This is what Eliot means when, in "The Dry Salvages," he refers to the still point as "The point of intersection of the timeless with time."

The still point is a kind of spiritual center, and the whole of *Four Quartets* is a search for various means of union with that center. The moment in the rose-garden symbolizes one way of reaching the still point, by the ecstatic moment, which is referred to throughout the *Four Quartets* in the line: "Quick now, here, now, always—." "Burnt Norton" is an attempt to reach the still point by recapturing the ecstatic moment, and a lament that such moments (in which lie the sole meaning and justification of one's existence) are so rare as to make the majority of one's life seem wasted:

> Sudden in a shaft of sunlight
> Even while the dust moves
> There rises the hidden laughter
> Of children in the foliage
> Quick now, here, now, always—
> Ridiculous the waste sad time
> Stretching before and after.

The ecstatic moment, though it is the most immediate, is not the only way to the still point, however; "Burnt Norton," Part III, suggests another way—Agatha's way, "across a whole Thibet of broken stones"—and thus foreshadows the development of the remaining quartets. For some, the way to the still point may be the way up; for others, the way down. It may be, for some, a choice of action; for others, abstention from action. But whatever the variation, the way is essentially the same, a lifetime's effort, involving, first of all, a descent into "the world of perpetual solitude."

> World not world, but that which is not world,
> Internal darkness, deprivation
> And destitution of all property,
> Desiccation of the world of sense,
> Evacuation of the world of fancy,
> Inoperancy of the world of spirit;
> This is the one way, and the other
> Is the same, not in movement
> But abstention from movement . . .[35]

The tone and implications of "East Coker" are religious, and the way it presents is the opposite of ecstasy; it is the way of agony:

> Whisper of running streams, and winter lightning.
> The wild thyme unseen and the wild strawberry,
> The laughter in the garden, echoed ecstasy
> Not lost, but requiring, pointing to the agony
> Of death and birth.[36]

What is required, in this case, is discipline and renunciation:

I said to my soul, be still, and wait without hope
For hope would be hope of the wrong thing; wait without love
For love would be love of the wrong thing; there is yet faith
But the faith and the love and the hope are all in the waiting.
Wait without thought, for you are not ready for thought:

So the darkness shall be the light, and the stillness the dancing.

As Eliot stated in *The Idea of a Christian Society*, "the alternative to hell is purgatory." [37] For the average, lost, soul the way to the still point is through purgatory, and the first step along the way is a "dark night of the soul"—the same "dark night of the soul" that St. John of the Cross described and that Eliot portrayed in "Ash-Wednesday." As with the still point itself, this way is defined in paradoxical terms:

Shall I say it again? In order to arrive there,
To arrive where you are [real being], to get from where you
   are not,
   You must go by a way wherein there is no ecstasy.
In order to arrive at what you do not know
   You must go by a way which is the way of ignorance.
In order to possess what you do not possess
   You must go by the way of dispossession.
In order to arrive at what you are not
   You must go through the way in which you are not.
And what you do not know is the only thing you know
And what you own is what you do not own
And where you are is where you are not. [38]

"East Coker" develops not only a new way but a new idea: that the ecstatic moment need not be isolated, but can be diffused into all moments, all time if, Eliot implies, one has a sense of history, a sense of the continuity of past and present, and of the universality of human suffering and human striving:

           . . . Not the intense moment
   Isolated, with no before and after,
   But a lifetime burning in every moment
   And not the lifetime of one man only
   But of old stones that cannot be deciphered.

In the realm of the spirit, all time is eternally present; *here* and *now* do not matter. All that matters is that

We must be still and still moving
Into another intensity
For a further union, a deeper communion
Through the dark cold and the empty desolation,
The wave cry, the wind cry, the vast waters
Of the petrel and the porpoise. In my end is my beginning.

"East Coker" is essentially a parallel to "Ash-Wednesday." It is Part VI of the latter that first describes "the time of tension between dying and birth," the time when one must learn "to care and not to care," and "to sit still"—the forms of self-discipline and self-surrender required to escape a dark night of the soul and find "Our peace in His will." In "East Coker" the struggle toward God becomes a struggle toward eventual union with the still point. One must move through various times of tension (from one to "another" intensity), surrender himself to other and "further" unions which will bring one closer to the still point. Final union brings the kind of peace described in "Ash-Wednesday" as "Our peace in His will," the peace of final surrender; the still point itself, however, cannot be defined in terms of peace alone. The still point involves peace and ecstasy, just as it involves balance and tension. The divine harmony or peace one finds at the still point is a kind of balance; and the ecstasy, a kind of tension—a reconciling force as well as a source of energy.

The "sudden illumination" that Eliot refers to in "The Dry Salvages," Part II, is again the ecstatic moment—for most of us the only way in which we ever reach the still point in this life, by chance, and a rare chance at that. The difficulty is that when we have the experience, we miss the meaning:

The moments of happiness—not the sense of well-being,
Fruition, fulfilment, security or affection,

Or even a very good dinner, but the sudden illumination—
We had the experience but missed the meaning,
And approach to the meaning restores the experience
In a different form, beyond any meaning
We can assign to happiness. . . .

To reach the still point and to understand it is "an occupation for the saint." [39] For most of us, the ecstatic moment remains "unattended," for even at best, the sudden illuminations and outward signs are but "hints and guesses."

For most of us, there is only the unattended
Moment, the moment in and out of time,
The distraction fit, lost in a shaft of sunlight,
The wild thyme unseen, or the winter lightning
Or the waterfall, or music heard so deeply
That it is not heard at all, but you are the music
While the music lasts. These are only hints and guesses,
Hints followed by guesses; and the rest
Is prayer, observance, discipline, thought and action.[40]

Even though the goal cannot be fully reached except by a few (the saints), it is necessary that all men strive toward it—by "prayer, observance, discipline, thought and action." The important thing is to keep trying: "Not fare well,/ But fare forward, voyagers." That is the message of "The Dry Salvages."

In "Little Gidding" both the concept of the still point and the suggested means of reaching it are restated. As the spiritual center, the source of all pattern, movement, and meaning, the center at which all things are unified, all paradoxes resolved, it can be reached not only by the ecstatic moment but, more important, by a way of life, a religious quest, during which one learns first to sit still, and then to fare forward. Ultimately this means that one must "be redeemed from fire by fire." For one can escape the fires of lust and the fires of destruction only by going through the fire of purgation, "that refining fire/ Where you must move in measure, like a dancer." [41]

"The dance," the pattern, is at the still point; and one must submit to the pattern to reach the still point. One has his glimpses of the still point; and one has his choice: to be simply moved in the movement, like a hollow man acted upon but not acting; to cut oneself off and do a brief, isolated dance which will end in spiritual destruction; or to move with and in the pattern, like the dancer—striving ever toward a goal impossible to reach in this life, but finding purpose and salvation in the striving. If one makes the last choice, "all shall be well and/ All manner of thing shall be well." For one will, in his ultimate being, reach that still point where the rose of earthly love becomes the rose of Divine Love; where the fires of lust, destruction, and purgation become the fire of illumination and Divine Love, "And the fire and the rose are one." [42]

One thing yet remains to be considered if one would understand Eliot's still point concept: Eliot's treatment of the Word of God, the word of the poet, and the relationship of both to the still point concept. Any reader of Eliot is familiar with the emphasis he places upon language in general, upon the word in particular, and upon poetry as a medium for the word. In *The Use of Poetry and the Use of Criticism*, Eliot defines poetry as a people's "highest point of consciousness, its greatest power and its most delicate sensibility." [43] In the same book, Eliot gives his well-known definition of the "auditory imagination":

> What I call the "auditory imagination" is the feeling for syllable and rhythm; penetrating far below the conscious levels of thought and feeling, invigorating every word; sinking to the most primitive and forgotten, returning to the origin and bringing something back, seeking the beginning and the end.

To write the kind of poetry that represents the "highest point of consciousness" of a people and re-establishes the connection between the individual and the race, the poet must develop an "auditory imagination" which can make the word serve as a link to the origin, to the beginning and the end. To put it another way, as Eliot does in "Poetry and Propaganda," the word should be "a sensuous embodiment." A poet should be judged not only by the philosophy he develops but also by the adequacy with which he realizes it:

> For Poetry—here and so far I am in accord with Mr. Richards—is not the assertion that something is true, but the making that truth more fully real to us; it is the creation of a sensuous embodiment. It is the making the Word Flesh, if we remember that for poetry there are various qualities of Word and various qualities of Flesh.[44]

Poetry, then, is the word made flesh, and an incarnation of the poet's beliefs, the poet's concept of reality, just as Christ is the Word made Flesh, and an incarnation of Divine principles. Eliot's poetry turns repeatedly to the problem and the meaning of the Word. In "Gerontion," the sign that is asked for (and subsequently ignored) is the infant Christ, "The word within a word, unable to speak a word,/ Swaddled in darkness." In "A Song for Simeon," Christ is similarly described:

Let the Infant, the *still* unspeaking and unspoken Word,
Grant Israel's consolation
To one who has eighty years and no to-morrow. (italics mine)

Here, as elsewhere in Eliot, "still" is used in the sense of "yet" and "silent" or "unmoving." And Christ, as the "unspoken" Word, is the yet unrealized promise of the state of real being, which He embodies.

In "Ash-Wednesday" Eliot considers both kinds of "words":

man's word, which has become so meaningless that it says
nothing; and the Divine Word, which is the sign that has
been ignored, the promise that has gone unheeded. The garden
of Part II represents not only the end of all earthly loves, and
hence the beginning of Divine Love, but also the end of
"Speech without word and/ Word of no speech," and therefore an approach to the meaning of God's Word, to be interpreted by the Lady who serves as spiritual guide in the
poem. But the knight is not yet worthy, so the Lady does not
speak, and the Word remains unheard. The Word is there, as
always, however, at the center of things, its meaning waiting
to be understood, its pledge waiting to be redeemed:

> If the lost word is lost, if the spent word is spent
> If the unheard, unspoken
> Word is unspoken, unheard;
> Still is the unspoken word, the Word unheard,
> The Word without a word, the Word within
> The world and for the world;
> And the light shone in darkness and
> Against the Word the unstilled world still whirled
> About the centre of the silent Word.[45]

As the foregoing passage clearly indicates, Eliot has begun,
in "Ash-Wednesday," to associate Christ and the Word with
a still point or center which embodies the same truths and the
same principles of which Christ himself is the incarnation.[46]
It is in the "Choruses" from *The Rock*, however, that one finds
Eliot's clearest statements concerning speech, the word of
man, and the Word of God. Here, man is urged to maintain
the church and religious tradition as a means of keeping alive
the Word of God; otherwise, he faces emptiness. Once he
separates himself from the church, "The Rock," and substitutes the word of man for the Word of God, man exchanges
a meaningful silence for a meaningless babble, a spiritual peace
for purposeless motion:

The endless cycle of idea and action,
Endless invention, endless experiment,
Brings knowledge of motion, but not of stillness;
Knowledge of speech, but not of silence;
Knowledge of words, and ignorance of the Word.
All our knowledge brings us nearer to our ignorance,
All our ignorance brings us nearer to death,
But nearness to death no nearer to God.[47]

The old framework is rotten; what man must do, the
Women suggest, is build a new church and a new speech.
Where the brick is crumbling

> We will build with new stone
> Where the beams are rotten
> We will build with new timbers
> Where the word is unspoken
> We will build with new speech
> There is work together
> A Church for all
> And a job for each
> Every man to his work.

The Workmen express their desire for a similar goal:

. . . In this street
There is no beginning, no movement, no peace and no end
But noise without speech, food without taste.
Without delay, without haste
We would build the beginning and the end of this street.
We build the meaning:
A Church for all
And a job for each
Each man to his work.

Part III describes what will happen to the world of "decent
godless people," who leave God's Word unspoken, unheard;

their civilization will become the decayed house of "Gerontion":

> There shall be left the broken chimney,
> The peeled hull, a pile of rusty iron,
> In a street of scattered brick where the goat climbs,
> Where My Word is unspoken.

In Part VII, Eliot summarizes man's spiritual development
from the beginning of the world. Blindly at first, man struggled toward God, struggled through darkness, worshiping
trees, snakes, devils, "crying for life beyond life, for ecstasy
not of the flesh." "And the spirit moved upon the face of the
water." Those who followed the Spirit followed the light,
invented Higher Religions, which led men to a knowledge
of Good and Evil, but which were still "surrounded and shot
with darkness"; so these came to an end:

> Then came, at a predetermined moment, a moment in time
>   and of time,
> A moment not out of time, but in time, in what
>   we call history: transecting, bisecting the
>   world of time, a moment in time but not like
>   a moment of time,
> A moment in time but time was made through
>   that moment: for without the meaning there
>   is no time, and that moment of time gave
>   the meaning.
> Then it seemed as if men must proceed from
>   light to light, in the light of the Word,
> Through the Passion and Sacrifice saved in spite
>   of their negative being;

But man ignored the light, the meaning of the moment, the
meaning of the Word, and something happened that had never
happened before: "Men have left God not for other gods, they
say,/ but for no god. . . ." [48] As a result, the Church has

been disowned, and man lives in "an age which advances progressively backwards."

To rebuild the house of God, man must learn "the way of penitence"; he must learn "the joyful communion of the saints"; and he must learn to create as the artist creates:

> The soul of man must quicken to creation.
> Out of the formless stone, when the artist united
>   himself with stone,
> Spring always new forms of life, from the soul
>   of man that is joined to the soul of stone;
> Out of the meaningless practical shapes of all
>   that is living or lifeless
> Joined with the artist's eye, new life, new form,
>   new colour.
> Out of the sea of sound the life of music,
> Out of the slimy mud of words, out of the sleet
>   and hail of verbal imprecisions,
> Approximate thoughts and feelings, words that
>   have taken the place of thoughts and feelings,
> There spring the perfect order of speech, and the
>   beauty of incantation.

The necessity of giving order to speech, and the struggle involved, if words are to have meaning, is emphasized again in *Four Quartets*. "Burnt Norton," Part V, deals with the slipperiness and imprecision of words; Part II of "East Coker" complains of "the intolerable wrestle/ With words and meanings," and Part V describes that wrestle as "a raid on the inarticulate"; and finally, the dead poet in Part II of "Little Gidding" phrases the purpose of his age as an effort to "purify the dialect of the tribe/ And urge the mind to aftersight and foresight."

In the beginning was the Word, and the Word was with God, and the Word was God. Eliot is concerned with words and meanings because it is the word of the poet which gives meaning to the

Word in speech, just as Christ gives meaning to the Word in the flesh. As "sensuous embodiments," both are incarnations of a kind, and Christ is *the* Incarnation of the Word, the living promise of that state of real being which man may achieve upon complete union with God:

The hint half guessed, the gift half understood, is Incarnation.
Here [in Christ] the impossible union
Of spheres of existence [temporal and spiritual] is actual,
Here the past and future
Are conquered, and reconciled,[49]

Ultimately, Eliot's "still point" is the intellectualized presentation of a Christian concept. Union with the still point is equivalent to union with God. Union with the still point is a self-surrender to, and identification with the spiritual center of creation, the center of reality, where all opposites are reconciled and the divine pattern created. Divine Love (embodied in Christ, the Word incarnated) is equivalent to Divine Energy, the tension that is the reconciling force at the still point. Both reconcile the boarhound and the boar, and create the pattern; both are unmoved yet moving. Christ is the Word made flesh by God; and the still point concept is Eliot's attempt to make the Word flesh by speech. Striving to reach the still point is striving toward God. The struggles involved and the conditions required are the same. And though one may reach the still point in isolated moments and experience momentary union, complete union with the still point is the product of a lifetime's effort, a lifetime's march. So Agatha described it, and so Eliot sums it up in the concluding passage of "Little Gidding":

We shall not cease from exploration
And the end of all our exploring
Will be to arrive where we started
And to know the place for the first time.

Through the unknown, remembered gate
When the last of earth left to discover
Is that which was the beginning;
At the source of the longest river
The voice of the hidden waterfall
And the children in the apple-tree
Not known, because not looked for
But heard, half-heard, in the stillness
Between two waves of the sea.
Quick now, here, now, always—
A condition of complete simplicity
(Costing not less than everything)
And all shall be well and
All manner of thing shall be well
When the tongues of flame are in-folded
Into the crowned knot of fire
And the fire and the rose are one.

NOTES

1 *Selected Essays*, p. 342; subsequent passage, p. 4.

2 *Murder in the Cathedral*, p. 69; *Collected Poems, 1909-1935*, p. 180; passage following, "Choruses" from *The Rock*, *Collected Poems*, p. 179.

3 "'Ulysses,' Order, and Myth," *The Dial*, LXXV (November, 1923), 483.

4 *For Lancelot Andrewes: Essays on Style and Order*, p. 57; *The Idea of a Christian Society*, p. 64.

5 "Burnt Norton," *Four Quartets*, p. 5.

6 "The Metaphysical Poets," *Selected Essays*, p. 247.

7 *The Use of Poetry and the Use of Criticism*, p. 98.

8 *The Family Reunion*, p. 16; subsequent passage, p. 73.

9 *The Idea of a Christian Society*, p. 33.

10 *After Strange Gods: A Primer of Modern Heresy*, p. 53.

11 *Selected Essays*, p. 368.

12 *The Family Reunion*, p. 31; three subsequent passages, pp. 103, 18, 21.

13 See Eliot's *Notes Towards the Definition of Culture* for a detailed development of his theories of unity in relation to culture, religion, and society.

14 "East Coker," *Four Quartets*, p. 17.

15 *Selected Essays*, pp. 6-7.

[16] Elizabeth Drew, *T. S. Eliot: The Design of His Poetry*, p. xii; passage following, p. 106. Also see Genevieve W. Foster, "The Archetypal Imagery of T. S. Eliot," *PMLA*, LX (1945), 567-585.

[17] *The Idea of a Christian Society*, pp. 22, 56.

[18] See Canto XXXI of the "Purgatorio"; also see Eliot's reference to Dante's use of "the eyes" in "Dante," *Selected Essays*, p. 226.

[19] *The Family Reunion*, p. 23.

[20] *Murder in the Cathedral*, p. 13; subsequent passage, p. 66.

[21] *Notes Towards a Definition of Culture*, p. 23; subsequent passage, p. 83.

[22] *After Strange Gods*, p. 46.

[23] In *Notes Towards a Definition of Culture*, p. 31, Eliot writes: "When we consider the quality of the integration required for the full cultivation of the spiritual life, we must keep in mind the possibility of grace and the exemplars of sanctity in order not to sink into despair."

[24] See Leonard Unger, "T. S. Eliot's Rose Garden: A Persistent Theme," *The Southern Review*, VII (Spring, 1942), 667-689; and Louis L. Martz, "The Wheel and the Point: Aspects of Imagery and Theme in Eliot's Later Poetry," *The Sewanee Review*, LV (Winter, 1947), 126-147.

[25] *Selected Essays*, p. 234.

[26] *The Family Reunion*, pp. 99-100; two subsequent passages, pp. 103-104, 105.

[27] *Murder in the Cathedral*, p. 21; subsequent quotations, pp. 13, 20, 24. Eliot's use of the Wheel of Fortune, of Life, the Great Wheel of Buddhism from which man seeks release, gradually yields to the philosophers' wheel, whose revolving rim, centered upon a fixed point, supplies the figure for Eliot's still point metaphor. After *The Family Reunion*, though the metaphysical aspects of the concept change (the point of the intersection of time and eternity becoming an outside spiritual center), the basic image does not.

[28] *The Family Reunion*, p. 89.

[29] *The Idea of a Christian Society*, p. 22.

[30] "Leibniz's Monads and Bradley's Finite Center," *The Monist*, XXVI (October, 1916), 574.

[31] For this and passage following, see *Four Quartets*, p. 5.

[32] Drew, pp. 142-143. Jung's "Mandala" pattern, in the form of the wheel or circle, also appears in the works of Yeats and Lawrance as a symbol of the integrated self, the whole being.

[33] For this and subsequent passage, see *The Family Reunion*, p. 57.

[34] "Burnt Norton," *Four Quartets*, p. 3. The four quotations immediately following are also from "Burnt Norton," pp. 4, 4, 5, 8.

[35] "Burnt Norton," *Four Quartets*, p. 6.

[36] For this and passage following, see *Four Quartets*, p. 15.

[37] *The Idea of a Christian Society*, p. 22.

[38] "East Coker," *Four Quartets*, p. 15; two subsequent passages, p. 17.

[39] "The Dry Salvages," *Four Quartets*, p. 27. Notice the practical application of this idea in *The Cocktail Party* and *The Confidential Clerk*. Celia and

Colby alone are qualified for the way of the saint; the others must recognize their worldly selves for what they are and make the best of them.

⁴⁰ "The Dry Salvages," *Four Quartets*, p. 27.

⁴¹ *Four Quartets*, pp. 37, 35.

⁴² "Little Gidding," *Four Quartets*, p. 39.

⁴³ *The Use of Poetry and the Use of Criticism*, p. 5; passage following, p. 111.

⁴⁴ *The Bookman*, LXX (February, 1930), 601.

⁴⁵ *Collected Poems*, p. 118.

⁴⁶ See Miss Foster's discussion of "the Word" as the psyche's new center, "The Archetypal Imagery of T. S. Eliot," p. 582.

⁴⁷ *Collected Poems*, p. 179; four subsequent passages, pp. 183, 184, 190, 199-200.

⁴⁸ *Collected Poems*, p. 200; subsequent passages, p. 206.

⁴⁹ "The Dry Salvages," *Four Quartets*, pp. 27-28.

2

Coleridge and the Ecstatic Moment

"Descartes," Coleridge once protested with the vehemence of a D. H. Lawrence, and for the same reasons, "made nature utterly lifeless and godless" by considering it "as the subject of merely mechanical laws." [1] Realizing the blow that eighteenth-century Reason had dealt to faith and intuition, and the threat that science and reason offered to orthodox Christianity, Coleridge wished to construct a system of philosophy that would link reason and intuition so as to justify the latter and provide a rational basis for his own faith. To this end, he set forth certain theories which were to have formed the basis of his "system"; and in such works as *Aids to Reflection* and *The Statesman's Manual; or The Bible the Best Guide to Political Skill and Foresight* he offered a guide to the correct use and interpretation of the Scriptures—that he might help solve the rational difficulties impeding one's faith as a Christian. [2]

The "system" itself was never completed, but the defense of Trinitarian Christianity continued to be the main task of of Coleridge's last years; [3] and his attempts to make the Bible rationally acceptable laid the foundation for what has since become the "broad church" interpretation. [4] They also indicate the first cracks in a structure that continued to weaken under the ever-increasing bombardments of science. To my mind, Coleridge's defense of Christianity and his efforts to reconcile philosophy and religion by uniting reason and intuition, matter and spirit, mark the first stages in the development of the religio-philosophical problems that have particularly beset the twentieth century. And although Coleridge never formulated a complete philosophical system, what he did set down foreshadows many of the theories and concepts later expressed by our modern writers.

Unconsciously, Coleridge seems to have been moving toward an intellectualized concept of union with God, involving an ecstatic moment similar to that which, in Eliot's terms, leads one to the still point. This can best be seen, I believe, by considering certain aspects of Coleridge's theories of organic unity and the reconciliation of opposites (which form the basis of his philosophy), and by considering also his definition of symbol, his concept of joy, and the relation of the latter to the faculty of imagination.

Although Coleridge is sometimes inconsistent, sometimes contradictory in particular arguments and opinions, there is never any inconsistency or confusion about his general aim. As John Muirhead observes in his *Coleridge as Philosopher*:

> Whatever changes Coleridge's philosophical opinions underwent, one thing remained fixed and constant, the guiding star of all his wanderings, namely, the necessity of reaching a view of the world from which it could be grasped as the manifestation of a single principle, and therefore as a unity. The attempt to reach such a view was what he meant by Metaphysics, or philosophy in general.[5]

Coleridge's determination to grasp the world as "the manifestation of a single principle" expresses itself in his theories of organic unity and the reconciliation of opposites.[6] Quite simply, organic unity is symbolized by the growing plant:

the whole is greater than the mere sum of its parts and its (organic) form shaped from *within*, "evolved from the invisible central power." [7] Opposed to this, to be avoided and condemned, is mechanical form, as symbolized by "a child's garden of plucked flowers stuck in the earth" [8]—the garden being a mere collection of parts offering a lifeless "mechanical regularity" imposed from *without*.

The organic unity that Coleridge finds in nature, and advocates in art, is a living, active principle expressed by the conflict of opposites and dependent upon that conflict for its "living" quality. But "all opposition is a tendency to reunion"; hence, for Coleridge, the circle is complete.[9] If one would seek truth, says Coleridge, "seek first for the Unity as the only source of Reality, and then for the two opposite yet correspondent forms by which it manifests itself." [10]

The relationship between the *law of polarity* and organic unity is one that Coleridge considers at length in *Hints Towards the Formation of a More Comprehensive Theory of Life*, a tract containing one of the fullest statements we have concerning his philosophy. Here, Coleridge defines life as "the *power* which discloses itself from within as a principle of *unity* in the *many*."[11] Lest he be misunderstood, Coleridge expands the above to define life "*absolutely*, as the principle of unity in *multëity*, as far as the former, the unity to wit, is produced *ab intra;* but *eminently (sensu eminenti)*, I define life as *the principle of individuation*, or the power which unites a given *all* into a *whole* that is presupposed by all its parts. The link that combines the two, and acts throughout both, will, of course, be defined by the *tendency* to *individuation*."

The tendency to individuation is progressive, increasing in the higher forms of life, and reaching its peak in man. Like D. H. Lawrence, however, Coleridge insists that the tendency to individuation or "*detachment* from the universal life" is counteracted by the tendency to "*attachment* or reduction into" the universal life. "This tendency to individuate can not be conceived without the opposite tendency to connect, even as the centrifugal power opposes the centripetal, or as the two opposite poles constitute each other, and are the constituent acts of one and the same power in the magnet. We might say that the life of the magnet subsists in their union, but that it lives (acts or manifests itself) in their strife." Hence, pursuing the idea of the magnet a bit further, Coleridge defines the "highest law, or most general form" under which the tendency to individuation acts as "*polarity*, or the essential dualism of Nature."

The law of polarity, "which reigns through all nature," is "the manifestation of one power by opposite forces"; [12] and that one power, organic unity, is itself an expression of the "Supreme Reality," the absolute unity which is God. "Space is the ideal organ by which the soul of man perceives the *omnipresence* of the Supreme Reality . . . while the equal mystery of *Time* bears the same relation to his *Eternity*, or what is fully equivalent, his Unity." This Divine Unity is the secret and the center of life, and "the oneness of space and time . . . the predicate of all *real* being"—a oneness which Coleridge visualizes as a mid-point between opposite poles, "producing itself on each side." [13]

> In short, neither can the antagonists appear but as two forces of one power, nor can the power be conceived by us but as the equatorial point of the two counteracting forces. . . . To make it adequate, we must substitute the idea of positive production for that of rest, or mere neutralization. To the fancy alone it is the null-point, or zero, but to the reason it is the *punctum saliens*, and the power itself in its eminence.

It is significant that Coleridge conceives of reality in terms of unity, and unity in terms of opposing forces reconciled at a mid-point which, like Eliot's still point, is a source of energy. Coleridge's "equilibrium" is not mere neutralization but a pregnant stillness, a state of tension produced by the balance of opposing forces; in the human life, it is similar to "the time of tension between dying and birth" that Eliot describes in "Ash-Wednesday." It is in this "equilibrium" that one's moral being subsists:

> In all subjects of deep and lasting interest, you will detect a struggle between two opposites, two polar forces, both of which are alike necessary to our human well-being, and necessary each to the continued existence of the other. Well, therefore, may we contemplate with intense feelings those whirlwinds which are for free agents the appointed means, and the only possible condition of that equilibrium in which our moral Being subsists; while the disturbance of the same constitutes our sense of life.[14]

Still seeking to grasp the world as the manifestation of a single law, Coleridge applies the principle that he derived from Nature to the realm of Art and the concept of physical beauty, which he defines in terms of organic unity and reconciled opposites.

> The Beautiful, contemplated in its essentials, that is in *kind* and not in *degree*, is that in which the *many*, still seen as many, becomes one. Take a familiar instance, one of a thousand. The frost on a window-pane has by accident crystallized into a striking resemblance of a tree or a seaweed. With what pleasure we trace the parts, and their relations to each other, and to the whole! Here is the stalk or trunk, and here the branches or sprays—sometimes even the buds or flowers. Nor will our pleasure be less, should the caprice of the crystallization represent some object disagreeable to us, provided only we can see or fancy the component parts each in relation to each, and all forming a whole. . . .
>
> The most general definition of beauty, therefore is . . . Multëity in Unity.[15]

More specifically, "Beauty is harmony, and subsists only in composition"; and harmony is produced by the reconciliation of opposites, such as one finds in Raphael's "Galatea," which has "the balance, the perfect reconciliation, effected between these two conflicting principles of the FREE LIFE, and of the confining FORM!" [16]

Art *is* art, art has beauty, only when the parts are organically unified, the basic duality of life both expressed and reconciled. For it is the expression of organic unity that arouses one's "sense of beauty," which "*subsists in simultaneous intuition of the relation of parts, each to each, and of all to a whole: exciting an immediate and absolute complacency, without intervenence, therefore, of any interest, sensual or intellectual.*"

> The Mystics meant the same, when they define beauty as the subjection of matter to spirit so as to be transformed into a symbol, in and through which the spirit reveals itself; and declare *that* the *most* beautiful, where the most obstacles to a full manifestation have been most perfectly overcome.

In other words, the sense of beauty derives from the intuitive perception of the organic unity of an object (its "Multëity in Unity," its reconciliation of opposites); and the "absolute complacency," from the intuitive perception of that organic unity as a *symbol* of the "Supreme Reality," the unifying spirit (in and behind Nature) which is God.

To understand the interplay of Coleridge's ideas about art, nature, religion, and the relationship each bears to organic unity and the still point, it is essential to understand Coleridge's concept of symbol. *The Statesman's Manual*, in which Coleridge examines the connection between religion, nature, and symbol, describes the latter as

> characterized by a translucence of the special in the individual, or of the general in the special, or of the universal in the general; above all by the translucence of the

eternal through and in the temporal. It always partakes of the reality which it renders intelligible; and while it enunciates the whole, abides itself as a living part in that unity, of which it is the representative. [17]

Coleridge warns that only "a starvling and comfortless religion" is produced by an "idealess philosophy" which does not recognize the meaning or the value of symbol; the difficulty is that the revelations and symbolic truths offered in the Scriptures are considered so obvious as to be ignored:

> Truths of all others the most awful and mysterious and at the same time of universal interest are considered as so true as to lose all the powers of truth, and lie bedridden in the dormitory of the soul, side by side with the most despised and exploded errors.

Because of its accessibility and its seeming obviousness, man also ignores God's second book of Revelation, "the great book of His servant Nature," although it offers literal as well as figurative "correspondences and symbols of the spiritual world."

And the primary revelation, of course, is that of organic unity. In elementary nature, Coleridge finds "the natural symbol of that higher life of reason, in which the whole series (known to us in our present state of being) is perfected, in which, therefore, all the subordinate gradations recur. . . ." In its expression of organic unity, nature symbolizes the spiritual world and its unity. Because it "declares the being and attributes of the Almighty Father," nature also symbolizes that which man must become:

> It seems as if the soul said to herself: From this state hast thou fallen! Such shouldst thou still become, thyself all permeable to a holier power! thyself at once hidden and glorified by its own transparency, as the accidental and dividuous in this quiet and harmonious object [he is

looking at a flower in a meadow] is subjected to the life and light of nature; to that life and light of nature, I say, which shines in every plant and flower, even as the transmitted power, love and wisdom of God over all fills, and shines through, nature! But what the plant is by an act not its own and unconsciously—that must thou make thyself to become. . . .

That is, man must acquire the same transparency, the same qualities of symbol in regard to Divine Nature that the flower, or nature itself, has. Notice the emphasis on "permeable," "quiet," and "harmonious"; the parallel between the light of nature and the light of God; and the paradox of the self that is "at once hidden and glorified"—submerged into unity at the same time that it is radiantly individualized. The emphasis on light, harmony, and a kind of radiant quiescence recurs in Coleridge's poetry. Moreover, the state of the self which he describes as "at once hidden and glorified by its own transparency" is what Eliot would call the state of the individual who has reached "the still point."

How does one reach the Coleridgean still point? How does one attain those qualities of symbol which enable the self to become "at once hidden and glorified by its own transparency"?

In Chapter XII of *Biographia Literaria* Coleridge lays the groundwork for the philosophy which was to unite spirit and matter in such a way that neither would be sacrificed to prove the existence of the other. Philosophy he defines as "the science of BEING," and its postulate is "the heaven-descended KNOW THYSELF!" [18] But "all knowledge rests on the coincidence of an object with a subject." The sum of all that is "OBJECTIVE" Coleridge terms "NATURE," in its passive and material sense; the sum of all that is "SUBJECTIVE" he terms "SELF or INTELLIGENCE." The latter is conceived of as conscious; the former, as without consciousness.

"Truth is correlative to being." But there can be only one

absolute, original truth capable of being proved *a priori*. This Coleridge defines as the principle that "manifests itself in the SUM or I AM; which I shall hereafter indiscriminately express by the words spirit, self, and self-consciousness."

For Coleridge, self-consciousness is "not a kind of *being*, but a kind of *knowing* . . . the highest and farthest that exists for *us*." "In this, and in this alone, object and subject, being and knowing, are identical, each involving and supposing the other." But one must dissolve this identity to become conscious of it; and, by definition, the act of knowing requires the coalescence of an object and a subject. Hence, self-consciousness involves the act of "self-duplication" in which there is a unity of the self-as-subject with the self-as-object. "In the existence, in the reconciling and the recurrence of this contradiction consists the process and mystery of production and life." And, Coleridge suggests, self-consciousness itself "may be the modification of a higher form of being, perhaps of a higher consciousness, and this again of a yet higher. . . ."

Ultimately, "philosophy would pass into religion, and religion become inclusive of philosophy. We begin with the I KNOW MYSELF, in order to end with the absolute I AM. We proceed from the SELF, in order to lose and find all self in God."

"To lose and find all self in God" is equivalent to reaching the still point. To reach that goal and achieve a self "at once hidden and glorified by its own transparency," submerged into unity at the same time that it is radiantly individualized, one must develop that self-consciousness which is the highest kind of knowing. This, we have seen, involves the act of self-duplication, and it is the imagination that makes that act possible, for imagination is the faculty for unifying subject and object, the power that "reveals itself in the balance or reconciliation of opposite or discordant qualities: of sameness, with difference; of the general, with the concrete; the idea, with the image; the individual, with the representative. . . ." [19] Imagination is the "esemplastic power"—a term that Coleridge constructed from the Greek meaning "to shape into one." [20] Imagination is not only the prime agent of human perception; it "dissolves, diffuses, dissipates, in order to recreate." In Chapter XIII of *Biographia Literaria* Coleridge makes his famous distinction between the two "degrees":

> The Imagination then I consider either as primary, or secondary. The primary Imagination I hold to be the living power and prime agent of all human perception, and as a repetition in the finite mind of the eternal act of creation in the infinite I AM. The secondary Imagination I consider as an echo of the former, co-existing with the conscious will, yet still as identical with the primary in the *kind* of its agency, and differing only in *degree*, and in the *mode* of its operation. It dissolves, diffuses, dissipates, in order to recreate: or where this process is rendered impossible, yet still at all events it struggles to idealize and to unify.

Behind Coleridge's definition of the imagination lies the belief "that the productive power, which in nature acts as nature, is essentially one (that is, of one kind) with the intelligence, which is in the human minds above nature." [21] This is "the one Life within us and abroad," or as Wordsworth put it, the "something far more deeply interfused" that dwells in nature and in the mind of man: "A motion and a spirit, that impels/ All thinking things, all objects of all thought,/ And rolls through all things. . . ." [22] What both Coleridge and Wordsworth imply is a kind of "creative unconscious" similar to that which Lawrence describes. [23]

The unconscious is also implied in the union of thought and feeling that Coleridge considers requisite to revelation. "My opinion is thus," Coleridge wrote in 1801 to Thomas Poole: "that deep thinking is attainable only by a man of deep feeling, and that all truth is a species of revelation" [24]—the latter being a product of one's felt thought (here, also, Coleridge anticipates Eliot). The revelation occurs, the truth is perceived when, by means of the imagination, one recognizes nature as a symbol of the "Supreme Reality," becomes "all permeable to a holier power" and merges with the "Supreme Reality," or God.

Though he does not of course define it as such, Coleridge seeks what Eliot terms union with the still point. Eliot elaborates upon the means of reaching the still point; the ecstatic moment is but one of the means. Coleridge, on the other hand, as a Romantic who will never separate "deep feeling" from "deep thinking," seeks the still point *only* in terms of what Eliot calls the ecstatic moment. Joy serves as the bridge between the individual and the still point, for it is joy that activates the imagination (the faculty for unifying subject and object, the perceiver and the perceived) and makes possible the moment in which one is unified with the "Supreme Reality." To exemplify, let me turn now to a group of poems which reaffirm many of the ideas explicitly stated in the above prose writings and constitute Coleridge's fullest poetic expression of the ecstatic moment.

In "Religious Musings: A Desultory Poem, written on the Christmas Eve of 1794," Coleridge affirms: "There is one Mind, one omnipresent Mind,/ Omnific. His most holy name is Love." God is the omnipresent Mind; He is also the source of organic unity, the Supreme Reality "diffused through all, that doth make all one whole."

> 'Tis the sublime of man,
> Our noontide Majesty, to know ourselves
> Parts and proportions of one wondrous whole!
> This fraternises man, this constitutes
> Our charities and bearings. But 'tis God
> Diffused through all, that doth make all one whole;
> This the worst superstition, him except
> Aught to desire, Supreme Reality!

Once it has been awakened by Christ, the "drownséd Soul" is duty-bound to move toward a perfect union with God:

> From Hope and firmer Faith to perfect Love
> Attracted and absorbed: and centered there
> God only to behold, and know, and feel,
> Till by exclusive consciousness of God
> All self-annihilated it shall make
> God its Identity: God all in all!
> We and our Father one!

From the above, one can see that Coleridge's steps toward union are similar to the steps which Eliot urges for those who seek the still point; moreover, Coleridge describes the union *he* seeks—the complete union with God—in terms that might have come from Eliot himself.

"Hymn before Sunrise in the Vale of Chamouni" offers another example of the particular union Coleridge is seeking, as well as the ecstatic moment that leads to it. The poem is an apostrophe to Mont Blanc. Inspired by the immensity and the silence of that "most awful Form," which rises from its "silent sea of pines,/ How silently!" (in contrast to the two rivers which "rave ceaselessly" at its base), Coleridge experiences that ecstatic joy which invariably lifts him to the still point.

> O dread and silent Mount! I gazed upon thee,
> Till thou, still present to the bodily sense,
> Didst vanish from my thought: entranced in prayer
> I worshipped the Invisible alone.
>
> Yet, like some sweet beguiling melody,
> So sweet, we know not we are listening to it,[25]
> Thou, the meanwhile, wast blending with my Thought,
> Yea, with my Life and Life's own secret joy:
> Till the dilating Soul, enrapt, transfused,
> Into the mighty vision passing—there
> As in her natural form, swelled vast to Heaven!

Awake, my soul! not only passive praise
Thou owest! not alone these swelling tears,
Mute thanks and secret ecstasy! Awake,
Voice of sweet song! Awake, my heart, awake!
Green vales and icy cliffs, all join my Hymn.

The poem closes with Coleridge's command to Mont Blanc:

Rise like a cloud of incense from the Earth!
Thou kingly Spirit throned among the hills,
Thou dread ambassador from Earth to Heaven,
Great Hierarch! tell thou the silent sky,
And tell the stars, and tell yon rising sun
Earth, with her thousand voices, praises God.

Significantly, in the above poem, it is the "dread and *silent*
Mount" (italics mine) which inspires Coleridge's ecstatic joy.
For Coleridge, the stillness and silence of nature is not only
conducive to, but a necessary condition for the deep thinking
and deep feeling that produce an ecstatic moment. In "Fears
in Solitude" Coleridge exults that he has found:

A green and silent spot, amid the hills,
A small and silent dell! O'er stiller place
No singing sky-lark ever poised himself.

*   *   *

Oh! 'tis a quiet spirit-healing nook!

The value of nature's silence is that it promotes "a meditative
joy" and enables one to find "religious meanings in the forms
of Nature." But stillness is also necessary in the observer before the effect of nature as a symbol can be felt and the ecstatic
moment experienced. In "Fears in Solitude" the "green and
silent spot" fails to produce the accustomed "meditative joy";
no ecstatic moment is possible, because the observer is too
disturbed by fears of war and thoughts of human suffering to
achieve the kind of peace, the kind of stillness, necessary for experiencing the ecstatic moment that his other poems describe:

> My God! it is a melancholy thing
> For such a man, who would full fain preserve
> His soul in calmness, yet perforce must feel
> For all his human brethren— . . .

"Reflections on Having Left a Place of Retirement" describes the condition necessary for proper receptivity. Speaking of the sky-lark's song, Coleridge says to his beloved:

> . . . "Such, sweet Girl!
> The inobtrusive song of Happiness,
> Unearthly minstrelsy! then only heard
> When the Soul seeks to hear; when all is hush'd,
> And the Heart listens!"

With Coleridge, as with Eliot, "stillness" is used to convey more than one meaning. The stillness of nature may be the absence of sound, or the absence of motion; but in either case the important thing is that it produces an expectant stillness in the soul of the observer. Like Eliot's, also, is the paradox of stillness and ecstasy in the observer who experiences the ecstatic moment. In "This Lime-Tree Bower My Prison," unable to accompany his friends on their walk, Coleridge visualizes their progress and imagines the scenes which, in the past, have left him "silent with swimming sense." It is the ecstatic moment that Coleridge describes—the moment when, "struck with deep joy," he stood "silent with swimming sense"; it is the ecstatic moment that he wishes his friend, Charles Lamb, to experience:

> . . . So my friend
> Struck with deep joy may stand, as I have stood,
> Silent with swimming sense; yea, gazing round
> On the wide landscape, gaze till all doth seem
> Less gross than bodily; and of such hues
> As veil the Almighty Spirit, when yet he makes
> Spirits perceive his presence.

Nature awakens and stirs man's soul in the same way that the breeze stirs the strings of "The Eolian Harp" and in the same way that nature itself is stirred by "The one Life within us and abroad,/ which meets all motion and becomes its soul." Tranquilized and inspired by the stillness of nature ("the mute still air," and "the stilly murmur of the distant Sea" which "tells us of silence"), Coleridge muses:

> And what if all of animated nature
> Be but organic Harps diversely fram'd,
> That tremble into thought, as o'er them sweeps
> Plastic, and vast, one intellectual breeze,
> At once the Soul of each, and God of all?

Again in "The Nightingale" Coleridge uses the harp image to describe nature's awakening, an ecstatic awakening that comes after "a pause of silence," and reflects, in the last lines, the evocation of the ecstatic moment in the poet himself:

. . . and oft, a moment's space,
What time the moon was lost behind a cloud,
Hath heard a pause of silence; till the moon
Emerging, hath awakened earth and sky
With one sensation, and those wakeful birds
Have all burst forth in choral minstrelsy,
As if some sudden gale had swept at once
A hundred airy harps! And she [the "gentle Maid"] hath watched
Many a nightingale perch giddily
On blossomy twig still swinging from the breeze,
And to that motion tune his wanton song
Like tipsy Joy that reels with tossing head.

Awakened like the nightingale, the poet also expresses his ecstatic joy in song.

In an earlier quotation from *The Statesman's Manual* I

pointed to Coleridge's emphasis on the word "permeate," and his emphasis on light. The breeze that sweeps through the lute strings and awakens them is synonymous with the Life that permeates all animated nature; and both are synonymous with "light," and the "intellectual breeze" emanating from God. Compare Coleridge's prose statement of this idea in *The Statesman's Manual* with his poetic expression of the same idea in "The Eolian Harp":

> O what a mine of undiscovered treasures, what a new world of power and truth would the Bible promise to our future meditation, if in some gracious moment one solitary text of all its inspired contents should but dawn upon us in the pure untroubled brightness of an idea, that most glorious birth of the God-like within us, which even as the light, its material symbol, reflects itself from a thousand surfaces, then flies homeward to its Parent Mind enriched with a thousand forms, itself above form, and still remaining in its own simplicity and identity! [26]

> *   *   *

> O! the one life within us and abroad,
> Which meets all motion and becomes its soul,
> A light in sound, a sound-like power in light,
> Rhythm in all thought, and joyance everywhere—

The last quotation is more than the mere statement of an idea, however; it is an intellectualization of the ecstatic moment in which the poet has reached the still point and feels unified with the Spirit which permeates all life. One might go so far as to say that the theory of organic unity that Coleridge consistently applies to life and to art is but an intellectualization of what the poet *feels*, and the truth that the poet recognizes in the ecstatic moment.

In his *Coleridge on Imagination*, I. A. Richards defines the two doctrines concerning the intercourse of the mind with nature:

1. The mind of the poet at moments, penetrating "the film of familiarity and selfish solicitude," gains an insight into reality, reads Nature as a symbol of something behind or within Nature not ordinarily perceived.

2. The mind of the poet creates a Nature into which his own feelings, his aspirations and apprehensions, are projected.[27]

Coleridge's poems exemplify both doctrines; this is particularly true of "The Eolian Harp" for the former, and of "Dejection: An Ode" for the latter. "Dejection: An Ode" presents the negative side of the picture and in its way does more, perhaps, than any other single poem to explain Coleridge's concept of joy and its relationship to the ecstatic moment and to the creativity of the poet. Here, Coleridge sees nature, not as a symbol of the spiritual world, but as a product of his own mind and as a reflection of his own mood:

> O Lady! we receive but what we give,
> And in our life alone does Nature live:
> Ours is her wedding garment, ours her shroud!

Here Coleridge shifts from objective nature, which symbolizes the spiritual and evokes the poet's creativity, to the soul of the poet himself, recognizing that a certain condition of the soul, or a certain power, must pre-exist before the individual is capable of responding to nature as a symbol of anything:

> Ah! from the soul itself must issue forth
> A light, a glory, a fair luminous cloud
>   Enveloping the Earth—
> And from the soul itself must there be sent
>   A sweet and potent voice, of its own birth,
> Of all sweet sounds the life and element!

The soul's "voice" is the creative voice of the poet, and the "light" is the creative force itself, the poet's "shaping spirit of Imagination," which, for Coleridge, is usually brought into play by the sight of nature viewed as a symbol of that organic unity which, emanating from the Divine Spirit, pervades and unifies all. In "Dejection: An Ode," the poet lacks the necessary, pre-existent condition of the soul. He has lost the ability to see nature as a symbol, as he formerly did when he wrote:

> I seem to myself to behold in the quiet objects, on which I am gazing, more than an arbitrary illustration, more than a mere *simile*, the work of my own fancy. I feel an awe, as if there were before my eyes the same power as that of reason—the same power in a lower dignity, and therefore a symbol established in the truth of things. . . . Lo!—with the rising sun it commences its outward life and enters into open communion with all the elements, at once assimilating them to itself and to each other.[28]

As R. H. Fogle observes in his analysis of the poem, what the poet bemoans is his loss of the power of joy, joy and imagination being the "active agencies by which the mind creates, shapes, and unifies its vision of reality."[29] But what is required to bring these "active agencies" into play?

There is a significant parallel, in "Dejection: An Ode," to Toynbee's idea of withdrawal and return, challenge and response, and the eddying of the two opposites as the *basis* of movement and creation. The challenge, when it is not too great, is productive of creation:

> There was a time when, though my path was rough,
>   This joy within me dallied with distress,
> And all misfortunes were but as the stuff
>   Whence Fancy made me dreams of happiness:

But when the challenge is too great (as here the despair is too great), response becomes impossible and the creative power is lost:

> But now afflictions bow me down to earth:
> Nor care I that they rob me of my mirth;
> But oh! each visitation
> Suspends what nature gave me at my birth,
> My shaping spirit of Imagination.

The soul's eddyings are the basis of and the fountain of the mind's shaping, unifying power. At the end of the poem the poet says of the "Lady": "To her may all things live from pole to pole,/ Their life the eddying of her living soul!"

Though Coleridge is often inspired by nature to poetic creation, that inspiration is not possible unless certain conditions exist in the poet's inner self. "I may not hope from outward forms to win/ The passion and the life, whose fountains are within." For the proper condition, what Toynbee would require in the way of eddying forces is what Coleridge would describe as the reconciliation of opposites; and this is not so much a static condition as a balance of opposites, producing a state of tension which, while it seems to be a *still* point, is actually the source of movement. As Eliot says, "At the still point, there the dance is."

In "Dejection: An Ode," the dance, or the idea of movement, is expressed by Coleridge in various ways. Feeling is movement; the static condition to which Coleridge's despair has reduced him is lamented when, after looking at the moon, clouds, and stars, he says: "I see, not feel, how beautiful they are!" [30]

Creation is movement; but for Coleridge, that is dependent upon feeling, an *active* feeling, rather than the despair, the "grief without a pang," which is passive—"A stifled, drowsy, unimpassioned grief." In the past, Nature inspired him by giving an impulse to that active feeling:

Those sounds which oft have raised me, whilst they awed,
  And sent my soul abroad,
Might now perhaps their wonted impulse give,
Might startle this dull pain, and make it move and live!

But the active feeling itself must come from within. Like the clouds "that give away their motion to the stars," Coleridge has given away his motion, his creativity, to a despair, a passive "dull pain" unopposed by any counterbalancing force, and therefore incapable of producing motion.

Joy is movement; it *is* the active feeling that counterbalances distress, activates the imagination, unifies one with Nature, and produces creativity:

> O pure of heart! thou need'st not ask of me
> What this strong music in the soul may be!
> What, and wherein it doth exist,
> This light, this glory, this fair luminous mist,
> This beautiful and beauty-making power.
>   Joy, virtuous Lady! Joy that ne'er was given,
> Save to the pure, and in their purest hour,
> Life, and Life's effluence, cloud at once and shower,
> Joy, Lady! is the spirit and the power,
> Which wedding Nature to us gives in dower
>   A new Earth and new Heaven,
> Undreamt of by the sensual and the proud—
> Joy is the sweet voice, Joy the luminous cloud—
>   We in ourselves rejoice!
> And thence flows all that charms or ear or sight,
>   All melodies the echoes of that voice,
> All colours a suffusion from that light.

"That voice" is the creative voice of the poet, and "that light" is the combined power of imagination and joy, which Mr. Fogle calls the "active agencies, by which the mind creates, shapes and unifies its vision of reality." By counterbalancing distress and producing a pregnant stillness, a state of tension, joy moves the imagination, which, in turn, enables the poet to apprehend the natural world and its organic unity as a symbol of the spiritual world and the absolute unity of God. The recognition of nature's symbolic meaning intensifies his joy, inducing "deep, heartfelt, inward joy," [31] the Ecstatic Joy that lifts one to the still point, where one experiences momentary union with the "Supreme Reality" that is God. Coleridge must reach something approximating this still point in order to create, and the experience is in turn reflected *in* the creation, in his description of the ecstatic moment as it appears, for example, in the poems already discussed.

It is the combined power of joy and imagination that enables the poet to create his vision of reality; the combined power of joy and imagination which enables the self to merge with the "Supreme Reality"—to become "at once hidden and glorified by its own transparency." That the Coleridgean concepts of joy and imagination are inextricably linked is to be expected, for Coleridge is the man who believes deep feeling essential to deep thinking and insists that "all truth is a species of revelation."

Without joy, the imagination lies dormant. Without joy, the poet is incapable of responding to the outside world; without imagination, incapable of perceiving its symbolic meaning. It is joy that, "wedding Nature to us," makes it possible for the poet's imagination to recreate heaven and earth.[32] It is joy combined with imagination which, in the figure of "light" especially, is made almost synonymous with the creative force that Coleridge also described in terms of light in the passages already quoted from *The Statesman's Manual*. Joy and imagination—when Coleridge speaks of the one, he generally implies the other. But inextricably linked though they be, all hinges upon joy, the initiating power. In the poems previously discussed, it is joy which dominates the passages that reflect the ecstatic moment. In "The Night-

ingale" the bird perches giddily, "like tipsy Joy that reels
with tossing head." In "The Eolian Harp" the poet, when he
has reached the still point, reflects his experience in the lines:

> O! the one life within us and abroad,
> Which meets all motion and becomes its soul,
> A light in sound, a sound-like power in light,
> Rhythm in all thought, and joyance everywhere—

There is a noticeable parallel between certain ideas contained in Eliot's definition of the still point and Coleridge's
idea of contending opposites as the source of creation and
movement; by way of emphasis, let me again quote the lines
in which Coleridge's "Dejection: An Ode" laments the loss,
not of mirth itself, but of mirth or joy as a counterbalancing
of distress, the sort of balanced opposition that made him
creative before, and the lack of which leaves him static and
uncreative now:

> There was a time when, though my path was rough,
>   This joy within me *dallied* with distress,
> And all misfortunes were but as the stuff
>   Whence Fancy made me dreams of happiness:
> For hope grew round me, like the twining vine,
> And fruits, and foliage, not my own, seemed mine.
> But now afflictions bow me down to earth;
> Nor care I that they rob me of my mirth;
>   But oh! each visitation
> Suspends what nature gave me at my birth,
>   My shaping spirit of Imagination. (*italics mine*)

As the activator of the imagination, and thus the source of
movement, insight, and creativity, as well as the power that
unites one with Nature and God, joy is the finest thing that
Coleridge can wish for the "Lady" at the end of the ode:

Joy lift her spirit, joy attune her voice;
To her may all things live from pole to pole,
Their life the eddying of her living soul!
O simple spirit, guided from above,
Dear Lady! friend devoutest of my choice,
Thus mayest thou ever, evermore rejoice.

The union that Coleridge seeks—oneness with the "Supreme Reality," or God—is achieved when the individual not only recognizes nature as a symbol but *feels* himself become a symbol of the spiritual world and an integral part of its organic unity. The feeling and the revelation of its meaning occur when the poet experiences what Eliot terms the ecstatic moment; herein lies the only way in which Coleridge can reach the kind of still point he is seeking. And the bridge from the individual to the ecstatic moment and the still point is joy.

NOTES

[1] *The Philosophical Lectures, Hitherto Unpublished*, ed. K. Coburn, pp. 376-377.

[2] See "The Author's Address to the Reader," *Aids to Reflection*, in *The Complete Works of Samuel Taylor Coleridge*, ed. William Shedd, I, 111.

[3] E. K. Chambers, *Samuel Taylor Coleridge*, p. 310.

[4] See Coleridge's "Confessions of an Inquiring Spirit," Shedd, V, 576, 606; ed. posthumously by H. N. Coleridge, this is a collection of "Seven letters to a Friend concerning the bounds between the right, and the superstitious use and estimation of the Sacred Canon." Concerning the Divinity of the Bible, Coleridge advises one to accept as sacred all but the parts or passages "as seem to you irreconcilable with known truths, and at variance with the tests given in the Scriptures themselves. . . ."

[5] John H. Muirhead, *Coleridge as Philosopher*, p. 60.

[6] For detailed studies of these principles, see Alice D. Snyder, *The Critical Principle of the Reconciliation of Opposites as Employed by Coleridge;* and Gordon McKenzie, *Organic Unity in Coleridge.* For historical development, see James V. Baker, *The Sacred River: Coleridge's Theory of the Imagination;* and James Benziger, "Organic Unity: Leibniz to Coleridge," *PMLA*, LXVI (1951), 24-48.

[7] See *Aids to Reflection*, Shedd, I, 359.

[8] *Coleridge's Shakespearean Criticism*, ed. T. M. Raysor, I, 231.

[9] *The Friend*, Shedd, II, 91. Like D. H. Lawrence, Coleridge considered love a manifestation of the "tendency to re-union" and defined it as "a desire

of the whole being to be united to some thing, or some being, felt necessary to its completeness. . . ." (*Coleridge's Shakespearean Criticism*, II, 142.)

10 From Coleridge's marginal notes on Kant's *Allgemeine Naturgeschichte*, quoted by J. H. Muirhead, *Coleridge as Philosopher*, p. 86.

11 Shedd, I, 386; subsequent passage, p. 387; for quotations in paragraph following, see p. 391.

12 *The Friend*, Shedd, II, 434.

13 Shedd, I, 393, for this and preceding quotation; passage following, pp. 393-394.

14 *The Table Talk and Omniana of Samuel Taylor Coleridge*, Oxford ed., pp. 416-417.

15 For this and quotations in the following discussion, see Coleridge's third essay "On the Principles of Genial Criticism Concerning the Fine Arts," *Samuel Taylor Coleridge: Selected Poetry and Prose*, ed. Elizabeth Schneider, pp. 373-374, 375, 376, 379, 380.

16 "All harmony," Coleridge says in a selection from *Table Talk*, "is founded on a relation to rest—on relative rest. Take a metallic plate, and strew sand on it; sound a harmonic chord over the sand, and the grains will whirl about in circles, and other geometrical figures, all, as it were, depending on some point of sand relatively at rest. Sound a discord, and every grain will whisk about without any order at all, in no figures, and with no points of rest." Here, as in the reference to the magnet, and the figure of the mid-point between two poles, Coleridge seems to anticipate the metaphorical form as well as certain metaphysical aspects of Eliot's still point concept. See Schneider, p. 465.

17 For passages in following discussion, see Shedd, I, 437-438, 434, 461, 463, 461, 462.

18 For quotations in this paragraph, see Shedd, III, 335, 342, 344; in two paragraphs following, see pp. 349, 347, 349, 348.

19 *Biographia Literaria*, Ch. XIV, Shedd, III, 374.

20 See *Biographia Literaria*, Ch. X, Shedd, III, 272; passage following, pp. 363-364.

21 *The Friend*, Shedd, II, 449.

22 "The Eolian Harp," l. 26; "Tintern Abbey," ll. 96-102.

23 Coleridge was perhaps more aware of this implication than we realize, for he praised Shakespeare for "directing self-consciously a power and an implicit wisdom deeper than consciousness." *Coleridge's Shakespearean Criticism*, I, 224.

24 *Letters of Samuel Taylor Coleridge*, ed. E. H. Coleridge, I, 351.

25 Cf. "The Dry Salvages," Part V, where Eliot speaks of "music heard so deeply/ That it is not heard at all, but you are the music/ While the music lasts." In both of the moments described, one finds a fusion of thought and feeling, the perceiver and the perceived; and a revelation of the eternal in the temporal. And in Eliot's case, the moment described offers one of the "hints and guesses" leading to the still point.

[26] Shedd, I, 450-451.

[27] I. A. Richards, *Coleridge on Imagination*, p. 145.

[28] *The Statesman's Manual*, Shedd, I, 462.

[29] R. H. Fogle, "The Dejection of Coleridge's Ode," *ELH*, XVII (1950), 75.

[30] As Coleridge explains in Chapter XVII of *Biographia Literaria* (Shedd, III, 409), it is "the property of passion . . . to set in increased activity." Thus Coleridge, like Lawrence, condemns "the thinking disease . . . in which the feelings instead of embodying themselves in *acts*, ascend and become materials of general reasoning and intellectual pride." (*Anima Poetae: From the Unpublished Note-Books of Samuel Taylor Coleridge*, ed. E. H. Coleridge, p. 143.)

[31] Coleridge makes an implicit distinction between two levels or degrees of joy, just as Eliot distinguishes between the two kinds of still points. There is a lesser "joy," a term that indicates a more superficial or secular emotion; then there is a "deep, heartfelt, inward joy" (see the poem "To Nature"), which indicates a religious emotion, the ecstatic joy that lifts one to *the* still point. Such is the "joy" to which Coleridge refers in the lines above.

[32] In "The Lake Poets in Somersetshire," *Transactions of the Royal Society of Literature of the United Kingdom*, 2d series, XX (1899), 120, E. H. Coleridge says: "Coleridge had a shorter name for this indispensable condition of creative genius. He called it joy, meaning thereby not mirth or high spirits, or even happiness, but a consciousness of entire and therefore well being, when the emotional and intellectual faculties are in equipoise."

3

Yeats and His System

The end for art is the ecstasy awakened by the presence
before an ever-changing mind of what is permanent in
the world, or by the arousing of that mind itself into the
very delicate and fastidious mood habitual with it when
it is seeking those permanent and recurring things. There
is a little of both ecstasies at all times, but, at this time
we have a small measure of the creative impulse itself,
of the divine vision . . . perhaps because all the old
simple things have been painted or written, and they will
only have meaning for us again when a new race or a new
civilization has made us look upon all with new eye-
sight.[1]

It was Yeats's recognition of a modern "Waste Land" and
his attempts to recapture something of "the divine vision"
that permitted Eliot to describe him as "one of those few
whose history is the history of our own time, who are a part
of the consciousness of their age, which cannot be understood
without them."[2] Yeats not only shared the general disillusionment of his age, he pioneered in the use of myth as a way of
bringing order and tradition into a chaotic and traditionless

world. For Yeats, like Eliot, looked upon the transition from the Middle Ages to the present as one in which the "whole" man had been lost.

> Somewhere about 1450, though later in some parts of Europe by a hundred years or so, and in some earlier, men attained to personality in great numbers, "Unity of Being," and became like a "perfectly proportioned human body," and as men so fashioned held places of power, their nations had it too, prince and ploughman sharing that thought and feeling. . . . Then the scattering came, the seeding of the poppy, bursting of pea-pod, and for a time personality seemed but the stronger for it.[3]

The apparent strengthening of "personality" did not last, however, and as time went on both society and the individual personality became more and more fragmented. Looking back upon the world he himself grew up in, Yeats says:

> Doubtless because fragments broke into even smaller fragments we saw one another in the light of bitter comedy, and in the arts, where now one technical element reigned and now another, generation hated generation, and accomplished beauty was snatched away when it had most engaged our affections. One thing I did not foresee, not having the courage of my own thought: the growing murderousness of the world.

His use of myth and his later development of a system was, then, Yeats's personal protest against the growing chaos of his world, and his personal solution to the problems of unity and coherence that so plague the modern artist; for the "system" was simply a way of ordering experience so as to provide himself with a firm foundation, a frame of reference for his art Writing to Edmund Dulac in 1937, after completing the second edition of *A Vision*, Yeats says:

I do not know what my book will be to others—nothing perhaps. To me it means a last act of defense against the chaos of the world, & I hope for ten years to write out of my renewed security.[4]

In his need for and consequent emphasis upon unity, pattern, and tradition, Yeats is, as Eliot has termed him, representative of his age. It was this need coupled with a firm belief in the dualistic nature of the universe, and some distinctly Yeatsian theories regarding art, personality and self-expression, the imagination and the passions, that led to the final development of the "system." Of the basic ideas involved, first and foremost is tradition, the cornerstone of Yeats's system as well as a kind of substitute for religion. In the 1927 autobiography Yeats writes:

> I was unlike others of my generation in one thing only. I am very religious, and deprived by Huxley and Tyndall, whom I detested, of the simple-minded religion of my childhood, I had made a new religion, almost an infallible church of poetic tradition, of a fardel of stories, and of personages, and of emotions, inseparable from their first expression, passed on from generation to generation by poets and painters with some help from philosophers and theologians. I wished for a world, where I could discover this tradition perpetually, and not in pictures and in poems only, but in tiles round the chimney-piece and in the hangings that kept out the draught. I had even created a dogma: "Because those imaginary people are created out of the deepest instinct of man, to be his measure and his norm, whatever I can imagine those mouths speaking may be the nearest I can go to truth." When I listened they seemed always to speak of one thing only: they, their loves, every incident of their lives, were steeped in the supernatural.[5]

Like Eliot, Yeats sees both the individual man and the individual work of art as a product of and continuation of the past. In "First Principles," written in 1904, Yeats asserts that "art, in its highest moments, is not a deliberate creation, but the creation of intense feeling, of pure life; and every feeling is the child of all past ages and would be different if even a moment had been left out." [6] Later, in the 1938 autobiography:

> Supreme art is a traditional statement of certain heroic and religious truths, passed on from age to age, modified by individual genius, but never abandoned. The revolt of individualism came because the tradition had become degraded, or rather because a spurious copy had been accepted in its stead. Classical morality—not quite natural in Christianized Europe—dominated this tradition at the Renaissance, and passed from Milton to Wordsworth and to Arnold, always growing more formal and empty until it became a vulgarity in our time. . . . But Anarchic revolt is coming to an end, and the arts are about to restate the traditional morality. [7]

As Sir William Rothenstein notes in *Scattering Branches*, Yeats had no use for extreme individualism. "He held the reaction against tradition to be tiresome. We have to accept the conditions we find in our time; within their discipline we can still remain free enough to be ourselves." [8]

He was equally impatient of cosmopolitanism in literature, for he believed that the writer's tradition has its roots in his own racial and national heritage. This explains Yeats's intense nationalism, his continued use of Celtic lore and Celtic themes, and his condemnation of Irish writers who ignore their heritage. "Creative work has always a fatherland." "Whenever an Irish writer has strayed away from Irish themes and Irish feeling, in almost all cases he has done no more than make alms for oblivion. There is no great literature without nationality, no great nationality without literature." [9]

As with Eliot, Yeats's belief in tradition led him to defend a class, as opposed to a classless, society, and to elevate both the aristocracy and the peasantry above the middle class, which he came to despise; for the aristocracy offered a family tradition and the peasantry a folklore tradition, whereas the middle class offered nothing beyond material values. And like James, he emphasized the necessity of wealth for the maintenance of an aristocracy and the making of a gentleman:

> Ireland has grown sterile, because power has passed to men who lack the training which requires a certain amount of wealth to ensure continuity from generation to generation, and to free the mind in part from other tasks. A gentleman is a man whose principal ideas are not connected with his personal needs and his personal success.[10]

Closely allied to his need for tradition is Yeats's desire for pattern and ritual; ritual appealed to his sense of tradition, and pattern—like tradition—offered a defense against a chaotic world. He regretted the passing of pre-Raphaelitism, and objected to Henley's poetry and to the current use of *vers libre;* what Yeats wanted was a metrical form offering a definite pattern, and *that* rooted in past tradition.

> With the exception of some early poems founded upon old French models I disliked his [Henley's] poetry, mainly because he wrote in *vers libre*, which I associated with Tyndall and Huxley, and Bastien-Lepage's clownish peasant staring with vacant eyes at her great boots; and filled it with unimpassioned description of an hospital ward where his leg had been amputated. I wanted the strongest passions, passions that had nothing to do with observation, and metrical forms that seemed old enough to have been sung by men half-asleep or riding upon a journey.[11]

Both in life and in art Yeats demanded "a deliberate shaping of all things."[12] And, as with Eliot, his insistence upon tradition, pattern, and ritual was but the manifestation of a more basic desire for unity—so were his efforts toward a politically and culturally united Ireland.

> A conviction that the world was now but a bundle of fragments possessed me without ceasing. . . . I had been put into a rage by the followers of Huxley, Tyndall, Carolus Duran and Bastien-Lepage, who not only asserted the unimportance of subject whether in art or literature, but the independence of the arts from one another. Upon the other hand, I delighted in every age where poet and artist confined themselves gladly to some inherited subject matter known to the whole people, for I thought that in man and race alike there is something called "Unity of Being," using that term as Dante used it when he compared beauty in the *Convito* to a perfectly proportioned body.[13]

Comparing the "old" with the "new" art of 1909, Yeats observes:

> The old art, if carried to its logical conclusion, would have led to the creation of one single type of man, one single type of woman; gathering up by a kind of deification a capacity for all energy and all passion, into a Krishna, a Christ, a Dionysus; and at all times a poetical painter, a Botticelli, a Rossetti, creates as his supreme achievement one type of face, known afterwards by his name. The new art can create innumerable personalities, but in each of these the capacity for passion has been sacrificed to some habit of body or of mind. . . . Some limiting environment or idiosyncrasy is displayed; man is studied as an individual fact, and not as that energy which seems measureless and hates all that is not itself. It is a powerful but prosaic art, celebrating the "fall into division" not the "resurrection into unity."[14]

What Yeats wanted was a politically and culturally united people, out of which would come an art expressing their "Unity of Being"; and what could better serve these ends than their inherited folklore or mythology?

> Have not all races had their first unity from a mythology, that marries them to rock and hill? We had in Ireland imaginative stories, which the uneducated classes knew and even sang, and might we not make those stories current among the educated classes, rediscovering for the work's sake what I have called "the applied arts of literature," the association of literature, that is, with music, speech, and dance; and at last, it might be, so deepen the political passion of the nation that all, artist and poet, craftsman and day-labourer would accept a common design? [15]

When one remembers Yeats's emphasis upon the folk elements of tradition and their association with the supernatural, one can see the direction in which Yeats was going and the way in which his search for pattern, tradition, and unity led him first to myth, then from myth to the occult and the supernatural. In order to understand that transition, however—a transition that led him away from general concepts which he shares with men like Eliot to concepts that are purely Yeatsian—one must consider Yeats's theory of art in relation to the passions, symbolism, and the imagination.

Early in his youth, Yeats decided that if one set down the thoughts and emotions that occurred in a moment of passionate intensity, they would be, not an expression of ego, but an expression of truth. The idea came to him upon reading some newspaper verses in which a dying emigrant, returning from political exile, described Ireland's shores:

> They had moved me because they contained the actual thoughts of a man at a passionate moment of life, and when I met my father I was full of the discovery. . . .

Personal utterance, which had almost ceased in English
literature, could be as fine an escape from rhetoric and
abstraction as drama itself. But my father would hear of
nothing but drama; personal utterance was only egotism.
I knew it was not, but as yet did not know how to explain the difference. I tried from that on [sic] to write out
of my emotions exactly as they came to me in life, not
changing them to make them more beautiful.

From this, Yeats developed the theory that the impersonal is
to be reached by exhausting personal emotion, and that it is
the transition from personal to impersonal that produces art.
Speaking of "the strange, precocious genius of Beardsley,"
Yeats asks:

Does not all art come when a nature, that never ceases
to judge itself, exhausts personal emotion in action or
desire so completely that something impersonal, something that has nothing to do with action or desire, suddenly starts in its place, something which is as unfore-
seen, as completely organized, even as unique, as the
images that pass before the mind between sleeping and
waking?

Eventually, Yeats's belief in the inseparability of art and the
passions became so fixed that he could make this categorical
statement: "It is not permitted to a man, who takes up pen
or chisel, to seek originality, for passion is his only business. . . ." [16]

For Yeats, symbolism is as essential to great art as the passions; one of the chief reasons for his strong feeling of kinship
with Blake is that the latter had been "the first writer of
modern times to preach the indissoluble marriage of all great
art with symbol." [17]

Goethe has said, "Art is art, because it is not nature!"
It brings us near to the archetypal ideas themselves, and
away from nature, which is but their looking-glass.

Art brings one closer to the archetypal ideas by means of symbol, which Yeats—like Coleridge—is careful to distinguish from allegory:

> A symbol is indeed the only possible expression of some invisible essence, a transparent lamp about a spiritual flame; while allegory is one of many possible representations of an embodied thing, or familiar principle, and belongs to fancy and not to imagination: the one is a revelation, the other an amusement.

Both a product of and a stimulator of the imagination, the symbol reveals "a part of the Divine Essence."

> All art that is not mere story-telling, or mere portraiture, is symbolic, and has the purpose of those symbolic talismans which mediaeval magicians made with complex colours and forms, and bade their patients ponder over daily, and guard with holy secrecy; for it entangles, in complex colours and forms, a part of the Divine Essence.

As the passages on symbolism clearly indicate, Yeats shares a cardinal tenet of the Romantics, belief in the supremacy of the imagination. Nowhere is this more evident than in the essays entitled *Ideas of Good and Evil*, which appeared in 1903. The title itself, taken from a group of lyrics that Blake had intended to call "The Ideas of Good and Evil," emphasizes Yeats's acceptance of the Blakean concepts. Blake held that Reason created Ugliness and the other evils, in contradistinction to Imagination, which he associated with Beauty, goodness, and divinity. Similarly, Yeats's essays condemn the reasoning faculty and exalt the imagination. Evil is equated with that quality of the modern mind which has killed the old, imaginative beliefs in magic, folk legends, and superstitions; good is equated with imagination, and Blake's theory of the imagination hailed as a momentous discovery.

> He had learned from Jacob Boehme and from old al-
> chemist writers that imagination was the first emanation
> of divinity . . . and he drew the deduction, which they
> did not draw, that the imaginative arts were therefore
> the greatest of Divine revelations. . . .

"The Philosophy of Shelley's Poetry" again asserts the
supremacy of the imagination over reason. Referring to his
own boyhood discussions of philosophy and the "one un-
shakeable belief" he had even then, Yeats says:

> I thought, so far as I can recollect my thoughts after so
> many years, that if a powerful and benevolent spirit has
> shaped the destiny of the world, we can better discover
> that destiny from the words that have gathered up the
> heart's desire of the world, than from historical records,
> or from speculation, wherein the heart withers. Since
> then I have observed dreams and visions very carefully,
> and am now certain that the imagination has some way
> of lighting on the truth that the reason has not, and
> that its commandments, delivered when the body is still
> and the reason silent, are the most binding we can ever
> know.

The above passage reveals Yeats's growing tendency toward the occult and provides the link between his theories of
imagination and symbol and his simultaneously developed
theories of the Great Mind and the Great Memory. First of
all there is the suggestion that, to function perfectly, the
imagination must be freed, must be able to act independently;
and second, the implication that this freedom is to be obtained by a trance-like suspension of movement and thought.
Later, in *Per Amica Silentia Lunae*, Yeats states these ideas
explicitly.

Meanwhile, *Ideas of Good and Evil*, pointing the way toward
the later work, includes an essay on "Magic," which sums
up Yeats's theories about the Great Mind and Great Memory,

as he had then worked them out, and shows their relationship to his concept of imagination and symbol. Yeats begins by stating his belief in three doctrines which have been the "foundations of nearly all magical practices" from early times:

> (1) That the borders of our minds are ever shifting, and that many minds can flow into one another, as it were, and create or reveal a single mind, a single energy.
>
> (2) That the borders of our memories are as shifting, and that our memories are a part of one great memory, the memory of Nature herself.
>
> (3) That this great mind and great memory can be evoked by symbols.

Speaking of two visions that he and some friends had experienced simultaneously during an earlier experiment in the evocation of spirits, Yeats describes the sharing of visions as proof of the imagination's power to shape many minds into a single energy or force, and eventually concludes that the imagination seeks to "remake the world according to the impulses and patterns" of the Great Mind and the Great Memory.

Since Yeats had long believed that all emotions are part of an unending stream similar to that which forms the Great Memory, it is not surprising to find him arguing that whatever the emotions or passions of man have centered about, becomes a symbol in the Great Memory, and a real power in the hands of the artist able to evoke it:

> I cannot now think symbols less than the greatest of all powers whether they are used consciously by the masters of magic, or half unconsciously by their successors, the poet, the musician and the artist. At first I tried to distinguish between symbols and symbols, between what I called inherent symbols and arbitrary symbols, but the

distinction has come to mean little or nothing. Whether their power has arisen out of themselves, or whether it has an arbitrary origin, matters little, for they act, as I believe, because the great memory associates them with certain events and moods and persons. Whatever the passions of man have gathered about, becomes a symbol in the great memory, and in the hands of him who has the secret, it is a worker of wonders, a caller-up of angels or of devils.

It is here that one finds the greatest divergence between Yeats and other symbolist writers. For Coleridge (indeed, for Blake, also) the symbol is a kind of translucent medium for revealing the complex truths that lie behind or beyond nature. For Eliot, and for other modern symbolists, the symbol becomes a kind of "objective correlative," which serves both to unify the poetic work and to objectify the various mental and emotional states that the work presents. For Yeats, however, the symbol has, in addition to its traditional functions, all the powers of a magic charm capable of calling forth spirits and images from the past—spirits and images which dwell in the Great Memory and have, for him, an independent existence of their own.

From the first, Yeats had been drawn to the supernatural, particularly as expressed in ancient myths and stories. And when his conviction that all races attain their first unity from a mythology led him to study Irish folklore and popular poetry in an effort to further the national and literary unity of his country, what he learned was that the people of Ireland, the peasant class, "cannot separate the idea of an art or a craft from the idea of a cult with ancient technicalities and mysteries."

In addition to his studies of folklore and folk magic, Yeats had, during his formative years, experimented with, first, theosophy, then cabalism, and later, spiritualism. All combined to reinforce his natural love of ritual and to stimulate his search for some sort of mystical system by which he could explain and unify an otherwise chaotic world.

It was during the period from 1885 to 1890 that Yeats joined the two societies that had the greatest influence upon his work: the Theosophical Society of Madame Blavatsky, and the Hermetic Students of the Golden Dawn. Madame Blavatsky's group drew upon the wisdom of the East in an attempt to combine science, religion, and philosophy; and its four basic tenets, especially those regarding incarnation and polarity, reaffirmed some of Yeats's deepest beliefs. The theosophists' cardinal tenets were belief in "an Omnipresent, Eternal, Boundless, and Immutable Principle on which all speculation is impossible"; a universal law of polarity and a world understood as a conflict of opposites; the identity of all souls with a Universal Oversoul; an inescapable cycle of incarnation and spiritual evolution.[18] The Hermetic Students, on the other hand, combined Rosicrucianism and Christianity and followed the European practice of cabalistic magic, studying various symbols designed to call forth visions (not spirits). One will immediately recognize the elements which Yeats transferred from theosophy to his final "system," and from cabalism to his theory of symbols.

Per Amica Silentia Lunae (1918), which contains the clearest statements of Yeats's beliefs up to the 1925 publication of *A Vision*, explains the gradual emergence of his concepts of the Great Mind and the Great Memory.

> I have always sought to bring my mind close to the mind of Indian and Japanese poets, old women in Connaught, mediums in Soho, lay brothers whom I imagine dreaming in some mediaeval monastery the dreams of their village, learned authors who refer all to antiquity; to immerse it in the general mind where that mind is scarce separable from what we have begun to call "the subconscious."...[19]

In addition to his conscious attempt to immerse himself in the general thought stream of the past (by "murmured evocations"), Yeats discovered that, unconsciously, there came to him images which had also appeared to others whose works he had not previously read:

> Before the mind's eye whether in sleep or waking, came images that one was to discover presently in some book one had never read, and after looking in vain for explanation to the current theory of forgotten personal memory, I came to believe in a great memory passing on from generation to generation. But that was not enough, for these images showed intention and choice. They had a relation to what one knew and yet were an extension of one's knowledge.

Eventually Yeats came to think of the Great Memory as something very similar to what Jung has described as "the collective unconscious." [20] Yeats saw it as a kind of repository for archetypal ideas and images produced by the Great Mind. To receive the ideas or images, the whole vision, one must suspend both will and intellect so as to allow the imagination full reign; for it is the imagination that frees the personal unconscious (which Yeats terms the "subconscious"), enabling it to merge with "the collective unconscious" and thus draw up from the latter the complete vision of which it possesses only a fragment. For Yeats, at least, the completed vision or image was set apart from mere products of the imagination by the shock of revelation, "that sudden luminous definition of form. . . ."

> If you suspend the critical faculty, I have discovered, either as the result of training, or, if you have the gift, by passing into a slight trance, images pass rapidly before you. If you can suspend also desire, and let them form at their own will, your absorption becomes more complete

and they are more clear in colour, more precise in articulation, and you and they begin to move in the midst of what seems a powerful light. . . . You have discovered how, if you can but suspend will and intellect, to bring up from the "subconscious" anything you possess a fragment of. Those who follow the old rule keep their bodies still and their minds awake and clear, dreading especially any confusion between the images of the mind and the objects of sense; they seek to become, as it were, polished mirrors.

I had no natural gift for this clear quiet, as I soon discovered, for my mind is abnormally restless; and I was seldom delighted by that sudden luminous definition of form which makes one understand almost in spite of oneself that one is not merely imagining.[21]

One will immediately notice the similarity between the state of being at the Yeatsian moment of revelation—a condition Yeats would like to, but cannot often achieve—and the state of being Eliot describes at the moment of revelation which puts one in contact with the still point. Yeats has here achieved by means of trance a condition that Eliot achieves by means of ecstasy.

There is another very important similarity between Yeats and Eliot, a concept Yeats shares with Eliot, as well as with Romantics such as Blake and Coleridge; that of a dualistic world composed of opposites, which Eliot reconciles at the still point, and which Yeats makes the basis of his system as it appears in *A Vision*.

Yeats's dualistic concept of the universe is more than a belief; it is a reflection of conflicts within his own personality. As Richard Ellmann effectively argues in *Yeats: The Man and the Masks*, much of Yeats's work can be explained by the basic conflict within himself between the dreamer and the man of action; in his stories and plays, for example, his own self-division is often projected into such opposing pairs of characters as John Sherman and the Reverend William Howard, Michael Robartes and Owen Aherne. In "Estrangement, Extracts from a Diary Kept in 1909," Yeats acknowledges his vacillation between the life of action and the life of contemplation:

> I cry continually against my life. I have sleepless nights, thinking of the time that I must take from poetry . . . and yet, perhaps, I must do all these things that I may set myself into a life of action and express not the traditional poet but that forgotten thing, the normal active man.[22]

Again, in a poem significantly entitled "Vacillation," Yeats writes: "BETWEEN extremities/ Man runs his course." The "extremities" (or "antinomies," as he later defines them) that alternately attracted Yeats include not only action and contemplation, life and art, but also the simple and the complex, the subjective and objective, the ideal and the actual, the natural and the supernatural.

Yeats's vacillating point of view is nowhere more obvious than in three of his better-known poems: "A Dialogue of Self and Soul," "Sailing to Byzantium," and "Byzantium." In the first, alternating stanzas are allotted to "The Soul" and to "The Self," the spiritual world of *being* as opposed to the materialistic world of *becoming;* but the arguments are inconclusive. "The Self" is allowed the last (which is also the longest) speech, an affirmation of life and the world of becoming; but even this cannot be taken as a definite conclusion since "The Soul" and "The Self" have an equal number of speeches beginning with the former. One cannot be sure whether Yeats, by permitting "The Self" to have the final word, is indicating a conclusion or merely balancing the argument.

"Sailing to Byzantium" and "Byzantium," on the other hand, both deal with the conflict between art and life, but draw opposite conclusions. In the first, and earlier, poem Yeats contrasts the changing and imperfect world of nature with the changeless and perfect world of art, intellect, and spirit. His concluding stanza is a rejection of nature for the perfection of art, a rejection of the flawed and impermanent for the flawless, permanent world that the golden bird symbolizes.

> Once out of nature I shall never take
> My bodily form from any natural thing,
> But such a form as Grecian goldsmiths make
> Of hammered gold and gold enamelling
> To keep a drowsy Emperor awake;
> Or set upon a golden bough to sing
> To lords and ladies of Byzantium
> Of what is past, or passing, or to come.

Yeats's repeated use of Byzantium as a setting for and a symbol in his poetry reflects his own yearnings for unity and perfection; he is drawn to Byzantium and its golden age because he feels that they represent a kind of unity and perfection such as the world has never known before or since:

> I think if I could be given a month of Antiquity and leave to spend it where I chose, I would spend it in Byzantium a little before Justinian opened Saint Sophia and closed the Academy of Plato. . . .
> I think that in early Byzantium, maybe never before or since in recorded history, religious, aesthetic and practical life were one, that architect and artificers—though not, it may be, poets, for language had been the instrument of controversy and must have grown abstract—spoke to the multitude and the few alike. The painter, the mosaic worker, the worker in gold and silver, the illuminator of sacred books, were almost impersonal, almost perhaps without the consciousness of individual design, absorbed in their subject-matter and that the vision of a whole people.[23]

In his second poem dealing with Byzantium, however, Yeats is more interested in life and its imperfect manifestations of the ideal than in the ideal itself. The "dome" in the first stanza is a symbol for the transcendental world of the spirit; as such,

> A starlit or a moonlit dome disdains
> All that man is,
> All mere complexities,
> The fury and the mire of human veins.

In like manner, the golden bird of stanza two, a symbol for the perfect, changeless world of art, disdains the common bird and scorns:

> In glory of changeless metal
> Common bird or petal
> And all complexities of mire or blood.

However, Yeats does not, as in the earlier Byzantine poem, reject the world of nature for its opposite. Instead, he centers his attention and admiration upon the human artificers, the "smithies" who can, by a creative act of the imagination, "Break bitter furies of complexity" and forge from materials of the time world that which is timeless and enduring. Here, in contrast to the first Byzantine poem, Yeats is more concerned with the workman's act of creation than with the object created. What is important is the creative act of the imagination by which the human artist triumphs over the imperfect time world and creates an object belonging to the perfect, changeless world of art.[24]

> Astraddle on the dolphin's mire and blood,
> Spirit after spirit! The smithies break the flood,
> The golden smithies of the Emperor!

Thus the poem becomes an acceptance of the physical world, "That dolphin-torn, that gong-tormented sea," and a glorification of the human imagination, which can resolve life's complexities in the creative fire, just as the "blood-begotten spirits" of stanza three resolve those same complexities in "An agony of trance."

Undoubtedly the conflicting desires and conflicting views that Yeats found within himself are partly responsible for his insistence upon a dualistic universe and perhaps explain why his greatest emphasis is usually upon conflict and the meaning of conflict, rather than upon reconciliation. When Hanrahan is on the verge of dying ("The Death of Hanrahan"), he hears "the music of Heaven"; that "music" is the sound of war. Again, when Martin receives his vision of heaven in *The Unicorn from the Stars*, he says that "the battle goes on always, always. That is the joy of Heaven, continual battle." [25]

In *Per Amica Silentia Lunae* one finds the earliest summary of Yeats's ideas concerning the conflict of opposites and the meaning of that conflict. The poem "Ego Dominus Tuus" sets the tone of the book by stating Yeats's theory of the anti-self: that one completes himself by finding his antithesis. Yeats not only believes that one must find his anti-self in order to complete his personality, he also believes that one must assume another self in order to improve his personality. "Active virtue" means the wearing of a mask:

> If we cannot imagine ourselves as different from what we are and assume that second self, we cannot impose a discipline upon ourselves, though we may accept one from others. Active virtue as distinguished from the passive acceptance of a current code is therefore theatrical, consciously dramatic, the wearing of a mask. It is the condition of arduous full life. [26]

"Active virtue" means the struggle between the self one is and the self one wants to be (and therefore deliberately assumes). Such a struggle produces character; it also produces poetry: "We make out of the quarrel with others, rhetoric, but of the quarrel with ourselves poetry." [27] Or to put it another way, as Yeats did in a letter to Dorothy Wellesley, August, 1936:

> We have all something within ourselves to batter down and get our power from this fighting. I have never "produced" a play in verse without showing the actors that the passion of the verse comes from the fact that the speakers are holding down violence or madness—"down Hysterica passio." All depends on the completeness of the holding down, on the stirring of the beast underneath. . . . Without this conflict we have no passion only sentiment and thought. [28]

Since Yeats believed that passion is essential to poetry, it is inevitable that he should define poetry in terms of conflict, a "quarrel with ourselves"; for he saw both passion and personality as outgrowths of opposition. History, also. In "A People's Theatre," an essay published in *The Irish Statesman* in the autumn of 1919, Yeats writes:

> as I read the world, the sudden changes, or rather the sudden revelation of future changes, are not from visible history but from its anti-self. Blake says somewhere in a Prophetic Book that things must complete themselves before they pass away, and every new logical development of the objective energy intensifies in an exact correspondence a counter-energy, or rather adds to an always deepening unanalysable longing. That counter longing, having no visible past, can only become a conscious energy suddenly, in those moments of revelation which are as a flash of lightning. Are we approaching a supreme moment of self-consciousness, the two halves of the soul separate and face to face? [29]

Yeats came more and more to see history in terms of opposite phases, each of which must complete itself before the pendulum swung in the other direction. He was convinced, moreover, that the period which began with the birth of Christ was nearing its end and that "The Second Coming," the antithetical phase, was about to begin. Yeats's second edition of *A Vision* is prefaced by an open letter to Ezra Pound in which he says:

> I send you the introduction of a book which will, when finished, proclaim a new divinity. Oedipus lay upon the earth at the middle point between four sacred objects, was there washed as the dead are washed, and thereupon passed with Theseus to the wood's heart until amidst the sound of thunder earth opened, "riven by love," and he sank down soul and body into the earth. I would have him balance Christ who, crucified standing up, went into the abstract sky soul and body. . . .

> What if Christ and Oedipus or, to shift the names, Saint Catherine of Genoa and Michael Angelo, are the two scales of a balance, the two butt-ends of a seesaw? What if every two thousand and odd years something happens in the world to make one sacred, the other secular; one wise, the other foolish; one fair, the other foul; one divine, the other devilish? What if there is an arithmetic or geometry that can exactly measure the slope of a balance, the dip of a scale, and so date the coming of that something? [30]

A Vision is Yeats's attempt to develop a system that can "exactly measure" the cyclic phases of personal and world history. Based upon the images and concepts Yeats received through the automatic writing of his wife (which began shortly after they were married in 1917), the system hinges upon four basic figures: the cone, the gyre, the wheel, and the sphere. In his first edition of *A Vision* (1925) Yeats explains "the geometrical foundation of the wheel":

A line is the symbol of time, and expresses a movement, symbolizing the emotional subjective mind without extension in space; a plane, cutting the line at right angles, is spatial, the symbol of objectivity and intellect. A gyre is a combination of line and plane, and as one tendency or the other must always be stronger the gyre is always expanding or contracting. The gyre is drawn as a cone *which represents sometimes the individual soul and its history, sometimes general life.* For this cone two cones are substituted since neither the soul of man or nature can be expressed without conflict.[31] (italics mine)

The resulting figure, a gyre composed of two revolving cones, one waxing as the other wanes, thus becomes a symbol of conflicting opposites and their alternating ascendancy. The second, revised edition of 1937 proceeds to a fuller explanation of the wheel and the relationships of the four figures involved. The *smaller* gyres or cycles are seen as phases of a *larger* gyre or wheel representing twenty-eight incarnations, the peak of which is a phase producing temporary "Unity of Being"; and twelve such wheels form a single *great cone*. According to Yeats, the twelve divisions within the great cone may be described as months, wheels, or cones; and all cycles revolve toward a final "Unity of Being," which is achieved upon reaching a "Thirteenth Cone" or "phaseless sphere," signifying one's complete delivery from "the twelve cycles of time and space."

Regarding the Great Wheel of twenty-eight incarnations, Yeats goes on to explain:

> This wheel is every completed movement of thought or life, twenty-eight incarnations, a single incarnation, a single judgment or act of thought. Man seeks his opposite or the opposite of his condition, attains his object so far as it is attainable, at Phase 15 and returns to Phase I again.[32]

Beginning with Phase I, which is described as "complete
objectivity" and "complete plasticity," the soul moves toward the fifteenth incarnation or phase, which is described
as "complete subjectivity" and "complete beauty," then
back to Phase I again, and the cycle is complete. Phase 8 is the
struggle to find personality; Phase 22, the struggle to lose it.
Since they are ideal rather than real states of being, Phases I
and 15 are called "supernatural incarnations"; it is at Phase
15, moreover, that the soul achieves the Unity of Being which
it can perpetually maintain only when it has completed its
various cycles and passed into the "phaseless sphere." At
Phase 15, will and thought, effort and attainment have become one, and the soul's condition is that of an "immovable
trance."

> As all effort has ceased, all thought has become im-
> age. . . . All that the being has experienced as thought
> is visible to its eyes as a whole, and in this way it per-
> ceives . . . all orders of existence. Its own body pos-
> sesses the greatest possible beauty, being indeed that
> body which the soul will permanently inhabit, when all
> its phases have been repeated according to the number
> allotted: that which we call the clarified or Celestial
> Body.[33]

In regard to general history, "A Great Wheel of twenty-
eight incarnations is considered to take, if no failure compels
repetition of a phase, some two thousand odd years, and
twelve such wheels or gyres constitute a single great cone or
year of some twenty-six thousand years." The twelve cycles
constituting the great year or great cone are considered
"months" of the great year:

> The twelve months or twelve cycles can be considered
> not a wheel but as an expanding cone, and to this is op-
> posed another cone which may also be considered as

divided into twelve cycles or months. As the base of each cone has as its center the apex of the other cone the double vortex is once more established.

One cone represents human life; and the other, the "spiritual objective" of that life. When the spiritual objective is attained, man is considered to have reached a thirteenth cycle or "phaseless sphere."

> I shall consider the gyre in the present expanding cone for the sake of simplicity as the whole of human life . . . and the contrasting cone as the other half of the antinomy, the "spiritual objective." Although when we are in the first month of this expanding cone we are in the twelfth of the other . . . and so on, that month of the other cone which corresponds to ours is always called by my instructors the Thirteenth Cycle or *Thirteenth Cone*, for every month is a cone. It is that cycle which may deliver us from the twelve cycles of time and space. The cone which intersects ours is a cone in so far as we think of it as the antithesis to our thesis, but if the time has come for our deliverance it is the phaseless sphere, sometimes called the Thirteenth Sphere, for every lesser cycle contains within itself a sphere that is, as it were, the reflection or messenger of the final deliverance.

The distinction between the "phaseless" or "Thirteenth Sphere" and its corresponding "Thirteenth Cone" is simply a distinction between the ideal and the actual. "The ultimate reality because neither one nor many, concord nor discord, is symbolized as a phaseless sphere, but as all things fall into a series of antinomies in human experience it becomes, the moment it is thought of, what I shall . . . describe as the thirteenth cone."

In the figure of the sphere Yeats had at last found a symbol that gave meaning to the dualistic conflicts he saw everywhere in life, and at the same time provided for their ultimate resolution. "The whole system is founded upon the belief that the ultimate reality, symbolized as the sphere, falls in human consciousness . . . into a series of antinomies." Again, "My instructors identify consciousness with conflict, not with knowledge, substitute for subject and object and their attendant logic a struggle towards harmony, towards Unity of Being." Thus consciousness itself becomes a struggle toward the Unity of Being that one attains by progressing through a series of cyclic phases, or "incarnations," leading to the sphere where all opposites are reconciled, complete unity achieved, and "ultimate reality" experienced.

The further details of Yeats's elaborately contrived and often confusing "system"—with its Four Faculties, Four Principles, tables of dominating parts (Body, Heart, Mind, Soul), each with its period of ascendancy, corresponding to the various cycles of sun and moon—do not concern us here. What is important is the purpose involved: to trace the "history" of the soul, in its struggle toward unity, and to provide for its eventual completion in the "phaseless sphere"—"the final place of rest."

Hitherto, Yeats had seen life in terms of forces that merely alternated their periods of ascendancy; one waxed as the other waned. The development of his system, however, led him to a concept of unity which converts alternation to reconciliation, and changes the wheel, or cycle, into the sphere. Yeats describes just such a conversion in the poem "Chosen":

> I struggled with the horror of daybreak,
> I chose it for my lot! If questioned on
> My utmost pleasure with a man
> By some new-married bride, I take
> That stillness for a theme
> Where his heart my heart did seem
> And both adrift on the miraculous stream
> Where—wrote a learned astrologer—
> The Zodiac is changed into a sphere.

The transformation of the Zodiac signifies that momentary, but perfect unity which two lovers achieve through physical union. Elsewhere, in a letter to Mrs. Shakespear, May 25, 1926, Yeats comments on the similarity between sexual love and the mystic vision: "One feels at moments as if one could with a touch convey a vision—that the mystic vision & sexual love use the same means—opposed yet parallel existences." [34]

Yeats seems to have shared D. H. Lawrence's belief that physical union can lead to mystical union, and that the brief reconciliation it offers is the only one possible between men and women. This is the theme of his later "Crazy Jane" poems, but it is also present as early as 1904 in the play *On Baile's Strand*, when Cuchulain speaks of his former relationship to Aoife:

> I have never known love but as a kiss
> In the mid-battle, and a difficult truce
> Of oil and water, candles and dark night,
> Hillside and hollow, the hot-footed sun
> And the cold, sliding, slippery-footed moon—
> A brief forgiveness between opposites
> That have been hatreds for three times the age
> Of this long-'stablished ground. [35]

The theme reappears in the short poem "Solomon and the Witch," where the world "ends" during the moment of physical union. It is the material world, the world of disunity and conflict, which ends, giving way for the moment to that spiritual or supra-natural world wherein perfect unity is possible and the irreconcilables are reconciled:

> . . . the world ends when these two things,
> Though several, are a single light,
> When oil and wick are burned in one;
> Therefore a blessed moon last night
> Gave Sheba to her Solomon.'

It is the "moment of intensity" that reconciles the irreconcilables and produces spiritual union from a physical one, a moment of intensity "when the ecstasy of the lover and the saint are alike, and desire becomes wisdom without ceasing to be desire." [36] During such a moment, both the lover and the saint are permitted a glimpse of that "divine order" which is visible to the dead and to souls in ecstasy:

> This beauty [Intellectual Beauty], this divine order, whereof all things shall become a part in a kind of resurrection of the body, is already visible to the dead and to souls in ecstasy, for ecstasy is a kind of death.

Since his youth, Yeats had been convinced that both creation and revelation are the products of a single moment of intense feeling or passion. In *Per Amica Silentia Lunae* he had considered, as well, the possibility of attaining complete self-possession (elsewhere called self-realization, or Unity of Being) in a single moment of intensity, a moment of vision, a moment of reality.

> After so many rhythmic beats the soul must cease to desire its images, and can, as it were, close its eyes.
>
> When all sequence comes to an end, time comes to an end, and the soul puts on the rhythmic or spiritual body or luminous body and contemplates all the events of its memory and every possible impulse in an eternal possession of itself in one single moment. That condition alone is animate, all the rest is phantasy, and from thence come all the passions, and some have held, the very heat of the body. [37]

Yeats's works contain many references to such a moment, for example the story of "Hanrahan's Vision." Hanrahan has been plucking rose leaves, which go fluttering down into the valley below; when the moment of vision comes and the spirit of Dervagilla reveals the truth about herself and her dead lover, Hanrahan screams.

But a little below the edge of the rock, the troop of rose leaves still fluttered in the air, for the gateway of Eternity had opened and shut again in one beat of the heart.[38]

In the preceding passage Yeats not only emphasizes the time element of the revelation—a single, intense moment—but, like Eliot, suggests that reality is too much for humankind to bear. In "The Death of Synge: Extracts from a Diary Kept in 1909," Yeats is more explicit:

I think that all happiness depends upon the energy to assume the mask of some other self; that all joyous or creative life is a re-birth as something not oneself, something which has no memory and is created in a moment and perpetually renewed. We put on a grotesque or solemn painted face to hide us from the terrors of judgment, invent an imaginative Saturnalia where one forgets reality . . . where one loses the infinite pain of self-realization. Perhaps all the sins and energies of the world are but its flight from an infinite blinding beam.[39]

Two earlier works show how closely Yeats's moment of intensity resembles Eliot's ecstatic moment. The first, "The Heart of Spring," is a story about an old hermit and his servant boy, to whom he explains his lifelong quest for the moment of ecstasy, the moment of reality:

I have sought through all my life to find the secret of life. . . . I read in my youth, in a Hebrew manuscript I found in a Spanish monastery, that there is a moment after the Sun has entered the Ram and before he has passed the Lion, which trembles with the Song of the Immortal Powers, and that whosoever finds this moment and listens to the Song shall become like the Immortal Powers themselves. . . .[40]

The hermit believes that the moment is coming at the close of the first hour of dawn, and as a last request—for he expects to receive eternal youth, thus will need the boy's services no longer—he sends the boy out gathering rushes, lilies, and roses to decorate his house for the occasion. At the appointed hour, "Gradually the birds began to sing, and when the last grains of sand were falling, everything suddenly seemed to overflow with their music. It was the most beautiful and living moment of the year; one could listen to the spring's heart beating in it." The boy runs to his master, but upon finding him dead—a mass of roses and lilies clasped in his arms—concludes that the old man has failed in his quest. Just then, at the window, a thrush begins to sing. Yeats leaves us there, but the implication is that the old man *has* experienced his "moment" and become one with the Immortal Powers; for as Yeats has said elsewhere, the "divine order, whereof all things shall become a part in a kind of resurrection of the body," is visible alike to the dead and to souls in ecstasy, ecstasy itself being a kind of death.

In the play *The Unicorn from the Stars*, Yeats's ecstatic moment is much more clearly defined and its similarity to Eliot's much more obvious. Martin, a dreamer, is given to trance-like comas—a freeing of the spirit from the body—which he describes in terms of ecstasy.[41] Acting upon an incomplete dream or vision, Martin thinks it his mission to effect a Nietzschean "reformation" of the world by destroying all its existing institutions. When his vision is finally completed, he realizes his mistake. His dream is concerned, not with reformation, but with revelation, the kind of revelation that one receives in a "fiery moment."

> I was mistaken when I set out to destroy Church and Law. The battle we have to fight is fought out in our own mind. There is a fiery moment, perhaps once in a lifetime, and in that moment we see the only thing that matters. It is in that moment the great battles are lost and won, for in that moment we are a part of the host of Heaven.

It is by no accident that the moment of ecstasy, of reality, of divine revelation, the moment of transcendence is described as a "fiery" one, for as he indicates in the following passage from *Per Amica Silentia Lunae*, Yeats associates fire with an other-world harmony reconciling all opposites—with the same condition of "rest" that one achieves upon reaching the "phaseless sphere."

> There are two realities, the terrestrial and the condition of fire. All power is from the terrestrial condition, for there all opposites meet and there only is the extreme of choice possible, full freedom. And there the heterogeneous is, and evil, for evil is the strain one upon another of opposites; but in the condition of fire is all music and all rest.[42]

The "fiery moment" in which one becomes "a part of the host of Heaven" would be, in Eliot's terms, the moment of intersection of the timeless with time in which one reaches *the* still point, the outside, spiritual center. Yeats seems to have had in mind a concept similar to Eliot's intersection of time and eternity and its attendant unity, for which—prior to *A Vision*—he used that protean symbol of his, the rose.[43] In *The Shadowy Waters*, a play which first appeared in 1911, the rose appears at the point where opposites are reconciled. Forgael says:

> I can see nothing plain; all's mystery.
> Yet sometimes there's a torch inside my head
> That makes all clear, but when the light is gone
> I have but images, analogies,
> The mystic bread, the sacramental wine,
> The red rose where the two shafts of the cross,
> Body and soul, waking and sleeping, death, life,
> Whatever meaning ancient allegorists
> Have settled on, are mixed into one joy.[44]

The 1913 essay "Poetry and Tradition" suggests that the artist must reach a kind of still point, "the trysting-place of mortal and immortal, time and eternity," in order to conceive and recreate that perfect union of opposites which alone produces the "red rose."

> the nobleness of the arts is in the mingling of contraries, the extremity of sorrow, the extremity of joy, perfection of personality, the perfection of its surrender, overflowing turbulent energy, and marmorean stillness; and its red rose opens at the meeting of the two beams of the cross, and at the trysting-place of mortal and immortal, time and eternity. No new man has ever plucked that rose, or found that trysting-place, for he could but come to the understanding of himself, to the mastery of unlocking words after long frequenting of the great masters, hardly without ancestral memory of the like.[45]

The rose symbolizes an absolute unity, an ultimate reality that Forgael is able to see only when there is a "torch" inside his head—that is, during a "fiery moment," a moment of revelation. And the rose opens, blooms, completes its being, only when and where the spiritual and the temporal are united and reconciled—at "the trysting-place" of time and eternity, at "the two beams of the cross." In like manner the soul completes its being when it has reached the "phaseless sphere" where all opposites are reconciled. In Yeats's "system" the concepts formerly symbolized by the rose are incorporated into and further clarified by the symbol of the sphere.

One other symbol has a close connection with Yeats's system and its sphere: that of the dance, which so often appears in Yeats's poetry. At times he uses it, as does Eliot, to indicate patterned movement, at times to indicate joyous energy. On occasion he also associates it with the kind of "immovable trance" that he uses to describe the state of the soul in Phase 15, and with the kind of unity that is represented by the sphere. It is the last two associations that concern us most. In his poem, "Upon a Dying Lady," the woman's soul "flies to the predestined dancing-place." The "predestined dancing-place," of course, brings to mind all that is traditionally associated with a heavenly afterlife—perfect joy, perfect peace, and perfect unity. The concept of unity is again invoked by the symbol of the dance in the much-quoted final stanza of "Among School Children":

> Labour is blossoming or dancing where
> The body is not bruised to pleasure soul,
> Nor beauty born out of its own despair,
> Nor blear-eyed wisdom out of midnight oil.
> O chestnut tree, great rooted blossomer,
> Are you the leaf, the blossom or the bole?
> O body swayed to music, O brightening glance,
> How can we know the dancer from the dance?

The first four lines depict a heavenly or ideal state of balance and unity; the last four shift the focus to life itself with the suggestion that one cannot separate the part from the whole, nor being from becoming, nor body from spirit. In both poems the ideal state associated with the symbol of the dance is that which is elsewhere represented by the sphere.

The fourth stanza of "Byzantium" equates the dance with the trance, which (like the sphere) releases human beings from the conflicts and complexities of earthly life, promoting them from "the terrestrial condition" to "the condition of fire":

> At midnight on the Emperor's pavement flit
> Flames that no faggot feeds, nor steel has lit,
> Nor storm disturbs, flames begotten of flame,
> Where blood-begotten spirits come
> And all complexities of fury leave,
> Dying into a dance,
> An agony of trance,
> An agony of flame that cannot singe a sleeve.

To understand the significance of the trance, one must remember that Yeats considers it a prerequisite to the freeing of imagination from will and intellect so that the individual can receive images coming from the Great Memory. The dance has a similar function. In "Rosa Alchemica," Robartes tells his would-be initiate that before he can complete his initiation and join the secret order he must learn the steps of an ancient dance: "I had to join three times in a magical dance, for rhythm was the wheel of Eternity, on which alone the transient and accidental could be broken, and the spirit set free." [46] Yeats says much the same thing in his 1900 essay on "The Symbolism of Poetry":

> The purpose of rhythm, it has always seemed to me, is to prolong the moment of contemplation, the moment when we are both asleep and awake, which is the one moment of creation, by hushing us with an alluring monotony, while it holds us waking by variety, to keep us in that state of perhaps real trance, in which the mind liberated from the pressure of the will is unfolded in symbols. [47]

Yeats's essay on "The Celtic Element in Literature" suggests another reason why the dance appeals to him as a symbol. The men of ancient times

> worshipped nature and the abundance of nature, and had always, as it seems, for a supreme ritual that tumultuous dance among the hills or in the depths of the woods, where unearthly ecstasy fell upon the dancers, until they seemed the gods or the godlike beasts, and felt their souls overtopping the moon; and, as some think, imagined for the first time in the world the blessed country of the gods and of the happy dead.

By its trance-inducing rhythm the dance serves to prolong the moment of creation, of revelation, of vision—the "fiery mo-

ment"; and its joyous energy leads to that "unearthly ecstasy" which lifts man out of himself into a momentary rebirth as a divine being, allowing him, for the moment, to
experience that Unity of Being which he can permanently
achieve only when he has reached the "phaseless sphere"—
the Yeatsian "still point." This, like Eliot's, is an outside,
spiritual center, permanently reached in Eliot's case by a
Christian way of life; in Yeats's, by a series of incarnations
that eventually free one from the Great Wheel and allow
one's soul to escape into the Great Sphere. What is important
is not the various phases and cycles involved in reaching the
"phaseless sphere," but the metaphysical aspect of the sphere
itself, and the spiritual goal it represents—for this amounts
to a redefinition of what is traditionally described as union
with God.

Mechanically, Yeats's system was simply his way of giving
shape to experience and of maintaining a grasp on reality.
When he had finished the second edition of *A Vision* and completed his system, Yeats had this to say of it:

> now that the system stands out clearly in my imagination
> I regard them [cycles of sun and moon] as stylistic ar-
> rangements of experience comparable to the cubes in the
> drawing of Wyndham Lewis and to the ovoids in the
> sculpture of Brancusi. They have helped me to hold in a
> single thought reality and justice.[48]

Where Eliot used Christian dogma as the basis for his grasp
of reality, Yeats used the occult; where Eliot drew consciously
upon ancient literature and mythology for his symbols, Yeats
used trance, dream, and automatic handwriting as a means of
drawing images from the "Great Memory."

As Yeats explains in the first edition of *A Vision:*

> Some were looking for spiritual happiness or for some
> form of unknown power, but I had a practical object. I

wished for a system of thought that would leave my imagination free to create as it chose and yet make all that it created, or could create, part of one history, and that the soul's.[49]

That history, for Yeats, is the soul's journey through various cycles and phases until it reaches the phaseless sphere, its still point, where, "free and yet fast," it can "sink into its own delight at last." [50]

NOTES

[1] *The Cutting of an Agate*, pp. 95-96.

[2] Quoted by Joseph Hone, *W. B. Yeats: 1865-1939*, p. 514. From an address made in connection with the Dublin Memorial Service held for Yeats following his death in 1939.

[3] *Autobiographies: Reveries over Childhood and Youth, and The Trembling of the Veil* (1927), p. 359; subsequent passage, p. 238.

[4] From an unpublished letter quoted by Richard Ellmann, *Yeats: The Man and the Masks*, p. 291.

[5] *Autobiographies* (1927), pp. 142-143.

[6] *Plays and Controversies*, p. 102.

[7] *The Autobiography of William Butler Yeats, Consisting of Reveries over Childhood and Youth, The Trembling of the Veil, and Dramatis Personae* (1938), pp. 418-419.

[8] *Scattering Branches: Tributes to the Memory of W. B. Yeats*, ed. Stephen Gwynn, p. 51.

[9] *Letters to the New Island*, ed. Horace Reynolds, pp. 74, 103-104.

[10] *Autobiography* (1938), p. 417.

[11] *Autobiographies* (1927), p. 154.

[12] *Cutting of an Agate*, p. 127. It is because they recognized his need for the conscious creation of form or pattern that Yeats's friends could excuse his personal and artistic idiosyncrasies. In his contribution to *Scattering Branches*, Edmund Dulac justifies the elaborate system and occult symbols of Yeats the poet as a "desire for evidence of some sort of order in the world," and defends the "pose" of Yeats the man as part of the ritual by which Yeats sought to identify himself with "the hidden forces that shape our universe," pp. 138-139.

> He came into the room with slow, deliberate steps, his hand raised in a gesture between a salute and a blessing. . . . The raised hand was part of the ritual. Part of the ritual also, his love of the village craftsman, the untrained performer—images in his mind of the types when art sprang from a more intimate contact between the artist and the hidden forces that shape our universe.

[13] *Autobiographies* (1927), pp. 234-235.

[14] *Autobiography* (1938), p. 427.

[15] *Autobiographies* (1927), p. 240; two subsequent passages, pp. 127, 410.

[16] *Per Amica Silentia Lunae*, p. 36.

[17] This and nine subsequent passages are from Yeats's *Ideas of Good and Evil*, pp. 176, 152, 176, 230, 170, 90-91, 29, 68, 65, 13. Yeats shared not only many of Blake's theories about the imagination but also many of his ideas concerning symbols, the passions, and the oppositions of "contraries." This in part explains his long-termed interest in, and feeling of kinship for the poet-engraver; see *The Works of William Blake, Poetic, Symbolic, and Critical*, ed. and interpreted by W. B. Yeats and E. J. Ellis.

[18] See H. P. Blavatsky, *The Secret Doctrine: The Synthesis of Science, Religion, and Philosophy*, I, 14-17.

[19] *Per Amica Silentia Lunae*, p. 45; subsequent passage, p. 50.

[20] In *Wheels and Butterflies*, pp. 107-108, Yeats writes: "We may come to think that nothing exists but a stream of souls, that all knowledge is biography, and with Plotinus that every soul is unique; that these souls, these eternal archetypes, combine into greater units, as days and nights into months, months into years, and at last into the final unit that differs in nothing from that which they were at the beginning: everywhere that antinomy of the One and the Many. . . ."

[21] *Per Amica Silentia Lunae*, pp. 47-49.

[22] *Autobiography* (1938), p. 420.

[23] *A Vision* (2d ed. revised, 1937), pp. 279-280. Future references to *A Vision* will be to the 1937 ed. unless otherwise stated.

[24] For Yeats, the imagination was the mediator between the ideal and the actual. In his preface to Volume I of the Yeats and Ellis edition of Blake, Yeats writes: "In Imagination only we find a Human Faculty that touches nature on one side and spirit on the other. Imagination may be described as that which is sent bringing spirit to nature, entering into nature and seemingly losing its spirit, that nature being revealed as symbol may lose the power to delude."

[25] *Early Poems and Stories*, p. 456; *Collected Plays*, p. 382.

[26] *Autobiography* (1938), pp. 400-401; quoted by Yeats in *Per Amica Silentia Lunae*, p. 28.

[27] *Per Amica Silentia Lunae*, p. 21.

[28] *Letters on Poetry from W. B. Yeats to Dorothy Wellesley*, ed. Dorothy Wellesley, pp. 94-95.

[29] *Plays and Controversies*, pp. 217-218.

[30] *A Vision* (1937), pp. 27, 28-29.

[31] *A Vision* (1925), p. 129.

[32] *A Vision* (1937), p. 81; seven subsequent passages, pp. 136, 202, 209, 210, 193, 187, 214.

[33] In *Collected Poems*, see "The Phases of the Moon"; see also Yeats's use of the fifteenth phase in "The Double Vision of Michael Robartes."

³⁴ *The Letters of W. B. Yeats*, ed. Allan Wade, p. 715.

³⁵ *Collected Plays*, p. 259.

³⁶ *Ideas of Good and Evil*, pp. 70, passage following, p. 101.

³⁷ *Per Amica Silentia Lunae*, pp. 71-72.

³⁸ *Early Poems and Stories*, p. 447.

³⁹ *Autobiography* (1938); p. 429; cf. Yeats's play *The Resurrection* in the scene where the Greek screams when he touches the risen Christ and discovers that He is real.

⁴⁰ *Early Poems and Stories*, pp. 355-356; subsequent passage, p. 358.

⁴¹ In Act I of *The Unicorn from the Stars, Collected Plays*, p. 343, referring to his trick of slipping away in spirit, Martin says: "That is what they call ecstasy, but there is no word that can tell out very plain what it means. That freeing of the mind from its thoughts; when we put those wonders into words, those words seem as little like them as blackberries are like the moon and sun." Subsequent passage, p. 378.

⁴² *Per Amica Silentia Lunae*, pp. 70-71.

⁴³ In the following selections, the rose indicates both the point of intersection and the absolute unity produced by the intersection of time and eternity (the reconciliation of opposites). The Hermetic Students, which Yeats joined in 1890, had the rose as their central symbol; Yeats also used the rose at various times as a symbol of beauty, love, reality, divinity, etc. See Ellmann's *Yeats: The Man and the Masks*, pp. 90-95, for a discussion of the various meanings.

⁴⁴ *Collected Plays*, p. 152. In Act II of *Unicorn from the Stars, Collected Plays*, p. 362, Martin says: "Events that are not begotten in joy are misbegotten and darken the world, and nothing is begotten in joy if the joy of a thousand years has not been crushed into a moment." This is the ecstatic moment, which, as Yeats suggests in "Poetry and Tradition," produces creativity.

⁴⁵ *Cutting of an Agate*, p. 131.

⁴⁶ *Early Poems and Stories*, p. 489.

⁴⁷ *Ideas of Good and Evil*, p. 247; passage following, p. 279. In *Unicorn from the Stars*, Martin associated ecstasy with a trance-like "freeing of the mind"; and in his *Autobiography* (1938 ed., p. 402), Yeats says that ecstasy comes "from the contemplation of things vaster than the individual and imperfectly seen, perhaps, by all those that still live," and suggests that ecstasy may be "some fulfilment of the soul in itself, some slow or sudden expansion of it like an overflowing well."

⁴⁸ *A Vision* (1937), p. 25.

⁴⁹ *A Vision* (1925), p. xi.

⁵⁰ "All Souls' Night: Epilogue to 'A Vision,' " *A Vision* (1937), p. 304.

4

The Jamesian Moment of Experience

Like Yeats and Eliot, Henry James exhibits that attitude of mind we call "modern." For, as Stephen Spender puts it, "beneath the stylistic surface, the portentous snobbery, the golden display of James's work, there lurk forms of violence and chaos. His technical mastery has the perfection of frightful balance and frightful tension: beneath the stretched-out compositions there are abysses of despair and disbelief: *Ulysses* and *The Waste Land*." [1] James himself once acknowledged, "I have the imagination of disaster—and see life indeed as ferocious and sinister." [2]

This "imagination of disaster" is reflected throughout James's work. His novels are usually concerned with destruction in one form or another; and in the conflict of good and evil, it is generally evil that triumphs—at least upon the surface. In *Roderick Hudson*, the artist hero is destroyed by a love of beauty which makes him the victim of an enervating, futile passion, and by an overripe culture that demoralizes what it was supposed to inspire. *The Portrait of a Lady* and *The Awkward Age* depict the inevitable destruction that occurs when a strong personality tampers with the freedom and self-development of a weaker one. In *The Princess Casamassima*, Hyacinth Robinson is pushed to self-destruction by two stronger wills representing subterranean, anarchistic forces that threaten the existing order of society. Newman, *The American*, loses the battle for his chosen wife because, at a crucial point, his sense of honor ties his hands, giving an advantage—and the victory—to the girl's unscrupulously clever family, who oppose him. Isabel Archer is similarly victimized by her husband and his former mistress, who do not hesitate to turn her goodness and innocence to their own ends. Again, Fleda Vetch, in *The Spoils of Poynton*, is hobbled by a moral sense that will not allow her to do as her opponent does and seize what she wants at any cost. Pitted against an unscrupulous adversary, Fleda's defeat is a foregone conclusion; most of James's heroes are similarly doomed. Though the good and the innocent may achieve success in the world of moral beauty, it is usually the evil, the clever and unscrupulous, who win in the material world of the immediate and the tangible. As James himself remarked in a discussion of Turgenev's pessimism,

> Life *is*, in fact, a battle. On this point optimists and pessimists agree. Evil is insolent and strong; beauty enchanting but rare; goodness very apt to be weak; folly very apt to be defiant; wickedness to carry the day; imbeciles to be in great places, people of sense in small, and mankind generally, unhappy. But the world as it stands is no illusion, no phantasm, no evil dream of a night; we wake up to it again for ever and ever; we can neither forget it nor deny it nor dispense with it. We can welcome experience as it comes, *and give it what it demands*, in exchange for something which it is idle to pause to call much or little so long as it contributes to swell the volume of consciousness.[3] (italics mine)

To a rudderless age James offered his aesthetic ideal as a guiding principle; to the individual he offered the goal of a "*cultivated* consciousness"[4] capable of understanding and

serving the aesthetic ideal. The development or extension of
consciousness was to be achieved by what James termed the
"process of vision": the gradual accumulation of separate
moments of experience, "the happy moments of our consciousness" that Nash would save "from the dark gulf," moments
that Vereker and, later, Maggie describe as "pearls on a
string"; a succession of lesser moments leading to the moment
of vision, the moment of full consciousness—a moment of
acute mental and emotional awareness similar to Eliot's timeless moment of illumination. Such is "the final flash of the
light under which he [Marcher] reads his lifelong riddle and
sees his conviction proved." [5]

For a religious ideal James substituted an aesthetic ideal, a
concept involving most if not all of the ideas and attitudes
that the world considers typically Jamesian. What I am here
concerned with is, first, the way in which James's basic ideas
are related to his concept of the aesthetic ideal, and, second,
the way in which the moment of experience is related to the
extension of consciousness and the achievement of the aesthetic ideal.

To begin with, James's dissatisfaction with the present
led him, like Eliot and like Yeats, toward the past. But, unlike Yeats, he rejected regional characteristics in favor of a
general tradition:

> I have not the least hesitation in saying that I aspire to
> write in such a way that it would be impossible to an out-
> sider to say whether I am at a given moment an American
> writing about England or an Englishman writing about
> America . . . and far from being ashamed of such an
> ambiguity I should be exceedingly proud of it, for it
> would be highly civilized. [6]

James's sense of the past and his yearning for lost values
and a lost tradition are everywhere evident. A sense of the
past is the dominant note of the sketches called *English Hours,*

as it is also of its American counterpart, *The American Scene*, wherein James laments the fading of Newport's aristocracy and the loss of Boston's intellectual spirit. James's fiction reflects his sense of the past in both characters and themes. Adam Verver, of *The Golden Bowl*, derives a spiritual satisfaction from his collection of art treasures. In *The Spoils of Poynton*, it is Fleda's appreciation of Poynton's fine old pieces that attracts the attention of Mrs. Gareth and involves Fleda in the battle over their future ownership. And Strether's sacrifice in *The Ambassadors* hinges upon a recently acquired awareness of what old-world Europe has to offer, echoes of "the world of Chateaubriand, of Mme. de Staël, of the young Lamartine: a stamp impressed on sundry small objects, ornaments and relics." [7]

Like Eliot and like Virginia Woolf, James believed that by reaching back to the past and reliving it, one intensifies the present moment. "The Turn of the Screw" shows past evil returning to distort the present; here, James is concerned with the negative effects of the past upon the present. *The Sense of the Past*, which, though unfinished, remains James's most extensive treatment of the subject, offers the positive effects of the past upon the present; here, a contemporary tries to live in the eighteenth century, only to discover that he is better off in his own time, provided that he retains the best of the past to enrich it.

Yet another trait that James shares with Eliot and Yeats is his insistence upon form. His letters to A. C. Benson continually chide his friend for not striving for a tighter form in his lyrics; and he repeatedly urged the young novelist Hugh Walpole to take his art seriously, to concentrate on form and selection, its very essence:

> Don't let anyone persuade you . . . that strenuous selection and comparison are not the very essence of art, and that Form *is* (not) substance to that degree that there is

absolutely no substance without it. Form alone *takes*, and holds and preserves substance. . . .[8]

James actually rejoiced whenever his French translator, Auguste Monod, found his work too difficult to render. When Monod complained of difficulties with *A Small Boy and Others*, James replied:

> The new volume [*Notes of a Son and Brother*] will complete that defiance and express for me how much I feel that in a literary work of the least complexity the very form and texture are the substance itself and that the flesh is in-detachable from the bones! Translation is an effort . . . to *tear* the hapless flesh, and in fact to get rid of so much of it that the living thing bleeds and faints away![9]

James is advancing a theory of organic unity similar to Coleridge's. In fact, James was so obsessed with the idea that he made it the subject of a short story: "The Figure in the Carpet." Vereker cannot explain the meaning of his books, what they are written "for," because his meaning is as much a matter of the form and texture as of the content; that is what he wants his readers to recognize. When questioned about the "secret" of his writing, Vereker says:

> It stretches, this little trick of mine, from book to book, and everything else, comparatively, plays over the surface of it. The order, the form, the texture of my books will perhaps someday constitute for the initiated a complete representation of it.[10]

In art, James saw an opportunity to achieve form, order, and unity—values that his contemporary world denied him. His entire life became the pursuit of artistic perfection; his entire judgment, the application of aesthetic standards. His objection to the "Vox Americana," for example, was its lack of beauty.[11] And for James, the real tragedy of Lincoln's death was the aesthetic loss. Lincoln had a "commanding style," which his successor lacked; Lincoln was a great, therefore beautiful, figure, which Johnson was not. The tragedy, the aesthetic tragedy, lay in the replacement of a man like Lincoln by a man like Johnson: "the immediate harvest of our loss was almost too ugly to be borne—for nothing more sharply comes back to me than the tune to which the 'Esthetic Sense' . . . recoiled in dismay from the sight of Mr. Andrew Johnson perched on the stricken scene." As for the latter's impeachment, James felt that, whatever the public reasons, "the grand inward logic or mystic law had been that we really couldn't go on offering each other before the nations the consciousness of such a presence." [12]

Jamesian novels and Jamesian characters rarely take a stand upon philosophy, religion, or politics. Art is another matter. James not only permitted his people to philosophize about art; he based many of his stories upon questions of art and the artist. F. O. Matthiessen collected an entire volume of such stories (*Stories of Writers and Artists*); and among James's novels are two which examine problems of the artist. James's first successful novel, *Roderick Hudson*, traces the downfall of a young sculptor whose exposure to Rome encourages moral disintegration rather than creativity; qualities essential to him as an artist contribute to his downfall as a man.

The Tragic Muse, written fourteen years after *Roderick Hudson*, deals with the conflict of life and art in another form. Here, the problem is not that of the artist who loses himself by plunging too deeply into life, but the inner conflict of a man who, from the start, is uncertain which life to plunge into, that of the man, or that of the artist. To provide for his family, Nick must be a success in politics, and this involves marriage to his beautiful cousin, Julia Dallow, who has both the money and the political influence necessary to give him his start; once he has made the initial effort, that is, a proposal to Julia, his father's old friend, Mr. Carteret, will provide whatever financial assistance he needs for a *political* career—and make Nick his heir.

Nick is attracted to Julia; to the political world, also. But neither can satisfy the artist in him. "He was conscious of a double nature; there were two men in him, quite separate, whose leading features had little in common and each of whom insisted on having an independent turn at life." [13] After winning the seat at Harsh and announcing his engagement to Julia, Nick feels let down and escapes to his London studio, where he eventually frees himself from the world of politics. Once he has renounced all for art, however, doubts assail him; for "He had incontestably been in much closer relation to the idea a few months before than he was today: it made up a great deal for the bad side of politics that they were after all a clumsy system for applying and propagating the idea."

The truth of the matter, of course, is that Nick is an idealist; in practice, neither politics nor art come up to his expectations. What is worse, Nick realizes that he is merely second-rate; unlike Roderick Hudson, he lacks the genius that would have made him certain of his choice. He is rather like Colby Simpkins in Eliot's *The Confidential Clerk*, and like Colby, makes his final choice in spite of, rather than because of, his limited talent, deciding that it is enough to contribute whatever he can in his own small way. Each man's effort helps, for as Nick has long ago remarked to his sister Biddy, "All art is one." "It's the same great, many-headed effort, and any ground that's gained by an individual, any spark that's struck in any province, is of use and suggestion to all the others. We are all in the same boat." [14]

In *The Tragic Muse*, as in no other book, James preaches the aesthetic ideal. Nick dedicates his life to its pursuit. Nash, the aesthete, is its promoter; as an artist he accomplishes little, but as a mouthpiece for James he is extremely valuable. It is he who persuades Nick to become an artist; and it is he who most often speaks for James himself. To Nick he insists that each man has his own pipe to play; his first duty is to determine which pipe is his, then to play it as best he can. When Nick asks, "And what might your instrument be?" Nash replies, "To speak to people just as I am speaking to you."

Even Nick's cousin Peter serves the aesthetic ideal, by worshiping and promoting Miriam, the actress who symbolizes the aesthetic ideal. She is not only "the Tragic Muse," whom Nick desires to paint; she is an embodiment of the ideal itself, "a rare incarnation of beauty. Beauty was the principle of everything she did and of the way she unerringly did it." Peter finds it "a supreme infallible felicity, a source of importance, a stamp of absolute value. To see it in operation, to sit within its radius and feel it shift and revolve and change and never fail, was a corrective to the depression, the humiliation, the bewilderment of life." [15]

And Nash says of her: "She's a capital girl, and I quite admit that she'll do for a while a lot of good. She will have brightened up the world for a great many people; she will have brought the ideal nearer to them, held it fast for an hour, with its feet on earth and its great wings trembling."

By brightening up the world for a time, Miriam performs a service like that of the novelist. "The great thing to say for them [novelists] is surely that at any given moment they offer us another world, another consciousness, an experience that, as effective as the dentist's ether, muffles the ache of the actual and, by helping us to an interval, tides us over and makes us face, in the return to the inevitable, a combination that may at least have changed." [16]

The kind of escapism one finds in James is the kind Sir Claude describes in *The Confidential Clerk* as "an escape into living,/ Escape from a sordid world to a pure one." [17] It is what Adam Verver hopes to offer the people of American City when he builds the "palace of art": a "release from the bondage of ugliness," and "a monument to the religion he wished to propagate, the exemplary passion, the passion for perfection at any price." [18] Like Sir Claude, Verver is a collector whose artistic appreciation compensates for his lack of creativity and places him, in his own eyes, only a little lower than the original artists themselves. And like Sir Claude's, his aesthetic appreciation becomes a kind of private religion. His joy upon discovering in himself the spirit of the connoisseur is a religious joy; his aesthetic passion burns like a holy flame.

> It was all, at bottom, in him, the aesthetic principle, planted where it could burn with a cold, still flame; where it fed almost wholly on the material directly involved, on the idea (followed by appropriation) of plastic beauty, of the thing visibly perfect in its kind. . . .

Except where art, the aesthetic ideal, and its application are concerned, Jamesian characters seldom reflect their author's ideas, for James was too meticulous a craftsman to reduce his creatures to mere spokesmen for himself. Where they do reflect his aesthetic beliefs (echoing themes from his nonfiction), these beliefs are made an integral part of the characters themselves. That they rarely reflect any particular views upon philosophy, religion, or politics is perhaps because James *had* no particular theories on these matters. As Stuart Sherman notes in "The Aesthetic Idealism of Henry James," James offers "a purely aesthetic criticism of modern society and modern fiction," and approaches all experience with an "aesthetic consciousness." [19] James says as much himself. To H. G. Wells, who remarked that he and James had totally different attitudes toward life and literature, James wrote:

> But I *have* no view of life and literature, I maintain, other than that our form of the latter in especial is admirable exactly by its range and variety, its plasticity and liberality, its fairly living on the sincere and shifting experience

of the individual practitioner. . . . It is art that *makes* life, makes interest, makes importance . . . and I know of no substitute whatever for the force and beauty of its process.[20]

Literary art must "live on" individual experience, individual life; yet James insists that it is art that *"makes"* life—a seeming contradiction which "The Art of Fiction" helps clarify. "The only reason for the existence of a novel," James says here, "is that it does attempt to represent life." It does so by presenting direct, personal impressions: "that, to begin with, constitutes its value, which is greater or less according to the intensity of the impression." [21] And it follows that one must write from experience, for that is where personal impressions are obtained.

> What kind of experience is intended, and where does it begin and end? Experience is never limited, and it is never complete; it is an immense sensibility, a kind of huge spider-web of the finest silken threads suspended in the chamber of consciousness, and catching every air-borne particle in its tissue.

Experience is an attitude of mind, a sensitivity to impressions; in fact, impressions *are* experience—a conclusion that James himself comes to in a succeeding paragraph of the essay:

> The power to guess the unseen from the seen, to trace the implication of things, to judge the whole piece by the pattern, the condition of feeling life in general so completely that you are well on your way to knowing any particular corner of it—this cluster of gifts may almost be said to constitute experience, and they occur in country and in town, and in the most differing stages of education. If experience consists of impressions, it may be said that impressions *are* experience, just as . . . they are the very air we breathe.

To be an artist one must have a sensibility open to impressions and enough imagination to catch their implications, understand their full meaning. The artist must experience, then transmit what James calls "felt life"; [22] for in this way he extends the limits of consciousness so that it, in turn, may become more and more sensitive, more capable of experiencing life.

> His case, as I see it, is easily such as to make him declare that if he were not constantly, in his commonest processes, carrying the field of consciousness further and further, making it lose itself in the ineffable, he shouldn't in the least feel himself an artist. [23]

Life *is* consciousness. [24] Therefore, as James remarked in the letter to H. G. Wells, art *makes* life—by extending consciousness. In fact, as James wrote in his preface to *The American*, the creative process constitutes "the greatest extension, beyond all others, of experience and of consciousness." [25] It also provides the antithesis of chaos. "Oh art, art, what difficulties are like thine; but, at the same time, what consolation and encouragements, also, are like thine? Without thee, for me, the world would be, indeed, a howling desert." [26]

By selection, art imposes order and shape upon raw life, which is "all inclusion and confusion"; searches the unformed mass for its latent values, "the merest grain, the speck of truth, of beauty, of reality," and "in the face of the *constant* force that makes for muddlement," creates that which is eternal, that which is indestructible. [27]

For James, art was all encompassing, all satisfying.

> It appears to me that no one can ever have made a seriously artistic attempt without becoming conscious of an immense increase—a kind of revelation—of freedom. One perceives in that case—by the light of a heavenly ray— that the province of art is all life, all feeling, all observa-

tion, all vision. As Mr. Besant so justly intimates, it is all experience.[28]

As a confirmed believer in what Percy Lubbock calls "the sanctity and sufficiency of the life of art," [29] James felt that since it offers all, art should demand all, that whatever renunciations it requires are justified. To become an artist worthy of the name, one must be willing to dedicate himself as single-mindedly as a priest to his religion.

The duties of the critic are only a little less exacting than those of the artist, for the critic must be a "helper of the artist, a torch-bearing outrider, the interpreter, the brother." Like the artist, he must be sensitive to and a collector of impressions; he must develop his understanding and his perception to "the pitch of passion" in order that he, too, can serve the aesthetic ideal, and "add the idea of independent beauty to the conception of success." [30]

James applies his aesthetic ideal not only to art but to life, for he sees life in terms of art. He requires of the layman the same qualities, the same sacrifices that he demands of the critic and artist, and for the same end: that each serve the aesthetic ideal insofar as he can. The artist must renounce, must free himself for the creation of artistic beauty. The Jamesian character must renounce, must free himself for beauty of action that will lead to beauty of being. "Life's nothing—" says James, "unless heroic and sacrificial." [31] Although Newman possesses information that would most certainly force his prospective in-laws to withdraw their opposition to his suit, he fails to use it; rather than stoop to blackmail, he sacrifices love for honor, surrendering his chosen bride by default. Because of equally fine scruples, Fleda Vetch, when placed in such a position that she cannot with honor retrieve either her love or the "spoils of Poynton," renounces both; and Strether, refusing to benefit from a mission he cannot honestly complete to the satisfaction of those who have sent him, turns his back on a world and a way of life he has just learned to appreciate. In each case, the renunciation is an act of moral beauty, one that exemplifies what Nash described as "the beauty of having been disinterested and independent; of having taken the world in the free, brave, personal way."

James demands of his heroes and heroines what he demands of his artists: an intelligent and imaginative perceptivity, that they may continually extend their limits of consciousness and further their ability to "experience" life. And "Experience," James wrote in his preface to *The Princess Casamassima*, "is our apprehension and our measure of what happens to us as social creatures. . . ." [32]

Where Eliot depends upon Christianity in his approach to reality, and Yeats employs the occult, James turns to a study of human relations. His primary concern is not for a general, outside reality, but for an inner, personal one. His characters' motives, states of mind, degrees of consciousness, are revealed through a central consciousness, which may remain fixed, as in *The Ambassadors*, or may shift from one character to another, as in *The Wings of the Dove* and *The Golden Bowl*. James's "social creatures" come from the upper middle class and belong to the cultured few. They share a similar attitude of mind—James believed culture to be "a matter of attitude quite as much as of opportunity" [33]—and each seeks a similar goal, the chance to develop himself and his consciousness to its fullest: "To be what one *may* be, really and efficaciously . . . to feel it and understand it, to accept it, adopt it, embrace it. . . ." [34]

"To be what one *may* be" requires not only the qualities of mind necessary to "experience" life but the freedom to live fully: financial freedom from the tedious hand-to-mouth struggle of everyday existence, and personal freedom from the interference of others. Very often the two freedoms conflict. In *The Tragic Muse*, Nick is offered financial freedom at the expense of his personal freedom; he must choose between them, knowing that *full* freedom requires both. Kate Croy faces a similar problem in *The Wings of the Dove*. If she wishes to retain her aunt's favor and the financial freedom provided thereby, Kate must reject her penniless lover, of whom her aunt disapproves. Seeking an escape from the dilemma, and a chance to live fully Kate maneuvers in such a way that she sacrifices another's rights, another's freedom, to obtain her own, and thus commits what James considers the greatest of crimes.

"To be what one may be" involves not only the question of freedom but the question of personal identity—what one really is in himself. The inner conflict of Nick Dormer, in *The Tragic Muse*, arises from his own uncertainty as to what he really is, an artist trying to be a politician, or a politician trying to be an artist. Again, in *The Portrait of a Lady*, Madame Merle raises the problem of identity:

> What shall we call our "self"? Where does it begin? Where does it end? It overflows into everything that belongs to us—and then it flows back again. I know a large part of myself is in the clothes I choose to wear. I've a great respect for *things!* One's self—for other people—is one's expression of one's self; and one's house, one's furniture, one's garments, the books one reads, the company one keeps—these things are all expressive.[35]

Because he thinks that no one can completely know another, James presents his characters (to us, and to each other) in such a way as to leave deliberate ambiguities. He acquaints us with his people gradually, by accumulated impressions which lead by degrees toward a further, but never a complete, understanding of his characters.

James was concerned not only with the problem of determining one's real self but also with the problem of *maintaining* that self. He feared any loss of personal identity; for this reason he preserved, in his own life, a kind of aesthetic distance or detachment. In a letter to John Bailey, he once remarked, "I am a mere stony, ugly monster of *Dis*sociation and Detachment." In another letter, he warned Grace Norton not to immerse herself too much in the general mass.

> You are right in your consciousness that we are all echoes and reverberations of the *same*, and you are noble when your interest and pity as to everything that surrounds you, appears to have a sustaining and harmonizing power. Only don't, I beseech you, *generalize* too much in these sympathies and tendernesses—remember that every life is a special problem which is not yours but another's, and content yourself with the terrible algebra of your own. Don't melt too much into the universe, but be as solid and dense and fixed as you can.[36]

The Sense of the Past, one of James's two unfinished novels, was to have dealt with loss of identity. The hero is a young American whose sense of the past is so strong that, for a time, he actually projects himself into it, exchanging identities with one of his ancestors who had longed for the future. His problem becomes the recovery of his own identity, once he has realized how much of himself he has lost by his "immersion."

> He feels, after he has a bit taken things in, the particular things about him, he feels *cut off*, as I say, and lost: he is only too much immersed and associated and identified, and that . . . fills him with an anguish that it seems to him he can neither betray nor supress.

James was at once fearful of immersion and desirous of it; like Strether, he felt that he had missed too much of life by his detachment. In his notebook, one finds James urging himself to "let go," as the only way to experience life fully and "affirm one's self *sur la fin*." [37] And the essence of *The Ambassadors* lies in Strether's advice to Little Bilham: "Live all you can; it's a mistake not to." James offers the same advice to Hugh Walpole, admitting that, in his old age, he regrets "certain occasions and possibilities I didn't embrace." [38]

The desire to experience life and the desire to keep his personal identity intact produced a conflict that James reflects in his works—a fact which Elizabeth Stevenson justifiably emphasizes in her study of James, *The Crooked Corridor*. Referring to the letter warning Grace Norton not to "melt too much into the universe," Miss Stevenson observes:

> His stories bear out this thought. They exhibit a tension between the conscious individual and the raw material of life. That person has two duties in living: the first, to expose himself to as much of the great unconscious force of life as he is able to endure; the second, to hold firm to that irreducible core which is himself, to be what and who he is with all his might. Upon the one hand, there is the assault of the multiplied battery of life; and upon the other, the integrity of the individual; the link between the two being the necessary tension of the personal consciousness. [39]

The Jamesian novel presents the conflict in two forms: the conflict between the individual and a certain tradition or culture, and the conflict between one individual and another. Old-world tradition and old-world culture are necessary for self-development; at the same time they tend either to hinder or distort it. *The American* offers an example of the former, and *Roderick Hudson* an example of the latter. Association with one's fellow creatures is also necessary for one's development, but the association often harms more than it helps, for one person's gain sometimes means another's loss. The loss-gain motif is the main theme in *The Sacred Fount*, and a minor theme in such novels as *The Wings of the Dove*, *The Portrait of a Lady*, and *The Tragic Muse*. Nick Dormer resents the pressure put upon him to choose a career that will bring financial security to his family but cost *him* his freedom; yet when the opportunity arises, he does not hesitate to urge his sister toward an unwanted suitor who is rich enough to provide for the family and thus ensure Nick's release.

What becomes most important in the James novel is the question of *how* one's goal is obtained, and whether it is *deliberately* achieved at another's expense. When Kate's conniving (her insistence that Densher pretend love for the dying heiress) inadvertently hastens Milly's death, Densher refuses to accept the fortune Milly leaves him, even though it would enable him to marry Kate. He is willing to give Kate the money and her freedom, or to marry her without the money; but he will not accept both Kate and the inheritance. For one thing, Milly's noble gesture toward those who have wronged her reveals a moral beauty which Densher now appreciates—so much so, that Kate accuses him of having fallen in love with the dead woman. For another thing, Densher cannot allow himself to benefit from a death he and Kate have hastened. Herein lies James's "aesthetic distinction" between right and wrong.

In an 1865 review setting Edmond Schérer above his fellow critic, Sainte-Beuve, the young James wrote:

> we prefer him because his morality is positive without being obtrusive; and because, besides the distinction of beauty and ugliness, the aesthetic distinction of right and wrong, there constantly occurs in his pages the moral distinction between good and evil; because, in short, we salute in this fact that wisdom which, after having made the journey round the whole sphere of knowledge, returns at last with a melancholy joy to morality.[40]

In two respects, the review foreshadows the mature James: the concept of a morality that is "positive without being obtrusive"; and the tendency to view moral and aesthetic values in terms of one another. Beauty and ugliness become the aesthetic equivalents of good and evil, and eventually the moral act becomes the beautiful one—James's aesthetic ideal applied to conduct and life.

For James the greatest beauty in life is a fully developed consciousness, a state of being in which one has the greatest possible awareness of the aesthetic ideal, its implications, and its applications. Freedom is necessary for the full development of consciousness; freedom is moral beauty. In *The Tragic Muse*, Nash urges his friend to give up politics for art, to be "on the side of beauty." When Nick replies that there will be little beauty if he produces nothing but daubs, Nash answers: "There will be the beauty of having been disinterested and independent; of having taken the world in the free, brave, personal way." [41]

In his study of character and of human relations, James is primarily concerned with a beauty of action which leads to beauty of being; the free act is a beautiful one, and the greatest good is to promote freedom—one's own or another's. When Ralph Touchett leaves his inheritance to Isabel so that she may be free to have a "go" at life, his act is both beautiful and good. The same is true when Milly Theale leaves her money to Densher with the full knowledge that it will enable him to marry another woman. What is beautiful is that each has offered *full* freedom, with no conditions. Mr. Carteret's offer to Nick Dormer is *not* beautiful, because it restricts Nick's personal freedom at the same time that it guarantees his financial freedom—and of the two, James considered personal freedom the more essential to self-development. Significantly, what James appreciated most in his own life was the freedom of self-development that Henry James, Sr., allowed his sons and the "magnanimity" of spirit that made it possible for them "to have all the benefit of his intellectual and spiritual, his religious, his philosophic and his social passion, without ever feeling the pressure of it to our direct irritation or discomfort." [42]

If beauty lies in freedom, and good in the promotion of

freedom, ugliness and evil are just the opposite; the greatest ugliness is a violation of the aesthetic ideal, and the greatest evil a violation of personal freedom. The Jamesian character is guilty of deliberate evil whenever he consciously interferes with another's free development. Dr. Sloper, of *Washington Square*, commits a moral wrong against his daughter by controlling her life—even after his own death—and preventing the only kind of marriage open to her. Evil, in *The Portrait of a Lady*, is represented by Madame Merle and Gilbert Osmond, who deliberately make use of Isabel to supply their illegitimate daughter with a home and a mother, and to guarantee Osmond the money necessary for a life of cultured ease. Opposed to this is Ralph Touchett's action, which gives Isabel the chance to be a free agent—and makes possible her subsequent mistake, her marriage to Osmond. In ironic contrast are the beauty of Ralph's act, the freedom he offers, and the ugliness and tyranny that result from Isabel's misuse of that freedom; the greatest irony lies in Isabel's final realization that she has never really been a free agent at any time, that the decision to marry Osmond was not her own, but something she was maneuvered into by those cleverer than she.

Of all James's novels and characters, none offers a clearer example of Jamesian evil than *The Awkward Age* and Mrs. Brookenham. "Mrs. Brook," as she is called, is suddenly faced with the problem of a daughter too old to be excluded any longer from adult society, but too young for Mrs. Brook's circle, where her naïveté will cramp her mother's style.

To the select, this style represents sophistication, "a fine freedom of mind" that will allow one to discuss anything and anybody. But to Mr. Longdon—a former suitor of Mrs. Brook's mother, and Nanda's would-be benefactor—this style reflects the degeneration of an age that has discarded many cherished values of the past.

Mrs. Brookenham's character reveals itself through her relationships with others and through a series of too-clever moves, which eventually prove her undoing. Her attitude toward her son is one of resigned boredom. That Harold is a monster who pockets whatever money is left lying about, borrows from his mother's friends, and is capable of a subtle but malicious blackmail, in itself reflects the social ambitions and pretenses of a woman who pushes her family into living beyond its means and must therefore "farm" out her children to whoever can be persuaded, or forced, to invite them. When Harold suggests that he would like to come home if he finds he is not wanted at Brander, her only answer is: "*Be* wanted, and you won't find it. You're odious, but you're not a fool."

Mrs. Brook disparages her husband, makes a fool of him in public, and rarely bothers to address him when they are alone. As for Nanda, Mrs. Brook urges early marriage, and encourages the young girl's visits to Tishy Grendon's, well aware of the immoral atmosphere, but anxious to have her daughter out of the way.

Mrs. Brook insists upon keeping the immoral and somewhat flighty Lady Fanny within her group of friends because she thinks Lady Fanny's immoralities and indecisions are amusing. She fences perpetually with the Duchess, the one person she cannot manipulate, and is forced to compete with her for Mitchy, a wealthy bachelor each has determined to secure: the Duchess for her niece, and Mrs. Brook for Nanda. A schemer herself, the Duchess sees through Mrs. Brookenham: "She favors Mr. Mitchett because she wants 'old Van' herself."

When it becomes clear that Nanda favors Van, and that Mr. Longdon will provide the financial assistance that would make Van a possible suitor, Mrs. Brook destroys the girl's chances by suggesting to Van that Nanda is too young, too naïve for him, then reversing herself (when that fails) with the implication that Nanda is not so nice, not so naïve, after all.

It is at Tishy Grendon's, however, that Mrs. Brook most

clearly reveals herself. At Nanda's urging, Mitchy has already married the Duchess' niece; Van has not yet declared himself, nor Longdon come forward with an offer. Mrs. Brook determines to force their hands. Announcing her attention to call Nanda in, keep her at home once more, she plays the situation in a way which convinces Van that Nanda "does know too much," thus is spoiled for him, and convinces Longdon that the girl must be permanently removed from such an immoral environment.

Of all James's novels, *The Awkward Age* comes closest to portraying evil in black and white terms, but even here, the colors shade. The reader cannot dismiss Mrs. Brookenham's motives as entirely selfish, for there is always the possibility of mixed motives, always the suggestion of a genuine concern for Nanda. This deliberate ambiguity is typical of James, who was more than usually aware of the complications involved in the question of good and evil.

To begin with, there is the way good people contribute to evil, sometimes doing the greatest harm where they intend the greatest good. Very often in James's stories the helpful confidant is actually the one who brings about the final catastrophe. By making it financially possible for Roderick Hudson to study art in Europe, his benefactor subjects him to influences that destroy his character and dissipate his talent; later, by pointing out Roderick's selfish neglect of those who love him—in an attempt to step in and protect those involved—he confronts Roderick with such a terrible picture-of-himself-as-others-see-him that the latter sets off for a lone climb in the Alps, where he accidentally, or deliberately, meets his death. Again, in "The Madonna of the Future," the narrator-friend decides that he must destroy Theobald's illusions, must make him see the truth about his painting, but instead of forcing the old painter to live in the present, his friend merely induces a shock which kills him. Similarly, in "The Author of Beltraffio," the narrator-confidant helps bring about the death of Mark Ambient's son; attempting to promote a better understanding of the author's work, the narrator gives Ambient's wife a book which convinces her that it would be better for her son to die than to live under the influence of her husband's pagan ideas.

In addition to harming where they wish to help, good people also contribute to evil simply by permitting it to function. James's one Ibsenesque play, *The Other House*, concerns a woman who drowns the small daughter of the man she loves (a widower), and casts the blame upon her rival. The reaction of the distraught father and his fiancée is typically Jamesian: each assumes the blame and attempts to cover up the deed so that Rose can make her getaway; for each recognizes that insofar as he failed to perceive the evil in Rose and take precautions against it, he has made the crime possible, thus is partly responsible. Similarly, in *The Golden Bowl*, Maggie blames herself for the adultery of the Prince and Charlotte; by her willful ignorance of their former relationship, and her failure to perceive their basic weaknesses, their attraction to each other, and the possibilities involved, she herself placed them in an association that made their adultery all but inevitable.

One must be aware of evil, or become its unwitting tool. Beauty of being requires full consciousness; and full consciousness requires the intelligence, the imagination, and the *willingness* to recognize the existence of ugliness and evil and to admit their necessary involvement with the beautiful and the good. Any lack of these qualities, any attempt to extract from life merely the beautiful or the good, without coming to terms with its opposite, constitutes in itself a kind of sin. Thus, the James character victimized by those cleverer than he, is *not* more sinned against than sinning; his very failure to perceive the true situation makes him share the responsibility for any evil done him.

To the innate moral sense must be added a "cultured" per-

ception—a point James frequently illustrates by opposing
the American and the European. The American has a strong
moral sense but no cultural background; the European, a cultural background as rich as it is degenerate. Prince Amerigo
is very much aware of this difference. Lacking the moral
sense, he has a "fear of being 'off' someday, of being wrong,
without knowing it." He confides his fear to Mrs. Assingham,
but she cannot imagine any "sense" which he does not possess; to this he answers:

> "The moral, dear Mrs. Assingham. I mean, always, as
> you others consider it. I've of course something that in
> our poor dear backward old Rome sufficiently passes for
> it. But it's no more like yours than the tortuous stone
> staircase—half-ruined into the bargain!—in some castle
> of our *quattrocento* is like the 'lightning elevator' in one
> of Mr. Verver's fifteen-storey buildings. Your moral
> sense works by steam—it sends you up like a rocket. Ours
> is steep and slow and unlighted, with so many of the
> steps missing that—well, that it's as short, in almost any
> case, to turn round and come down again." [43]

The American and the European each have something that
the other needs for his further development. *The Ivory Tower,*
James's last, unfinished, novel was to develop a hero who combines the best of both cultures. In most cases, however, James
presents conflict, not amalgamation, and the immediate suf-
ferer, the apparent loser, is usually the American. Christopher
Newman fails to obtain the wife he wants; and Isabel Archer
discovers that instead of being a free agent, she has been most
vilely used. In Jamesian terms, they have gained more than
they lost, however; for their moral sense remains intact and
their very defeat has developed the intelligent perceptivity
they formerly lacked.

In *The Golden Bowl* (to my mind, James's greatest novel
about the problem of good and evil and the conflict between

European culture and the American moral sense), the problem of good and evil is treated with great insight and complexity; and in the conflict between European and American, Maggie triumphs where James's other Americans fail—triumphs because she develops in time the insight required to save herself. In the beginning, Maggie lacks Amerigo's highly cultivated intelligence, his keen perception; the Prince lacks Maggie's strong moral sense. What brings about the novel's situation and bares their Achilles' heels is the reappearance of Charlotte Stant, the Prince's old flame and Maggie's former classmate, a penniless woman of the world in search of a wealthy husband. Her first appearance is for Maggie's wedding; she makes a return visit just when Maggie and her father have each decided that he should remarry. Maggie is worried about her father's loneliness; and Verver is worried about being a burden to his married daughter. Charlotte's arrival solves both their problems—as well as her own.

James devotes Book I to the Prince's gradual involvement with Charlotte; Book II, to Maggie's gradual development, and her handling of the situation once she suspects what is going on. The degree of Charlotte's guilt is never quite clear. She may have begun with good intentions—James refuses to say; but he strongly suggests that she is the huntress throughout, that she deliberately ensnares the Prince, using *his* good intentions as the means of drawing him in. On the eve of his marriage, she persuades the reluctant Prince to help her shop for Maggie's wedding gift, but later admits this was merely an excuse to see him alone. Ironically, it is the golden bowl, which the Prince refuses to let Charlotte buy because it is flawed, that eventually proves Maggie's suspicions about Amerigo and his mistress.

Throughout their involvement, it is Charlotte who makes the first moves. Once married to Verver, she draws the Prince into a friendly conspiracy. Later, she goes to the Prince's quarters alone, on the pretext of discussing their mutual obligation to protect the naïvely innocent Ververs; and when the Prince responds to her altruistic appeal with a hand-clasp, "for the full assurance and the pledge it involved," [44] she retains his hand until the Prince, described as more sensuous than most, responds by drawing her into an embrace. After that, he is lost.

But whatever Charlotte's motives, it is Maggie herself (Mr. Verver merely echoes and confirms Maggie's mistakes) who incurs major responsibility for the Prince's downfall. This is what emerges most clearly in the novel; for, given the weaknesses that are his, and put into the situation in which Maggie places him, the Prince's downfall is inevitable. Maggie fails to realize that her new relationship must alter the old. She expects the relationship with her father to continue as before. Though a married woman, she keeps her old room, and a wardrobe, at her father's house so that she may be as much at home there as ever. Her greatest concern is for her father, not her husband, and she spends the greater part of her time with the former. When she might use her son to strengthen the ties between husband and wife, she uses him instead to renew the bonds between father and daughter. Despite Verver's marriage to Charlotte, Maggie insists upon staying at home with him when he is ill, sending Charlotte to the party in her stead— with the Prince. By dismissing Charlotte's duties as wife, and exaggerating her own as daughter, Maggie robs Charlotte and the Prince of their right to feel needed. The only service they can perform is that of meeting all social obligations so that Maggie and her father can enjoy each other undisturbed. By continually demanding that service, Maggie exposes the Prince where he is most vulnerable, and convinces him that the "sposi" exist only to make life easier for Maggie and her father. Hence, Charlotte and the Prince come to feel that they have a right to whatever life they can make for themselves, as long as they keep the knowledge of it from the Ververs.

In her concern for her father, Maggie fails to recognize what she owes her husband. She makes no attempt to adjust to his needs, although she realizes that the quiet life she and her father lead must seem dull to someone who loves gaiety and society as the Prince does. Maggie's excessive concern for her father, and resulting lack of concern for her husband, spring from an excess of the moral sense which is, in itself, entirely unselfish. But James makes it clear that this moral sense is as much to be condemned as admired when it is unaccompanied by any equivalent sense of perception. Maggie's complete selflessness is inhuman; not only that, she expects others to be as selfless as she. Maggie takes it for granted that the Prince will approve her sacrifice to filial duty. She has never known pain or evil, simply because she has not the intelligence, the imagination, or the willingness to admit their existence. Herein has Maggie brought about her unhappiness.

Maggie might have learned about Charlotte's affair with the Prince when it happened—long before she met Amerigo; but as Mrs. Assingham points out, it was not the sort of thing that one could tell Maggie. "She'd be so frightened. She'd be, in her strange little way, so hurt. She wasn't born to know evil. . . ." [45] Later, in a conversation with her father, Maggie confirms this analysis. She tells him that Charlotte has suffered, has loved and lost, but admits that she is ignorant of the details and wishes to remain so. It is not until her husband commits adultery that Maggie is forced to recognize the *existence* of evil. *That*, for her, is the real shock: "the horror of finding evil seated, all at its ease, where she had only dreamed of good; the horror of the thing hideously *behind*, behind so much trusted, so much pretended, nobleness, cleverness, tenderness. It was the first sharp falsity she had known in her life, to touch at all, or be touched by. . . ."

Maggie's real development begins when pain and jealousy awaken her consciousness—when she becomes aware of both evil and good, ugliness and beauty, and the implications involved. What she has gained is an imaginative, intelligent perception that becomes her salvation. She not only handles the situation so as to preserve appearances—hold together the shattered pieces of the golden bowl—she at last arouses her husband's interest and makes him realize that her goodness is not mere dullness or stupidity; as a result, he is willing to help her pick up the pieces and begin again.

One serves the aesthetic ideal by developing full consciousness. For the artist, this involves an awareness of the implications of things; an awareness of the ugly as well as the beautiful, and the recognition of ugliness and beauty as counterparts. It is because it offers a *full* picture that great art is inspiring.

> To be completely great, a work of art must lift up the reader's heart; and it is the artist's secret to reconcile this condition with images of the barest and sternest reality. Life is dispiriting, art is inspiring; and a story-teller who aims at anything more than a fleeting success has no right to tell an ugly story unless he knows its beautiful counterpart.[46]

For the layman also, full consciousness involves the recognition of beauty and goodness as counterparts of ugliness and evil. Full consciousness occurs—briefly—during the moments when we have the greatest *sense* of life, when we most "experience" life, when our perception is "at the pitch of passion" and we apprehend fully "what happens to us as social creatures." James's moment of experience is a *single* moment of full consciousness, a passing moment of awareness, of insight, of revelation. Taken together, the various moments of experience, the moments of seeing into things, form the process of vision that leads toward the permanent state of full consciousness, which is James's goal for the individual. In his preface to *The Ambassadors*, James wrote: "the business of my tale and the march of my action, not to say the precious moral of everything, is just my demonstration of this process of vision." [47] "It's the very string," Vereker said, "that my pearls are strung on!" For the process of vision is *James's* "figure in the carpet," the "little trick" that stretches from book to book—a matter of form as well as of content. And nowhere is it better exemplified than in *The Golden Bowl;* here, as in no other work, James achieves a perfect amalgamation of form and content, through which he presents his clearest demonstration of the process of vision.

The novel is a gradual revelation, first of the general situation and of the original state of Maggie's consciousness, then of Maggie's gradual awakening through the accumulation of separate moments of experience, moments of an increasing awareness of the implications of things. Each extension of consciousness prepares for the next. Once Maggie experiences her first intuition of evil, her final, full consciousness of evil is inevitable; such is the "process" of vision.

When her husband returns from Matcham, Maggie senses that something is wrong. In the hope of discovering *what* it is that bothers her, and why, she analyzes certain moments that occurred the night of Amerigo's arrival:

> It fell, for retrospect, into a succession of moments that were *watchable* still; almost in the manner of the different things done during a scene on the stage, some scene so acted as to have left a great impression on the tenant of one of the stalls. Several of these moments stood out beyond the others, and those she could feel again most, count again like the firm pearls on a string, had belonged more particularly to the lapse of time before dinner— dinner which had been so late, quite at nine o'clock, that evening, thanks to the final lateness of Amerigo's own advent. [48]

With the conscious effort to deepen her perception, Maggie's growth begins. Lesser moments of experience lead to the great moment of *illumination*, when she achieves full consciousness and perceives the whole vision. In this moment she recognizes not only the full extent of her husband's crime but the full extent of her own. For the first time in her life, Maggie understands the meaning of good and evil.

The Golden Bowl involves more than one process of vision, though Maggie's of course is paramount. Book I is primarily concerned with the reader's process of vision, his awareness of the developing situation; Book II, with Maggie's process of vision, her awareness of a situation that has already developed—and to a lesser extent, with Amerigo's and Charlotte's gradual recognition of Maggie's perceptions.

James is a subtle artist, more interested in the *process* of vision than the final illumination; to detach and analyze the individual moments of "experience" is virtually useless. The meaning is in the pattern, the *succession* of moments; one cannot separate the figure from the carpet. Any second reading of a James novel, however, will reveal the deliberate plotting of lesser moments leading to a great moment of experience, and the "final flash" of light; in each case, the important thing is the state of *full consciousness* that one attains, rather than the particular illumination of a particular situation.

In *The Portrait of a Lady*, one finds Maggie's "pearls on a string," in the succession of moments that lead to Isabel's final understanding of the relationship between Madame Merle and Gilbert Osmond, and the extent to which she has allowed herself to be used. In *The Awkward Age*, primary emphasis is upon the reader's growing perception; this reaches its climax during the scene at Tishy Grendon's, where Van experiences *his* great moment also, realizing at last the kind of woman Mrs. Brookenham is and the kind of crime she has committed. In *The Wings of the Dove* the process of vision culminates, first, in the moment of full consciousness when Milly sees the truth about herself, about Kate, and about Densher; and second, in the moment when Densher finally understands the principle (the aesthetic ideal applied to conduct and life)

which Milly symbolizes, and refuses to accept the money she
has left him.

And James himself has declared of *The Ambassadors* that
"the precious moral of everything" is his demonstration of
the process of vision, which leads, in this case, to the moment
when Strether realizes the truth about Chad's relationship
with Madame de Vionnet. Here, as in the other James novels,
the painful recognition of ugliness and evil is compensated
for by the beauty of full consciousness, in itself an aesthetic
ideal, as well as that state of being which is James's ultimate
goal for the individual.

Full consciousness is "the artistic consciousness," which
alone, James suggests, is capable of such development in a
world "of brutality and vulgarity" and "the so easy non-
existence of consciousness." In "Is There a Life after Death?"
(written in his later years), James asks: "How can there be a
life 'after' for insensible souls not really 'living' here?"
"unless indeed it be pronounced conceivable that the possibility may vary from man to man . . . and that the quantity
or the quality of our *practice of consciousness* may have something to do with it" (italics mine). "The question is of the
personal experience, of course, of another existence; of its being
I my very self. . . ." For "it is my or your sensibility that is
involved and at stake," says James, who decides that the
whole question is one of desire rather than of belief, and admits that he finds it difficult to conceive of the complete ex-
tinction or "disconnection" of a consciousness one has spent
a lifetime developing.[49]

"The large and consecrated consciousness" that James hopes
to preserve is *personal* consciousness (what D. H. Lawrence
calls "mental" consciousness), which is "consecrated" precisely because it serves, and in its absolute form exemplifies an
aesthetic ideal. In James one finds no equivalent of *the* still
point, for there is no outside center. But one does find the
timeless moment of illumination, as well as the other mani-

festations of the still point concept: the concept of a certain absolute, a certain state of being (full consciousness) which alone can contain or reconcile certain opposites; and the insistence upon a conscious way of life (application of the aesthetic ideal to life and art) which alone will enable one to attain the desired state.

Where Eliot offers an outside center, James offers full, personal consciousness as his source of life, vision, and experience; it is his means of reconciling beauty and ugliness, good and evil, and of bridging the gap between the individual and his fellow men, the individual and his world. It is in the Jamesian moment of experience that one is most alive, most real; for where the ecstatic moment leads Eliot to the still point, the Jamesian moment leads to full consciousness, through which one's inner, personal reality is achieved.

Where Eliot offers a metaphysical concept or ideal, James offers an aesthetic one. Where Eliot seeks an outside center, James would develop an inner one, personal consciousness. The kind of immersion that frightened Ralph Pendrel, James resisted to the last, insisting upon the isolated dance, upon preserving the personal identity which Eliot would merge in spiritual union with a God that James could not believe in.

NOTES

[1] Stephen Spender, *The Destructive Element*, p. 98. Spender views James's "snobbery" as an attempt at "imposing on a decadent aristocracy the greater tradition of the past"; see p. 11.

[2] *Letters to A. C. Benson and Auguste Monod*, ed. E. F. Benson, p. 35.

[3] *French Poets and Novelists*, pp. 250-251.

[4] *Notes on Novelists, with Some Other Notes*, p. 124. Experience must not be taken for granted; it demands a "*cultivated* consciousness."

[5] *The Art of the Novel: Critical Prefaces by Henry James*, ed. R. P. Blackmur, p. 247.

[6] *The Letters of Henry James*, ed. Percy Lubbock, I, 141-142.

[7] *The Ambassadors*, p. 170.

[8] *Letters*, II, 237.

⁹ *Letters to Benson and Monod*, pp. 117-118.

¹⁰ *Stories of Writers and Artists*, ed. F. O. Matthiessen, p. 287.

¹¹ See "The Question of our Speech," in *The Question of our Speech; The Lesson of Balzac: Two Lectures*.

¹² *Notes of a Son and Brother*, pp. 430-431, 432.

¹³ *The Tragic Muse*, p. 204; subsequent passage, p. 488.

¹⁴ *Tragic Muse*, p. 16; subsequent passage, p. 309.

¹⁵ *Tragic Muse*, p. 396; subsequent passage, p. 438. The opposition between life and art, and Miriam's significance as a representative of the aesthetic ideal, is further emphasized when Peter asks her to marry him and give up the stage; she protests that she is a "magnificent creature" on stage, but off stage, "a dull, ignorant, third-rate woman" (p. 544).

¹⁶ James, *Notes on Novelists*, p. 345.

¹⁷ See T. S. Eliot, *The Confidential Clerk*, p. 47.

¹⁸ *The Golden Bowl*, Bk. I, pp. 147, 148; subsequent passage, I, p. 200.

¹⁹ Stuart P. Sherman, "The Aesthetic Idealism of Henry James," *On Contemporary Literature*, pp. 235-236.

²⁰ *Letters*, II, 489-490. In *The American Henry James*, Quentin Anderson suggests that James created no philosophical system of his own because he had absorbed his father's and used it, however unconsciously, as a constant frame of reference.

²¹ *The Art of Fiction and Other Essays*, ed. Morris Roberts, p. 8; two subsequent passages, pp. 10-11, 11.

²² In his preface to *The Portrait of a Lady*, James speaks of "the perfect dependence of the 'moral' sense of a work of art on the amount of felt life concerned in producing it." *Art of the Novel*, p. 45.

²³ In *After Days: Thoughts on the Future Life*, contributions by W. D. Howells and others, p. 223.

²⁴ See *Letters*, I, 100, where James treats consciousness as synonymous with life.

²⁵ *Art of the Novel*, p. 29. Notice the similarity between James and Eliot, who defined poetry as a people's "highest point of consciousness, its greatest power and its most delicate sensibility," in *The Use of Poetry and the Use of Ciriticism*, p. 5.

²⁶ *The Notebooks of Henry James*, eds. F. O. Matthiessen and Kenneth Murdock, p. 68.

²⁷ See *Art of the Novel*, pp. 119-120, 149.

²⁸ *Art of Fiction*, p. 17.

²⁹ Percy Lubbock, "The Mind of an Artist," *The Question of Henry James: A Collection of Critical Essays*, ed. F. W. Dupee, p. 56.

³⁰ *Art of Fiction*, p. 218.

³¹ *Letters to Benson and Monod*, p. 23.

³² *Art of the Novel*, pp. 64-65.

³³ *Notes of Son and Brother*, p. 88.

³⁴ *Tragic Muse*, p. 308.

[35] *Portrait of a Lady*, I, 287-288. For a discussion of James's use of possessions to define character, see Edwin T. Bowden, *The Themes of Henry James*, pp. 48-60.

[36] *Letters*, II, 269; and *Letters*, I, 101. In *Henry James*, p. 134, F. W. Dupee says that once James was "Settled in England, a success and on his own, he began to evolve a vast inner structure of habit and scruple which rendered him firm, even hard, wherever he might be touched. It could give way surprisingly at times but it was always there: the sea-wall against a fearful fluidity within."

[37] *Notebooks*, p. 368; preceding passage, p. 106.

[38] *Ambassadors*, p. 149; *Letters*, II, 323.

[39] Elizabeth Stevenson, *The Crooked Corridor: A Study of Henry James*, p. 33.

[40] *Notes and Reviews*, ed. Pierre de Chaignon la Rose, pp. 105-106.

[41] *Tragic Muse*, p. 144.

[42] See *Notes of Son and Brother*, pp. 156-157.

[43] *Golden Bowl*, Bk. I, p. 32.

[44] *Golden Bowl*, Bk. I, p. 316.

[45] *Golden Bowl*, Bk. I, p. 80; subsequent passage, p. 243.

[46] *Notes and Reviews*, pp. 225-226.

[47] *Art of the Novel*, p. 308.

[48] *Golden Bowl*, Bk. II, p. 11.

[49] For preceding quotations, see *In After Days*, pp. 228, 207, 201, 204. James refers vaguely to the "feeling" of being "scented with universal sources" ("quâ imagination and aspiration") and immersed "in the fountain of being," but quickly reduces this experience to "an adventure of our personality" (p. 228).

5

Virginia Woolf's Moment of Reality

In "The Narrow Bridge of Art," which considers the problems of contemporary writers, Virginia Woolf describes "the modern" writer as one who

> follows every thought careless where it may lead him.
> He discusses openly what used never to be mentioned even
> privately. And this very freedom and curiosity are per-
> haps the cause of what appears to be his most marked
> characteristic—the strange way in which things that
> have no apparent connection are associated in his mind.
> Feelings which used to come single and separate do so no
> longer. Beauty is part ugliness; amusement part disgust;
> pleasure part pain. Emotions which used to enter the
> mind whole are now broken up on the threshold.
> For example: It is a spring night, the moon is up, the
> nightingale singing, the willows bending over the river.
> Yes, but at the same time a diseased old woman is pick-
> ing over her greasy rags on a hideous iron bench. She
> and the spring enter his mind together; they blend but do
> not mix. The two emotions, so incongruously coupled,
> bite and kick at each other in unison. But the emotion
> which Keats felt when he heard the song of the nightin-

gale is one and entire, though it passes from joy in beauty to sorrow at the unhappiness of human fate. He makes no contrast. In his poem sorrow is the shadow which accompanies beauty. In the modern mind beauty is accompanied not by its shadow but by its opposite. The modern poet talks of the nightingale who sings 'jug jug to dirty ears'. There trips along by the side of our modern beauty some mocking spirit which sneers at beauty for being beautiful; which turns the looking-glass and shows us that the other side of her cheek is pitted and deformed. It is as if the modern mind, wishing always to verify its emotions, had lost the power of accepting anything simply for what it is.[1]

A "modern" herself, Virginia Woolf felt "that science and religion have between them destroyed belief; that all bonds of union seem broken," and that "it is in this atmosphere of doubt and conflict that writers have now to create." Because she recognized the twentieth century as "an age clearly when we are not fast anchored where we are," her works are riddled with the questions: What is the meaning of life? Who am I? Where am I? What is truth? What is reality? For Mrs. Woolf these eventually become one question: What is reality? And her writings become a study of reality as it is experienced in certain moments of time.

Although Mrs. Woolf's moment of reality is more clearly isolated than James's moment of experience, and metaphysically closer to Eliot's ecstatic moment, there is a definite similarity between the Jamesian moments in which one experiences his greatest sense of living, and the moments in which one experiences his greatest sense of reality; both are moments of a combined, intensely acute, mental and emotional awareness. Like James, Mrs. Woolf is fascinated by "the inexhaustible richness of human sensibility," and sees life in terms of "a myriad impressions," "an incessant shower of innumerable atoms." [2] In "Modern Fiction" she attacks the conventional techniques of Wells, Bennett, and Galsworthy because they fail to "catch" life and the innumerable impressions a single day entails:

> Life is not a series of gig lamps symmetrically arranged; but a luminous halo, a semi-transparent envelope surrounding us from the beginning of consciousness to the end. Is it not the task of the novelist to convey this varying, this unknown and uncircumscribed spirit, whatever aberration or complexity it may display, with as little mixture of the alien and external as possible? . . . Let us record the atoms as they fall upon the mind in the order in which they fall, let us trace the pattern, however disconnected and incoherent in appearance, which each sight or incident scores upon the consciousness. Let us not take it for granted that life exists more fully in what is commonly thought big than in what is commonly thought small. [3]

" 'The proper stuff of fiction' does not exist; everything is the proper stuff of fiction, every feeling, every thought; every quality of brain and spirit is drawn upon; no perception comes amiss."

Both James and Mrs. Woolf attempt to extend the limits of consciousness. James's ultimate goal, however, is an *aesthetic* appreciation of life, which can be achieved only by a consciousness so highly developed that it can "experience" life to the utmost; his "process of vision" is the development of such a consciousness. Mrs. Woolf's goal, on the other hand, is not appreciation but *understanding;* hers is an attempt not merely to experience life but to determine what life or "reality" *is.*

> What is meant by "reality"? It would seem to be something very erratic, very undependable—now to be found

in a dusty road, now in a scrap of newspaper in the street, now in a daffodil in the sun. It lights up a group in a room and stamps some casual saying. It overwhelms one walking home beneath the stars and makes the silent world more real than the world of speech—and then there it is again in an omnibus in the uproar of Picadilly. Sometimes, too, it seems to dwell in shapes too far away for us to discern what their nature is. But whatever it touches, it fixes and makes permanent. That is what remains over when the skin of the day has been cast into the hedge; that is what is left of past time and of our loves and hates. Now the writer, as I think, has the chance to live more than other people in the presence of this reality. It is his business to find it and collect it and communicate it to the rest of us.[4]

Mrs. Woolf spent her life trying to find and collect and communicate this reality. But unlike James, who centers reality in *personal* consciousness, Virginia Woolf goes beyond the inner, subjective reality in search of a broader, objective reality "residing in the downs or sky." Similarly, in her study of human relations and the problem of personal identity—what people really are in themselves—Mrs. Woolf probes a little deeper. Because she believes, like James, that no one can completely "know" another, she, too, presents her characters so as to leave deliberate ambiguities. They are defined, insofar as they can be defined, by their reactions toward others and the reactions of other people toward them; but the responses continually fluctuate and conflict, for one's viewpoint changes from moment to moment, and mood to mood—one's behavior, also. One minute Lily Briscoe considers Mr. Ramsey the greatest man she has ever known, and the most sincere; the next moment, she thinks him petty, egotistical, demanding, and given to self-dramatization. But was it his behavior that changed, or her mood, or both? Since neither the observer nor the observed is static, how can one fix another's personality and say that he is this or that? Mrs. Dalloway has an intuitive understanding of people, and yet, "she would not say of Peter, she would not say of herself, I am this, I am that." And Mrs. Ramsey observes:

> one after another, she, Lily, Augustus Carmichael, must feel, our apparitions, the things you know us by, are simply childish. Beneath it is all dark, it is all spreading, it is unfathomably deep; but now and again we rise to the surface and that is what you know us by.[5]

In James, the ambiguities arise from one person's attempt to know another; rarely from one's attempt to know himself. The Jamesian theme of self-development—"to be what one may be"—is based upon the assumption that the individual can discover what he is. In Virginia Woolf, however, the ambiguities arise as often from the attempt to know oneself, as another. Her characters perpetually ask themselves: Who am I? What am I? To those who complain, as Forster does, that "she could seldom so portray a character that it was remembered afterwards on its own account," Mrs. Woolf would answer that that is precisely her point.[6] She does not allow her characters to emerge in any definitive form because she does not believe that there *is* any answer to the question: Who am I? No fixed delineation is possible: first of all, one's personal self is always changing; and second, that personal self merges with and draws something from other personal selves, past and present.

One of the themes in *A Room of One's Own* is the continuity of consciousness.

> Without those forerunners [early female diarists and letter-writers], Jane Austen and the Brontës and George Eliot could no more have written than Shakespeare could have written without Marlowe, or Marlowe without

Chaucer, or Chaucer without those forgotten poets who paved the ways and tamed the natural savagery of the tongue. For masterpieces are not single and solitary births; they are the outcome of many years of thinking in common, of thinking by the body of the people, so that the experience of the mass is behind the single voice.[7]

The continuity of past and present is also the subject of *Orlando*, an imaginative "biography" of Mrs. Woolf's friend, the poetess Victoria Sackville-West. A sixteen-year-old boy in the Elizabethan Age, Orlando advances from century to century, changing social and literary styles in accordance with the customs of the period, and changing his official duties in accordance with certain facts in the Sackville-West family history. In the eighteenth century, when it is possible for a woman to write professionally (that is, after the advent of Aphra Behn), when it is possible for a woman to exhibit inclinations and characteristics consistent with the character of the present Victoria Sackville-West, Orlando changes from a man into a woman, and finally emerges in the twentieth century.

Virginia Woolf not only believes in the continuity of history, but also in the continuity of human nature. That human nature, despite its outward changes, remains basically the same is a theme of *Orlando* and also of her last novel, *Between the Acts*. In the latter, the continuity of history is suggested by means of a village pageant which interjects scenes from past history into present "scenes" comprised of the spectators themselves; and the continuity of human nature is suggested by Mrs. Swithin, who reads passages from *The Outline of History* which offer a subtle reminder that the prehistoric man is still alive, still "present" in the modern one. The final scene, between the estranged husband and wife, takes place just after Mrs. Swithin has retired to read more about prehistoric man. As the married couple face each other, the room becomes less and less like a room and more and more like a cave. There will be a reunion, suggests the author; they will embrace. "But first they must fight, as the dog fox fights with the vixen, in the heart of darkness, in the fields of night." [8] Like Eliot, Mrs. Woolf believes that the past is eternally present. This is what Bernard means in *The Waves*, when he speaks of "the eternal renewal, the incessant rise and fall and fall and rise again." This is what Eleanor means in *The Years*, when she asks: "Does everything then come over again a little differently?" [9] The past *is* eternally present; but as *Orlando* suggests, Mrs. Woolf is trying to say more than that. She is trying to show that character cannot be "fixed," that the problem of personal identity cannot be solved, precisely because it is a question of more than the immediate self.

The personal or immediate self is a partial one. It must draw something from the past and from other present or personal selves for completion. There is in Woolf's writings a theory of complementary souls; it appears in *Mrs. Dalloway* both as a theory of Clarissa's and as a means of unifying the book. Peter sums up Clarissa's beliefs on the subject:

> It was to explain the feeling they had of dissatisfaction; not knowing people; not being known. For how could they know each other? You met every day; then not for six months, or years. It was unsatisfactory, they agreed, how little one knew people. But she said, sitting on the bus going up Shaftesbury Avenue, she felt herself everywhere; not "here, here, here"; and she tapped the back of the seat; but everywhere. She waved her hand, going up Shaftesbury Avenue. She was all that. So that to know her, or any one, one must seek out the people who completed them; even the places. Odd affinities she had with people she had never spoken to, some woman in the street, some man behind a counter—even trees, or barns. It ended in a transcendental theory which, with her

horror of death, allowed her to believe, or say that she believed (for all her scepticism), that since our apparitions, the part of us which appears, are so momentary compared with the other, the unseen part of us, which spreads wide, the unseen might survive, be recovered somehow attached to this person or that, or even haunting certain places after death . . . perhaps—perhaps.[10]

It is by means of this theory that the two separate strands, the two separate worlds of the book are unified: the normal world of Clarissa, the socialite wife of a Conservative M.P., and the abnormal world of Septimus, the shell-shocked poet. For Clarissa sees Septimus as her complement. When, at her party, she learns of his suicide, she feels the shock of the pavement as though it were her own body that had been thrown from the window. She sees his death as a condemnation of her own life, for he threw away his life to preserve a personal integrity she has sacrificed to "success." It is her disaster, her disgrace; and yet, since he is her counterpart, her complement, it is also her triumph. For by his act, Septimus has kept intact his "privacy of soul," refusing to be remolded to someone else's ideas of "proportion." [11] Septimus has done what Clarissa does not have nerve enough to do; he has upheld a value she cherishes; he has acted for her. He has freed her from her own thoughts of death, made her feel, in the end, triumphant, made her feel the beauty of life. And so she is ready to return to her party, to resume her life, and to exercise her own particular gift—the ability to create social unity in a gathering of isolated individuals.

In *The Waves*, published six years after the appearance of *Mrs. Dalloway*, Mrs. Woolf's theory of complementary souls becomes the actual basis of the novel. Although it is expressed most often by Bernard, the "phrase maker" and spokesman for the group, the descriptive passages preceding each selection not only set the tone for each but confirm its contents in such a way as to make it clear that the author shares the views of her characters.

As Mrs. Woolf uses the term, "the waves" become a protean symbol for the flux and flow of life, the forces of life that pound upon the individual: the individual characters of the book, and the general mass of humanity. The progression of the waves and the changes in their appearance accord with the time of day and parallel the development of the book's characters. When the novel opens, the sea is indistinguishable from the sky; all is merged, unformed. Then, out of the vast sea which, day after day, century after century, continues to form new combinations, the individual waves begin to emerge. When the sun is at its height (temporally, the passages move from sunrise to sunset and from spring to winter), the waves appear separate and distinct; but as the sun begins its gradual decline, the waves seem to mingle and merge with each other in their approach to the shore. Then, as the day closes and night comes on, the sea becomes indistinguishable from the sky again. Finally, at the end of the book, after Bernard has summed up his life and the lives of his friends, the waves break on shore, and the individual peaks dissolve into the sea mass again. In like manner, the six characters progress from simplicity to complexity, to simplicity again, and emerge from impersonality to develop a definite personal identity which, in turn, is finally resolved into impersonality. This is the process to which Bernard refers when he speaks of "the eternal renewal, the incessant rise and fall and fall and rise again." Or, to put it another way, as Bernard does when he thinks of his children as an extension of himself and his own life, "we come up again differently, for ever and ever." Susan expresses the same thought when she thinks of her sons: "I shall go mixed with them beyond my body and shall see India." [12]

It is Bernard, the spokesman, who makes it clear that Mrs. Woolf is talking about more than mere *historical* continuity from generation to generation. There is an overflow of one self into another, a merging of identities that takes place among the living; for what one is, one's personal identity, is not confined to the self inclosed within his body; it includes not only elements from the past but also elements from other living selves who complement and thus confirm it. Bernard says repeatedly, "I am not one person only." And then, more explicitly, in his summing-up he states that which is the real basis, the main theme of the novel:

> Our friends, how seldom visited, how little known—it is true; and yet, when I meet an unknown person, and try to break off, here at this table, what I call "my life," it is not one life that I look back upon; I am not one person; I am many people; I do not altogether know who I am— Jinny, Susan, Neville, Rhoda, or Louis; or how to distinguish my life from theirs.[13]

Speaking of the reunion that the six have had at Hampton Court, Bernard says: "We saw for a moment laid out among us the body of the complete human being whom we have failed to be, but at the same time, cannot forget." The six friends are complementary souls; together, and only together, they make up the complete being that Percival—the well-rounded person, their ideal—symbolized for them while he lived. Each of the six completes some facet in another or supplies some lack. Bernard is the "phrase maker"—sociable, malleable, sympathetic—the "dangling wire" who cannot confine his interests to one idea or one person, and cannot endure solitude; he becomes a novelist who attempts to pattern life by weaving characters and events into stories. Neville, Louis, and Rhoda are "the renegades" who seek solitude. Neville is a perfectionist—intense, studious, fastidious—who seeks an ordered universe, and the love of "one person only"; he satisfies the former need by writing poetry and making

precise grammatical distinctions; the latter, by a succession
of male lovers, to compensate him for the loss of Percival,
for Neville is a man who cannot love women. Louis—intense,
belligerent, the best scholar of them all—is the successful
businessman who cannot find "natural happiness"; driven to
success by an inferiority complex—he comes from Brisbane
and speaks with an Australian accent—he keeps his old attic
room and, when Rhoda leaves him, installs a Cockney mistress who relieves his loneliness but affronts his sense of order
and decency by dropping soiled underclothes about the room.
Like Neville, he desires an ordered universe, but he admires
church and school authority, which Neville despises, and conceives his ordered universe in terms of a historical continuity
that he hopes to, but never does, express in writing. Rhoda is
the dreamer and the escapist who can find no solidity in life
and can achieve no sense of identity. Shy, afraid of people,
she sits apart; drawn to Louis by their mutual sense of inferiority, she lives with him for a time, then leaves him because she "feared embraces"; she, alone of the six, has no
purpose, "no end in view." Susan is the earthy, possessive,
maternal woman who achieves "natural happiness," who
loves and hates with equal intensity, and who wants the love
of one person only; hating the city and seeking a life in harmony with nature, she marries a farmer and shapes her life
according to the rhythm of the seasons. Jinny is the socialite,
the beauty, the dancer, the pure animal who lives entirely in
the world of the body, and who is determined never to be
confined to one person only. Like Bernard, she hates solitude;
she must have people, preferably men, who can give her the
attention and admiration she seeks. Febrile, mischievous,
perpetually dancing, she is in her element in the glitter and
whirl of London, where she flits from one man to another,
determined to enjoy all the physical ecstasy that life can offer.

None of the six is a complete person alone, for one needs
other human beings to round out his partial self and confirm

his sense of identity. Recognizing this, Bernard is grateful to his wife for giving him "that feeling of existing in the midst of unconsciousness." Recognizing this, Rhoda, who hates "all details of the individual life," and who fears personal contacts, returns again and again to join the others, to "go through the antics of the individual." [14] Alone, she slips off the world "into nothingness."

The paradox is that the very thing that the individual seeks, a sense of personal identity, must eventually be overcome if he is to have any real understanding of the larger, objective reality. As David Daiches puts it, in his study of Virginia Woolf, Mr. Ramsey's journey to the lighthouse is essentially a journey from egotism to impersonality: "To reach the lighthouse is, in a sense, to make contact with a truth outside oneself, to surrender the uniqueness of one's ego to an impersonal reality." [15] Similarly, Bernard achieves his final vision of that reality only after "All this little affair of 'being' is over." [16] For, in the final analysis, Mrs. Woolf considers personal identity an illusion—necessary to anyone who would go on living, but nevertheless an illusion which must inevitably dissolve when confronted with impersonal, objective reality.

Nowhere are Mrs. Woolf's views about personal reality more clearly stated than in the eighth section of *The Waves*, the reunion at Hampton Court. After dinner is over, the others wander off, leaving Rhoda and Louis to one of those meditative silences they so often share. During that silence, each experiences one of those moments of (objective) reality which characterize Mrs. Woolf's writings. " 'The still mood, the disembodied mood is on us,' said Rhoda, 'and we enjoy this momentary alleviation (it is not often that one has no anxiety) when the walls of the mind become transparent.' " [17] When the others return, however, the moment is disrupted and Louis and Rhoda are brought back to themselves, forced to resume their personal identities, the illusion which, Louis recognizes, none can live without:

"Something flickers and dances," said Louis. "Illusion returns as they approach down the avenue. Rippling and questioning begin. What do I think of you—what do you think of me? Who are you? Who am I?—that quivers again its uneasy air over us, and the pulse quickens and the eye brightens and all the insanity of personal existence without which life would fall flat and die, begins again."

Rhoda hates this business of *being*. Like Septimus, she feels that society's demands corrupt the soul and rob one of "the white spaces that lie between hour and hour"; but unlike Septimus, she has no real "self" to preserve. No other of Virginia Woolf's characters so emphasizes the necessity of "personal existence"; for Rhoda is the child who sees herself "outside the loop of time," the woman who keeps thinking, "I have no face." [18] She fears the impact of stronger egos; she flees personal contacts. Yet she is forced to seek her kind because they confirm her identity at the same time that they destroy it.

"Alone, I often fall down into nothingness. I must push my foot stealthily lest I should fall off the edge of the world into nothingness. I have to bang my hand against some hard door to call myself back to the body."

Because she has virtually no "self" of her own, Rhoda is always wanting to be Susan, to be Jinny; and because she does not know how to *be*, she copies the way they act, the way they dress. "They have friends to sit by. They have things to say privately in corners. But I attach myself only to names and faces; and hoard them like amulets against disaster."

There are moments, rare moments, when Rhoda feels that, beyond one's reach, some security, some pattern exists; and for the time, her sense of chaos, her fear of nothingness subsides. "But these pilgrimages, these moments of departure, start always in your presence, from this table, these lights,

from Percival and Susan, here and now." [19] The human contacts that are a source of terror for Rhoda are also a source of
peace, but the terror outweighs the peace; so, for Rhoda there
is only one answer, which she eventually seeks—by suicide.

In order to achieve understanding, to obtain a glimpse of
"reality," one must be able to escape self. Yet for everyday
living, one must have a self, a sense of personal identity;
Rhoda's failure to develop this leads to her destruction. These
two conflicting needs, a basic theme of *The Waves*, are also
expressed in an essay, "Street Haunting: A London Adventure," which Mrs. Woolf wrote in 1930. In London on a
trivial errand—to buy a lead pencil—the author imaginatively
projects herself into the selves of the various people who cross
her path. She enjoys her "escape," her "adventure," but when
the shopping tour is over, experiences a feeling of relief at
being enclosed within her own personality again:

> Into each of these lives one could penetrate a little way,
> far enough to give oneself the illusion that one is not
> tethered to a single mind, but can put on briefly for a few
> minutes the bodies and minds of others. . . .
> That is true: to escape is the greatest of pleasures;
> street haunting in winter the greatest of adventures.
> Still as we approach our own doorstep again, it is com-
> forting to feel the old possessions, the old prejudices,
> fold us round; and the self, which has been blown about
> at so many street corners, which has battered like a moth
> at the flame of so many inaccessible lanterns, sheltered
> and enclosed. [20]

At one moment Virginia Woolf sees man as a separate, distinct entity (from this view comes the sense of human loneliness that pervades all of her work); at another moment, she
sees him as an undefined, and undefinable, quantity, insepara-
ble from the general stream of humanity from which he arises

(from this view comes her theory that personal identity is an illusion). The first view is essential to one's existence; the second, to the development of one's understanding. Mrs. Woolf's concept of time involves similarly conflicting needs and viewpoints. There is "time on the clock and time in the mind," the moment that has an existence of its own and the moment that is so much a part of all time that it cannot be separated from the general stream.[21] The first view is necessary to one's sense of identity; the second, to the development of one's understanding. One view arises from Mrs. Woolf's sense of tradition, of continuity; the other, from her overwhelming sense of the transitoriness of human existence.

> Now is life very solid or very shifting? I am haunted by the two contradictions. This has gone on forever; will last forever; goes down to the bottom of the world—this moment I stand on. Also it is very transitory, flying, diaphanous. I shall pass like a cloud on the waves. Perhaps it may be that though we change, one flying after another, so quick, so quick, yet we are somehow successive and continuous we human beings, and show the light through. But what is the light? I am impressed by the transitoriness of human life to such an extent that I am often saying a farewell—after dinner with Roger for instance; or reckoning how many more times I shall see Nessa.[22]

Time, death, and the nature of personality are recurrent themes in Virginia Woolf's writings and so closely related that it is difficult to separate one from another. Death, like time, appears in contradictory terms. On the one hand, death is a complete cessation of time and personality—the dissolution into nothingness that Rhoda fears; on the other hand, it it is an escape into the timeless and enduring. Death is a destroyer; it is also a preserver. In *Jacob's Room*, death is the destroyer; at the end of the novel Jacob simply ceases to be, and his mother is left standing in the middle of his room wondering what to do with his shoes. In *The Voyage Out*, death again cuts off a young life just as it is beginning—but there are compensations. At Rachael's deathbed, Hewet realizes that death will preserve, flawless and intact, that perfect union he and Rachael have sought but could never have maintained. And when Septimus commits suicide, Mrs. Dalloway shifts from a fear of death the destroyer to an appreciation of death the preserver; for by his embrace of death, Septimus has secured a personal integrity, a "privacy of soul," which she must compromise in daily living: "A thing there was that mattered; a thing, wreathed about with chatter, defaced, obscured in her own life, let drop every day in corruption, lies, chatter. This he had preserved." [23]

"Fear no more the heat of the sun," say Clarissa and Septimus. For death offers the ultimate escape from life's trials, terrors, and decay—the only real security possible. The past offers a similar escape, a sense of continuity, permanence, and security; for the past is fixed and timeless, whereas the present is chaotic, shifting—and the future, threatening. "It is only when we look at the past and take from it the element of uncertainty that we can enjoy perfect peace." [24]

The sense of transitoriness that compelled Mrs. Woolf to seek positive values in time and death, is but one aspect of a general sense of insecurity and of impending destruction; for what James called "the imagination of disaster" Mrs. Woolf had to an overwhelming degree. It explains not only much of *what* she wrote, but often *why* she wrote. After a week's depression following the death of her friend Roger Fry, Mrs. Woolf observes: "the other thing begins to work—the exalted sense of being above time and death which comes from being again in a writing mood." As her diary indicates, writing seems to have offered Mrs. Woolf her chief escape from the periods of deep melancholy she often suffered:

Why is life so tragic; so like a little strip of pavement over an abyss. I look down; I feel giddy; I wonder how I am ever to walk to the end. But why do I feel this: Now that I say it I don't feel it. The fire burns; we are going to hear the Beggar's Opera. Only it lies about me; I can't keep my eyes shut. . . . Melancholy diminishes as I write.[25]

There is a strong similarity between Virginia Woolf and Rhoda—the girl who hung suspended above the earth, the girl who had to push her toes hard against the foot of the bed to convince herself that she, that life, was real. Like Rhoda, Mrs. Woolf felt that chaos and nothingness were continually pressing in upon life, threatening to dissolve it.

A saying of Leonard's comes into my head in this season of complete inanity and boredom. "Things have gone wrong somehow." It was the night C. killed herself. We were walking along that silent blue street with the scaffolding. I saw all the violence and unreason crossing in the air: ourselves small; a tumult outside: something terrifying: unreason—shall I make a book out of this? It would be a way of bringing order and speed again into my world.

The sense of an outside chaos surrounding and pressing in upon a small circle of beings, and the need to hold that chaos at bay by creating some sort of order or unity, is reflected throughout Mrs. Woolf's writings; the contrast of chaos and order, insecurity and security, the unknown and the known, is usually symbolized by darkness and light. For example, the childhood expedition for moths, described in "Reading":

The business of dinner now engrossing the grown-up people we made ready our lantern, our poison jar, and took our butterfly nets in our hands. The road that skirted the wood was so pale that its hardness grated upon our boots unexpectedly. It was the last strip of reality, however, off which we stepped into the gloom of the unknown. The lantern shoved its wedge of light through the dark, as though the air were a fine black snow piling itself up in banks on either side of the yellow beam. The direction of the trees was known to the leader of the party, who walked ahead, and seemed to draw us, unheeding darkness or fear, further and further into the unknown world. Not only has the dark the power to extinguish light, but it also buries under it a great part of the human spirit. We hardly spoke, and then only in low voices which made little headway against the thoughts that filled us. The little irregular beam of light seemed the only thing that kept us together, and like a rope prevented us from falling asunder and being engulfed.[26]

Later, in the same essay, Mrs. Woolf describes the moment of "shock" between "the hour of midnight and dawn": "Something definitely happens. The garden, the butterflies, the morning sounds, trees, apples, human voices have emerged, stated themselves. As with a rod of light order has been imposed upon tumult; form upon chaos. . . ." Light shares with joy and sorrow the power to effect a "sudden arrest of the fluidity of life." It does so by imposing form upon chaos, thus "fixing" one moment in a stream that is fluid and changing, and producing what Mrs. Woolf describes elsewhere as a "moment of reality."

This use of light is standard in Virginia Woolf's novels. It is light that reassures Hewet in *The Voyage Out*. At night, he looks up the hill at the Ambrose's brightly lit villa, and "There seemed to be at once a little stability in all this incoherence." [27] In *To the Lighthouse*, both Mrs. Ramsey and the lighthouse with which she is identified offer illumination, stability, and permanence in the midst of darkness, fluidity, and change; they serve as stakes in the stream to which whirling bits of humanity can cling for brief moments of respite before they are swept onward. The lighthouse image is again invoked when all are gathered around the dinner table. When the candles are lit, night is shut outside the windows, and the group which has been separate and discordant suddenly becomes a unified party, a solid island in the midst of fluidity, a circle of light in the midst of darkness: "Some change at once went through them all, as if this had really happened, and they were all conscious of making a party together in a hollow, on an island; had their common cause against that fluidity out there." [28]

Orlando pictures the carnival on the ice as a circle of light surrounded by darkness: "Above and around this brilliant circle like a bowl of darkness pressed the deep black of a winter's night." [29] Significantly, the darkness is pressing in upon, or threatening the light. In *The Waves*, darkness symbolizes the vast nothingness that threatens to absorb the individual—"the huge blackness of what is outside us, of what we are not." [30] The scene is again a dinner party, the reunion at Hampton Court. There is a lapse in conversation; silence falls and the vast, outside world of timelessness and space presses in upon them, dissolving their sense of personal identity. Louis says, "Our separate drops are dissolved; we are extinct, lost in the abysses of time, in the darkness." In another moment, everyday sounds call them back to the time-world again, back to solid ground where they recover themselves:

"Silence falls; silence falls," said Bernard. "But now listen, tick, tick; hoot, hoot; the world has hailed us back to it. I heard for one moment the howling winds of darkness as we passed beyond life. Then tick, tick (the clock); then hoot, hoot (the cars). We are landed; we are on shore; we are sitting, six of us, at a table."

As the dinner scenes suggest, in *To the Lighthouse* and *The Waves*, Mrs. Woolf considers social unity one of the means of opposing chaos. This explains in part why social gatherings so often form her setting and why her heroines are so often women whose chief talent is a gift for welding separate individuals into a unified group, a gift for creating social harmony out of discordant elements. As Martin says in *The Years*, "When a party worked all things, all sounds merged into one." [31] What Lily Briscoe and Miss la Trobe contribute in the world of art is contributed by Mrs. Ramsey and Clarissa Dalloway in the world of society. By combining and creating, they impose some kind of order and unity upon chaos. Human beings are so separate, lonely, isolated; Mrs. Dalloway wishes instinctively to gather them together and unite them. Pondering her general attitude toward life, especially her desire to give parties, Clarissa says:

> Oh, it was very queer. Here was So-and-so in South Kensington; some one up in Bayswater; and somebody else, say, in Mayfair. And she felt quite continuously a sense of their existence; and she felt what a waste; and she felt what a pity; and she felt if only they could be brought together; so she did it. And it was an offering; to combine, to create; but to whom?
>
> An offering for the sake of offering, perhaps. Anyhow, it was her gift. [32]

Mrs. Ramsey also makes her contribution to social unity and is even more successful than Clarissa, for of all Virginia Woolf's characters Mrs. Ramsey has the greatest depth and force. In the dinner scene, it is she who orders the candles lit, thereby making a success of the party and a close-knit unit of a group which has been jangling and discordant. For at the beginning of the scene, all felt that something was lacking: "Nothing seemed to have merged. They all sat separate. And the whole of the effort of merging and flowing and creating rested on her." [33] Looking back after Mrs. Ramsey's death, Lily Briscoe realizes that by producing harmony and unity among human beings, Mrs. Ramsey had created something "like a work of art."

> Mrs. Ramsey bringing them together; Mrs. Ramsey saying, "Life stand still here"; Mrs. Ramsey making of the moment something permanent (as in another sphere Lily herself tried to make of the moment something permanent)—this was of the nature of a revelation. In the midst of chaos there was shape; this eternal passing and flowing (she looked at the clouds going and the leaves shaking) was struck into stability. Life stand still here, Mrs. Ramsey said. "Mrs. Ramsey! Mrs. Ramsey!" she repeated. She owed it all to her.

Her sense of the chaotic and the transitory gave Mrs. Woolf an overpowering need to be convinced of the solidity of things. A diary entry (March, 1941) made shortly before her suicide reveals her struggle to avoid excessive introspection and escape melancholy, and suggests that, for her, it was as difficult as it was necessary to "gain a certain hold" on things.

> Occupation is essential. And now with some pleasure I find that it's seven; and must cook dinner. Haddock and sausage meat. I think it is true that one gains a certain hold on sausage and haddock by writing them down. [34]

Mrs. Woolf's concern for solidity led her to place great emphasis upon natural and inanimate objects. As various critics have pointed out, Virginia Woolf's world of things is often more vivid, more "real" than her world of people; *Jacob's Room* is a good example. The explanation lies in Mrs. Woolf's belief that inanimate objects have a solidity, hence a reality, that the human being does not, for their identity is fixed, their being complete. [35] It is not surprising, therefore, to find, in *To the Lighthouse*, a lighthouse as the central symbol of reality. In the same novel, Lily turns to some trees to help "stabilise her position" when she realizes that the personalities and events of the dinner party have called her own life and values into question. "Her world was changing: they were still." [36]

In *Orlando*, the oak tree and the house alone resist change; through the centuries they remain as landmarks and as a standard of measure. A willow tree performs a similar function in *The Waves*. When Bernard tries to review the past, he realizes that there is no real sequence, that his stories have been false, their patterns arbitrary. One's life, one's being perpetually changes, flowing this way, now that. "The tree alone resisted our eternal flux." Therefore, when he wishes to sum up the characters of his friends, Bernard places them against a fixed background, under the tree.

> "I was saying there was a willow tree. Its shower of falling branches, its creased and crooked bark had the effect of what remains outside our illusions yet cannot stay them, is changed by them for the moment, yet shows through stable, still, and with a sternness that our lives lack. Hence the comment it makes; the standard it supplies, and the reason why, as we flow and change, it seems to measure." [37]

Inanimate objects not only help stabilize or measure; they are, in themselves, proof of an outside reality. Herein, I think, lies their chief significance for Mrs. Woolf. One of her early short stories, "The Mark on the Wall," records the various speculations aroused by an unidentifiable spot on the wall. When these speculations become disagreeable and depressing, the narrator decides that he had better go look at the thing itself and end his uncertainty. This idea leads to another series of reflections about the kind of doubts and uncertainties that "things," solid objects, help resolve. "Thus, waking from a midnight dream of horror, one hastily turns on the light and lies quiescent, worshipping solidity, worshipping reality, worshipping the impersonal world which is a proof of some existence other than ours. That is what one wants to be sure of. . . ." [38]

A diary entry for February 27, 1926, reveals Mrs. Woolf's constant search for a certain quality or value in life: whatever it is that makes the-thing-in-itself seem satisfactory, complete; whatever it is in "the impersonal world" that proves "some existence other than ours."

> I enjoy almost everything. Yet I have some restless searcher in me. Why is there not a discovery in life? Something one can lay hands on and say "This is it"? My depression is a harrassed feeling. I'm looking: but that's not it—that's not it. What is it? And shall I die before I find it? Then (as I was walking through Russell Square last night) I see the mountains in the sky: the great clouds; and the moon which is risen over Persia; I have a great and astonishing sense of something there, which is "it." It is not exactly beauty that I mean. It is that the thing is in itself enough: satisfactory; achieved. A sense of my own strangeness, walking on the earth is there too: of the infinite oddity of the human position; trotting along Russell Square with the moon up there and those mountain clouds. Who am I, what am I, and so on: these questions are always floating about in me: and then I bump against some exact fact—a letter, a person, and come to them again with a great sense of freshness. And so it goes on. But on this showing, which is true, I think, I do fairly frequently come upon this "it"; and then feel quite at rest. [39]

Mrs. Woolf's final conclusion that "reality" is what she seeks is indicated by a later entry, written September 10, 1928, at her country house in Rodmell, Sussex:

Often down here I have entered into a sanctuary; a nunnery; had a religious retreat; of great agony once; and always some terror; so afraid one is of loneliness; of seeing to the bottom of the vessel. That is one of the experiences I have had here in some Augusts; and then got to a consciousness of what I call "reality": a thing I see before me: something abstract; but residing in the downs or sky; beside which nothing matters; in which I shall rest and continue to exist. Reality I call it. And I fancy sometimes this is the most necessary thing to me: that which I seek. But who knows—once one takes a pen and writes? How difficult not to go making "reality" this and that, whereas it is one thing.

For Mrs. Woolf, reality is an abstract quality residing outside oneself. It is the essence of life and experience—that which is permanent and enduring, that which "remains over when the skin of the day has been cast into the hedge." In it lies both the significance and the justification of life. It is most easily recognized as it appears in the physical world outside one, and most clearly apprehended in moments of acute mental and emotional awareness—Mrs. Woolf's "moments of reality." As an abstract quality, reality cannot be reduced to any final definition. One can recognize it when and where it appears, and experience it in certain moments, thus gaining some understanding of it; but that understanding is of the nature of revelation, of intuition, and is therefore as indefinable as reality itself. Woolf's only answer to the question, "What is meant by 'reality'?", is to suggest *where* it may be found, or experienced. To find and communicate it is the artist's task.

From about 1927 on, Mrs. Woolf became increasingly concerned with reality as it is experienced in a single moment of time,[40] for by confining her search to the single moment, she could best avoid "making 'reality' this and that" instead of just "one thing." Moreover, she seems always to have viewed the individual moment as a thing in itself.[41] The sketch "To Spain" (written in 1923 and included in the posthumous collection, *The Moment and Other Essays*) describes the effect that the moment of departure has upon one en route to the London docks to board a ship for Spain:

> Try to recall the look of London streets seen very early, perhaps very young, from a cab window on the way to Victoria. Everywhere there is the same intensity, as if the moment instead of moving lay suddenly still, because suddenly solemn, fixed the passers-by in their most transient aspects eternally. They do not know how important they have become. If they did, perhaps they would cease to buy newspapers and scrub doorsteps. But we who are about to leave them feel all the more moved that they should continue to do these homely things on the brink of that precipice—our departure.[42]

Like Eliot, Mrs. Woolf suggests that the moment of intensity produces a kind of still point in the flux and flow of time; she also suggests that the single moment has a life of its own. In "The Moment: Summer's Night" (an undated sketch), the author describes a moment of time and attempts to determine just what that moment, in itself, consists of:

> The night was falling so that the table in the garden among the trees grew whiter and whiter; and the people round it more indistinct. An owl, blunt, obsolete looking, heavy weighted, crossed the fading sky with a black spot between its claws. The trees murmured. An aeroplane hummed like a piece of plucked wire. There was also, on the roads, the distant explosion of a motor cycle, shooting further and further down the road. Yet what composed the present moment? If you are young, the future lies upon the present, like a piece of glass, making it tremble and quiver. If you are old, the past lies

upon the present, like a thick glass, making it waver, distorting it. All the same, everybody believes that the present is something, seeks out the different elements in this situation in order to compose the truth of it, the whole of it.

To begin with: it is largely composed of visual and of sense impressions. . . .

These visual and sense impressions arise in part from changes in the physical world as the day progresses from sunrise to sunset. As sunset approaches, the changes become more rapid and the quick succession of moments seems "to make an order evident."

One becomes aware that we are spectators and also passive participants in a pageant. And as nothing can interfere with the order, we have nothing to do but accept, and watch. . . .

But that is the wider circumference of the moment. Here in the center is a knot of consciousness; a nucleus divided up into four heads, eight legs, eight arms, and four separate bodies [the four people seated at the table in the garden]. They are not subject to the law of the sun and the owl and the lamp.

For the people at the garden table, the core of the moment is composed of their own expressions and impressions, actions and reactions. "All this shoots through the moment, makes it quiver with malice and amusement. . . ." The moment is characterized by their own mood; yet when their thoughts shift from present company to a husband who beats his wife, the moment itself spreads beyond the present circle and "runs like quicksilver on a sloping board into the cottage parlour"; for the moment includes both an outer, objective reality and an inner personal reality, and extends to all things and all persons having a simultaneous existence in time.

Mrs. Dalloway is the first of Virginia Woolf's novels to deal extensively with the single moment of time. Organization of the novel is based upon two kinds of transitions: The author shifts from character to character to show thoughts and actions that occur simultaneously at a given moment; or she remains within the mind of one character and shifts up and down the time scale to show how much the past is involved in any single moment of consciousness.[43]

In *Mrs. Dalloway* one also finds the moment of vision, of illumination, which Mrs. Woolf so thoroughly explores in the later *To the Lighthouse*. Clarissa's moments are most often initiated by her contacts with women. She can never resist the charm and appeal of women who come to her with some confession to make, and for a moment she feels drawn toward them as she images a man would feel:

> Only for a moment; but it was enough. It was a sudden revelation, a tinge like a blush which one tried to check and then, as it spread, one yielded to its expansion, and rushed to the farthest verge and there quivered and felt the world come closer, swollen with some astonishing significance, some pressure of rapture, which split its thin skin and gushed and poured with extraordinary alleviation over the cracks and sores! Then, for that moment, she had seen an illumination; a match burning in a crocus; an inner meaning almost expressed. But the close withdrew; the hard softened. It was over—the moment.[44]

Peter Walsh has his moments of vision, also, moments in which he senses some underlying pattern or meaning: "really it took one's breath away, these moments; there coming to him by the pillar-box opposite the British Museum one of them, a moment, in which things came together; this ambulance; and life and death." His moments are initiated by Clarissa—not by his actual meetings with her, which are usually painful, but by the recollection of those meetings, which, given time and distance, "flower out" into meaning: "There was a mystery about it. You were given a sharp, acute, uncomfortable grain—the actual meeting; horribly painful as often as not; yet in absence, in the most unlikely places, it would flower out, open, shed its scent, let you touch, taste, look about you, get the whole feel of it and understanding, after years of lying lost." [45] As Eliot put it, "We had the experience but missed the meaning."

The flowering of a past moment into present illumination, and the necessity of distance for that flowering, are ideas Mrs. Woolf further develops in *To the Lighthouse.* Here, Mrs. Woolf makes her fullest study of the moment of vision, which she now merges with the moment of reality. It is here, also, that she most fully explores the question of truth, and its relation to reality. In a broadcast delivered April 20, 1937, on the subject of "Craftsmanship," Mrs. Woolf designated three kinds of truth: "God's truth," "literary truth," and "home truth." [46] To put it another way, there is factual or absolute truth; imaginary or ideal truth; and relative or human truth, the truth of human relations. But for all practical purposes these can be reduced—as Mrs. Woolf reduces them in *To the Lighthouse*—to truths of the intellect and truths of the emotions; truths that are absolute and truths that are imaginary, idealized, or emotional. The first has to do with the thing in itself; the second, with the thing as it appears to and affects the individual human being. The first is an impersonal truth; the second, a personal one. [47]

In *To the Lighthouse*, Mr. Ramsey represents one kind of truth; Mrs. Ramsey, another. Mr. Ramsey is the philosopher who writes books about "subject, object and the nature of reality." His concern is for God's truth, absolute facts, impersonal truths. "He was incapable of untruth; never tampered with a fact; never altered a disagreeable word to suit the pleasure or convenience of any mortal being, least of all his own children. . . ." [48] So he dashes the hopes of his young son by insisting that the weather will be bad, that the trip to the lighthouse is out of the question. He is annoyed by his wife's irrationality; "she flew in the face of facts." He is particularly angry when, despite the facts, she leads James to hope that the weather may clear by morning. Yet this man who will not alter an objective fact to suit another's convenience, cannot bear to have it suggested that his books are not so good as they might be; he must have continual praise.

On the other hand, Mrs. Ramsey, who will not tell James that the voyage to the lighthouse is impossible, who will not tell her husband that his books are bad (because she knows he cannot face the personal truth about himself and his limitations), is angered that Mr. Ramsey should "pursue truth with such astonishing lack of consideration for other people's feelings." Her concern is for emotional truths, personal, human truths, and her approach is intuitive rather than rational. When it is a question of people, of human relations, "she knew without having learnt. Her simplicity fathomed what clever people falsified." She has an "instinct for truth," her kind of truth; and this she will not tamper with. She is honest with herself in a way that Mr. Ramsey cannot be. "For her own self-satisfaction was it that she wished so instinctively to help, to give, that people might say of her, 'O Mrs. Ramsey! dear Mrs. Ramsey . . . Mrs. Ramsey, of course!' and need her and send for her and admire her?" She forces herself to recognize the truth about herself and the truth about life. She is "aware of the pettiness of some part of her, and of human relations, how flawed they are, how despicable, how self-seeking, at their best." Despite her insistence that people must marry, that people must have children, despite the moments in which she feels "the rapture of successful creation," she knows that life is difficult, that life is sad, that all is "as ephemeral as a rainbow." Despite her desire to believe otherwise, "she had always seized the fact that there is no reason, order, justice: but suffering, death, the poor. There was no treachery too base for the world to commit; she knew that. No happiness lasted; she knew that." [49] Because of her uncompromising adherence to her kind of truth, Mrs. Ramsey's husband considers her pessimistic and sees a "sternness at the heart of her beauty." And because of this quality, Mrs. Ramsey identifies herself with the lighthouse and its beam—the lighthouse which becomes for all a symbol of truth and reality.

In James one finds a recognition of both truths. When, as a boy of sixteen, James finally makes the long-awaited voyage to the lighthouse, he is struck by the contrast between the lighthouse he has dreamed of and the lighthouse as it actually is, but he realizes that the imagined, the ideal lighthouse of his childhood is as "true" as the actual one: "For nothing was simply one thing." [50]

It is Lily Briscoe, however, the spokesman and interpreter in the final section of the book, who embodies both kinds of truth and reveals their relationship to "reality." Like Mr. Ramsey, Lily is concerned with an impersonal kind of truth, a pure or absolute truth. What he searches for in the realm of abstract ideas, she searches for in the realm of abstract form. He withdraws from the personal everyday world to consider the relationship of ideas, whereas she withdraws to consider the relationship of line, mass, and color; and there is more than a casual similarity between the hard, bare kitchen table which, for Mr. Ramsey, poses the philsophical problem of reality, and the "uncompromising white stare" of the canvas which, for Lily, poses the artistic problem of form.

> For what could be more formidable than that space? Here she was again, she thought, stepping back to look at it, drawn out of gossip, out of living, out of community with people into the presence of this formidable ancient enemy of hers—this other thing, this truth, this reality, which suddenly laid hands on her, emerged stark at the back of appearances and commanded her attention. [51]

But Lily also has an affinity with Mrs. Ramsey. She herself recognizes the similarity between Mrs. Ramsey's creative efforts and her own. Both are trying to create shape in the midst of chaos and to stem the "eternal passing and flowing" of life by "making of the moment something permanent." Lily's attitude toward her "ancient enemy," the blank space on the canvas, is similar to Mrs. Ramsey's attitude toward "her old antagonist, life"; each enemy represents a void that must somehow be filled, an infinitely blank space into which one must somehow insert shape if one would achieve order, meaning, and permanence.

Lily is as concerned with applied as with pure truth. In the last section of the book, at the same time that she is wrestling with artistic problems of line, mass, and color, Lily is also wrestling with human problems: the relationships of Cam, James, and their father, and the meaning of life—human life. Lily cannot complete her painting because her attention is divided; one moment she is watching the progress of the three Ramseys in their voyage to the lighthouse and meditating upon the significance of that voyage, and the next moment she is facing her canvas. "For whatever reason she could not achieve that razor edge of balance between two opposite forces; Mr. Ramsey and the picture; which was necessary." [52] It is a moment of sudden illumination that enables Lily to resolve the two worlds—the world of human values and the world of abstract values—into a unified whole, a complete vision. In that moment Lily achieves the "razor edge of balance" between life and art, personality and impersonality, the human and the abstract; in that moment she perceives the significance of the voyage and completes her picture.

Here, in the painting, the opposing forces are reconciled. Mr. Ramsey's truth is represented by the pattern, and within the pattern is Mrs. Ramsey, its human center. Both kinds of truth are necessary to complete the picture and create the illusion of reality. For nothing is simply one thing. There is personal truth and impersonal truth; personal reality and a greater, impersonal reality which includes the former, but goes beyond it. Recognition of this constitutes Lily's moment of illumination.

Reality must be grasped intuitively, if at all; and understanding comes by way of revelation. That is why Lily does not achieve her final vision, does not experience her great moment, until she has first understood the significance of the intuitive Mrs. Ramsey; that is why Mr. Ramsey does not experience his moment of reality until he reaches the lighthouse with which Mrs. Ramsey is identified. Distance and impersonality are essential; one must be removed from the immediate, in time, space, or mind, to achieve the necessary perspective. James and his father do not achieve understanding until they have made an actual journey from their personal world to the impersonal world of the lighthouse. Lily cannot understand about Mrs. Ramsey until after the latter has been removed in time and space—by death; nor can she perceive the full meaning of the voyage until the boat and its occupants have dissolved into a blue haze on the horizon. She reaches a final understanding of both in the same moment.

Although "the great revelation" does not occur until the end of the book, Lily has had her lesser ones—"little daily miracles, illuminations, matches struck unexpectedly in the dark. . . ." Lily's memories of Mrs. Ramsey have led to more than one moment of vision. "But always something—it might be a face, a voice, a paper boy crying *Standard, News*— thrust through, snubbed her, waked her, required and got in the end an effort of attention, so that the vision must be perpetually remade." [53] Greater or lesser, the revelation will fade, the moment recede; and the painting will eventually, Lily knows, be destroyed. The important thing is that she has had her vision; that is enough.

Insofar as Virginia Woolf may be said to have a message for struggling humanity, it is that "the vision must be perpetually remade." There is no final meaning in life, no lasting solution to the problems it poses. Moments of reality, of illumination, come and go. But for Mrs. Woolf, as for Bernard, "the moment was all; the moment was enough"; [54] therein lies the significance and the justification of life, the compensation for its doubts, fears, and sufferings. Recognition of this awakes in Mrs. Ramsey a feeling of ecstasy and of triumph. She has been watching the lighthouse beam, the finger of truth that reminds her of the stern facts of life; at the same time, it reminds her of the great moments, the intense happiness she has known: "and it silvered the rough waves a little more brightly, as daylight faded, and the blue went out of the sea and it rolled in waves of pure lemon which curved and swelled and broke upon the beach and the ecstasy burst in her eyes and waves of pure delight raced over the floor of her mind and she felt, It is enough! It is enough!" [55]

Moments of reality lead to peace as well as ecstasy; for, while the moment lasts, one finds the much-needed assurance of solidity and feels secure. Thus Miss Craye's "moment of ecstasy" becomes something which surrounds her like a cloak.[56] It is such a moment that Mrs. Ramsey experiences in the scene at the dinner table when, after lighting the candles, she succeeds in creating a unified circle of beings with a common cause against the fluidity, darkness, and chaos outside.

> Just now (but this cannot last, she thought, dissociating herself from the moment while they were all talking about boots) just now she had reached security; she hovered like a hawk suspended; like a flag floated in an element of joy which filled every nerve of her body fully and sweetly, not noisily, solemnly rather, for it arose, she thought, looking at them all eating there, from husband and children and friends; all of which rising in this profound stillness . . . seemed now for no special reason

to stay there like a smoke, like a fume rising upwards, holding them safe together. Nothing need be said; nothing could be said. There it was, all round them. It partook, she felt . . . of eternity; as she had already felt about something different once before that afternoon; there is a coherence in things, a stability; something, she meant, is immune from change, and shines out (she glanced at the window with its ripple of reflected lights) in the face of the flowing, the fleeting, the spectral, like a ruby; so that again tonight she had the feeling she had had once today, already, of peace, of rest. Of such moments, she thought, the thing is made that endures.[57]

The thing that endures is not the moment itself, for that passes; not the private vision one achieves, for that fades. What endures is that which, in passing, one contributes to the common cause, that which becomes a part of mankind's collective experience, collective understanding, and collective vision. Louis reaffirms this idea in *The Waves*. Of the six friends it is he who is most conscious of the continuity of human history. Like Mrs. Ramsey, all try in one way or another "to make of the moment something permanent"; but it is Louis who realizes that when one fails to fix the moment, "the meeting-place of past and present," he defrauds human history of a moment's vision.

"This is the first day of a new life, another spoke of the rising wheel. But my body passes vagrant as a bird's shadow. I should be transient as the shadow on the meadow, soon fading, soon darkening and dying there where it meets the wood, were it not that I coerce my brain to form in my forehead; I force myself to state, if only in one line of unwritten poetry, this moment; to mark this inch in the long, long history that began in Egypt, in the time of the Pharaohs, when women carried red pitchers to the Nile. I seem already to have lived many thousand years. But if I now shut my eyes, if I fail to realise the meeting-place of past and present, that I sit in a third-class railway carriage full of boys going home for the holidays, human history is defrauded of a moment's vision." [58]

Although *To the Lighthouse* contains Mrs. Woolf's fullest study of the moment of reality, three subsequent novels—*Orlando*, *The Waves*, and *The Years*—help clarify her concept. Like Eliot, and like Yeats, Mrs. Woolf seems to have believed that "human kind cannot bear very much reality." Twice in *Orlando*, the present moment—the moment in which one experiences reality—causes the heroine a severe shock. The first occurs when, after a terrific explosion, Orlando suddenly finds herself thrust from the Victorian period into the present: "For what more terrifying revelation can there be than that it is the present moment? That we survive the shock at all is only possible because the past shelters us on one side, the future on another." [59] A similar explosion, and resulting shock, occurs later when the present moment intrudes upon Orlando's thoughts of the past. She becomes intensely aware of the actual objects around her, and she feels as if she hung suspended in space. "Braced and strung up by the present moment she was also strangely afraid, as if every time the gulf of time gaped and let a second through some unknown danger might come with it. The tension was too relentless and too rigorous to be endured long without discomfort." She sees "with disgusting vividness" the raised, pink flesh of the carpenter's thumb where the nail is missing, and feels faint; for a moment, her eyelids flicker—and that, at last, relieves "the pressure of the present." But, though painful to endure, the moment of intense reality has brought Orlando closer toward understanding. " 'Yes,' she thought, heaving a deep sigh of relief, as she turned from the carpenter's shop to climb the

hill, 'I can begin to live again. . . . I am about to understand.
. . .' "

The moment of reality produces a kind of still point in the life of an individual. It is the same kind of still point that Agatha, Harry, and the Chorus of Women experience in Eliot's *The Family Reunion* and *Murder in the Cathedral;* it is *a* still point, which both Agatha and Becket distinguish from "another kind," the abstract, spiritual center that Eliot calls *the* still point. In Mrs. Woolf's writings there is the suggestion of a center outside oneself, which one occasionally reaches in a moment of reality. Mrs. Ramsey reaches just such a center during the scene at the dinner table: "Here, she felt, putting the spoon down, was the still space that lies about the heart of things, where one could move or rest. . . ." [60]

The still point or center that one finds in Virginia Woolf, however, never emerges as a clearly defined concept and never attains the religious significance of Eliot's. Mrs. Woolf's still point offers a kind of ecstatic peace that signifies the completion of one's partial self and the union of that self with an impersonal, objective reality; it does not, as in Eliot's case, involve union with the force that controls the universe, the "unmoved mover."

The relationship between self-completion and Mrs. Woolf's still point is most clearly seen in *Orlando.* One aspect of her theory of complementary souls has to do with the nature and function of the sexes: a belief that the sexes are basically opposite, each serving as a complement to the other; and that the mind itself is androgynous, the mature individual being either woman-manly or man-womanly, according to his sex.[61] *Orlando* illustrates both points. Most obvious, of course, is the device of the hero-heroine who changes sex. Equally important, however, is the marriage of the man-womanly Orlando to the woman-manly Shelmerdine, for Orlando does not find fulfilment until her union with the ideal husband, the perfect complement. Significantly, Shelmerdine (Orlando's self-fulfilment) comes to her only in moments of "dead calm," moments in which Orlando, like Mrs. Ramsey, reaches "the still space that lies about the heart of things." This is true of his first appearance as well as his return after their marriage.

> He was coming, as he always came, in moments of dead calm; when the wave rippled and the spotted leaves fell slowly over her foot in the autumn woods; when the leopard was still; the moon was on the waters, and nothing moved between sky and sea. It was then that he came.[62]

In *Orlando*, Mrs. Woolf's still point is symbolized by the "moment of dead calm" when Shelmerdine appears. In that moment, Orlando's partial self is completed; by union with her opposite, her complementary self, she achieves perfect integration, reaches the still point, and finds at last what she has searched for throughout the centuries. This of course is "reality," symbolized in *Orlando* by the wild goose.

Shortly before her husband's return, Orlando begins to think about the wild goose, which has haunted her and eluded her since childhood:

> "I've seen it, here—there—there—England, Persia, Italy. Always it flies fast out to sea and always I fling after it words like nets . . . which shrivel as I've seen nets shrivel drawn on deck with only sea-weed in them. And sometimes there's an inch of silver—six words—in the bottom of the net. But never the great fish who lives in the coral groves."

The wild goose is associated with Shelmerdine first in the passage in which Orlando cries out her husband's name, and the name "fell out of the sky like a steel blue feather." The nature of Shelmerdine's arrival further develops the association, for he comes out of the sky, quite suddenly, in an aeroplane, and as he leaps from it "a single wild bird" springs up over his head. " 'It is the goose!' Orlando cried. 'The wild goose. . . .' " [68] Later, Orlando receives her clearest vision of the wild goose during the moment of stillness, the moment of dead calm at midnight when she is reunited with her husband, the moment in which she has achieved integration and has reached the still point.

In *The Waves* one finds further clarification of the moment of reality and its relation to the still point. When Virginia Woolf first began working out her ideas for the book, she wrote in her diary (November 28, 1928):

> The idea has come to me that what I want now to do is to saturate every atom. I mean to eliminate all waste, deadness, superfluity: to give the moment whole; whatever it includes. Say that the moment is a combination of thought; sensation; the voice of the sea. Waste, deadness, come from the inclusion of things that don't belong to the moment; this appalling narrative business of the realist: getting on from lunch to dinner: it is false, unreal, merely conventional. Why admit anything to literature that is not poetry—by which I mean saturated? [64]

Straight poetry, Mrs. Woolf decided, was not the answer; it eliminates too much. What she wanted was a poetic form that would eliminate all but the moment, yet make the moment so inclusive that it communicates reality. Consequently, *The Waves* not only contains Mrs. Woolf's most poetic prose; it is also the one work of hers which deals exclusively with moments of reality. The novel is confined to a series of moments as they occur in the life development of six people; and the moments are greater or lesser according to the character of the individual involved, and the stage of growth he has reached at the time. Jinny seeks an ecstasy that is purely physical; as a result, her moments of vision never lead her beyond a sense of personal reality. Rhoda, on the other hand, is overwhelmed by impersonal reality. She lacks the power of concentration required to isolate one's moments—or one's identity; hence, she cannot withstand the onslaught of the infinite, cannot maintain her existence, and feels herself perpetually dissolving into nothingness, merging into that vast, human sea, the impersonal reality from which she came.

The remaining four, Susan, Neville, Louis and Bernard, all attempt with varying degrees of success to "fix" the moment, and each achieves some vision of a greater, impersonal reality that includes and extends beyond the personal. Bernard is the most successful in achieving a balance between the sense of personal reality, the illusion that is necessary to one's everyday existence, and the sense of impersonal reality, the vision that is necessary to one's understanding. It is he who serves as interpreter, and it is he who achieves the greatest moment of vision, comparable to Lily's final moment in *To the Lighthouse*. This final revelation Bernard himself foresees. In a moment illuminated by Percival's death, Bernard has a glimpse of the meaning, the significance of life, but the vision slips from him before he has really grasped it: "Something lies deeply buried. For one moment I thought to grasp it. But bury it, bury it; let it breed, hidden in the depths of my mind some day to fructify. After a long lifetime, loosely, in a moment of revelation, I may lay hands on it, but now the idea breaks in my hand." [65] As with Peter Walsh, Bernard's past moments flower into later illumination. The "great revelation" comes to Bernard when "all this little affair of 'being' is over"; when, like Mr. Ramsey, he makes the difficult voyage from personality to impersonality; when, after developing a personal self in order to exist, he transcends that personal self in order to understand. In that moment, Bernard has a vision of the meaning of life, of the general scheme of things—"the eternal renewal, the incessant rise and fall and fall and rise again"—and of his own place in the scheme. In that moment, Bernard's partial self is merged into a larger unity which completes it; he has reached the still point. What is essential, as Rhoda's failure illustrates, is that one must first develop a *self* to merge.

The Years represents Mrs. Woolf's most negative approach to the moment of reality. Here, she is not so much concerned with the moment itself, for none of the characters experiences a great moment or achieves a complete vision; what she is concerned with is their failure to do so and the reasons for it. Early in the novel, at her mother's funeral, Delia comes close to experiencing a moment of reality; but the moment is disrupted, her partial vision destroyed by the words of the preacher, giving lip service to a form that has ceased to have meaning:

> She stared down into the grave. There lay her mother; in that coffin—the woman she had loved and hated so. Her eyes dazzled. She was afraid that she might faint; but she must look; she must feel; it was the last chance that was left her. Earth dropped on the coffin; three pebbles fell on the hard shiny surface; and as they dropped she was possessed by a sense of something everlasting; of life mixing with death, of death becoming life. For as she looked she heard the sparrows chirp quicker and quicker; she heard wheels in the distance sound louder and louder; life came closer and closer. . . .
> "We give thee hearty thanks," said the voice, "for that it has pleased thee to deliver this our sister out of the miseries of this sinful world—"
> What a lie! she cried to herself. What a damnable lie! He had robbed her of the one feeling that was genuine; he had spoilt her one moment of understanding.[66]

In the last section of the novel, "Present Day," Delia's niece Peggy has a similar experience; the trivialities of everyday life interrupt her thoughts and destroy a vision that is just beginning to form. The scene is Delia's party, where a moment's laughter inspires Peggy with a moment's vision;

but by the time she gets the attention of those around her, it
is too late. They are in no mood to be serious, and their levity
has disrupted her moment; she can neither express nor hold
onto the vision. In frustration, she turns to her brother with
an angry remark about "living differently." "She stopped.
There was the vision still, but she had not grasped it. She had
broken off only a little fragment of what she meant to say,
and she had made her brother angry. Yet there it hung before
her, the thing she had seen, the thing she had not said."

At the party, Peggy's aunt Eleanor also comes close to
achieving a moment's vision. When Nicholas repeats something Eleanor has heard him say in the past, she wonders
vaguely if there is a pattern to life, a theme recurring like
music, "a gigantic pattern, momentarily perceptible." The
thought pleases her, and later, after falling asleep in her chair,
she returns to the question of life and its meaning.

> There must be another life, she thought, sinking back
> into her chair, exasperated. Not in dreams; but here and
> now, in this room, with living people. She felt as if she
> were standing on the edge of a precipice with her hair
> blown back; she was about to grasp something that just
> evaded her. There must be another life, here and now, she
> repeated. This is too short, too broken. We know noth-
> ing, even about ourselves. We're only just beginning,
> she thought, to understand, here and there. She hollowed
> her hands in her lap, just as Rose had hollowed hers
> round her ears. She held her hands hollowed; she felt
> that she wanted to enclose the present moment; to make
> it stay; to fill it fuller and fuller, with the past, the present
> and the future, until it shone, whole, bright, deep with
> understanding.[67]

Eleanor never manages "to enclose the present moment";
neither her desire nor her power of concentration is lasting
enough. She lacks the strength, the courage, and the deter-

mination to "coerce" her brain, as Louis did; as a result, she, like Delia and like Peggy, defrauds human history of a moment's vision.

The years have passed, and the old Victorian patterns have been destroyed; but they have not been replaced by any new vision. It is North, Peggy's brother, who suggests both an explanation and a solution. Impatient with would-be reformers, he decides that the only possible way to improve the world is to begin with the individual. He himself wishes to be a writer, to make sentences. "But how can I, he thought—he looked at Eleanor, who sat with a silk handkerchief in her hands—unless I know what's solid, what's true; in my life, in other people's lives?" [68] And how can one know what is solid and what is true when life continually interrupts the moment and dissolves the vision? And what can one gain by talk, when conversation is so rambling and confused, and real communication so difficult? [69] One must have "silence and solitude" North decides; for only in silence and solitude can one experience the moment of vision. One must also have courage—courage to seek the truth, to be oneself, and to live by one's vision. [70] Thus and only thus can one live in contact with that total reality "beside which nothing matters."

Unlike Eliot, Mrs. Woolf did not formulate any definite philosophical or religious system. She sees no final meaning in life and no final solution to its problems. The value of life is in the living of it; and one is most alive, lives most intensely, in moments when one has the greatest sense of reality—that abstract "something," "residing in the downs or sky," which Mrs. Woolf considers the essence of life. For Mrs. Woolf, as for Eliot, the understanding of reality is a matter of intuition and revelation; and for Mrs. Woolf, as for Eliot, the vision of reality is too intense for human kind to bear except in moments. These moments may be lesser or greater; the lesser ones (constituting *a* still point in the life of an individual) provide a glimpse of reality; the greater ones (leading to *the* still point) unite one with impersonal reality and signify the shift of one's ego from self to a center greater than and outside oneself.

The center Mrs. Woolf suggests is never clearly defined, for it is rarely isolated from the moment of reality that leads to it. Hers is a union with reality, wholly and simply; Eliot's signifies much more than that. Despite the greater complexity and significance of Eliot's concept, however, there are marked similarities between the ecstatic moment that lifts one to the still point, and the great moment that unites one with total reality. In each case the moment of union *is* a moment of reality—as well as of ecstasy. And like Eliot's still point, Mrs. Woolf's moment signifies "the point of intersection of the timeless with time," or as Louis puts it, "the meeting-place of past and present." It is the point at which the individual self is integrated, complete, and therefore most "real"; it is the point at which opposites are reconciled and the whole vision appears.

Personality integration and the achievement of the whole self do not mean the same thing for Mrs. Woolf as they do for Eliot. In *The Family Reunion*, for example, Harry is given the task of recovering his past self and the meaning of his past self, as the way toward wholeness of being; and *self-recovery* implies a definite, definable identity. For Mrs. Woolf, how-ever, personal identity is but a necessary figment of the imagi-nation.

Mrs. Woolf and Eliot also differ on the question of op-posites—an integral part of Eliot's concept. It is at the still point that opposites are completely reconciled; and that reconciliation is a kind of tension synonymous with Divine Energy, the source of all unity, pattern, movement, and crea-tion. Mrs. Woolf places less emphasis upon opposites and their reconciliation, as such; and with her, it is not so much a question of opposing forces as of conflicting views, or truths, about the same thing. There is the lighthouse as a symbol or ideal; and the lighthouse as fact; the lighthouse as it appears to Mrs. Ramsey and the boy James, and the lighthouse as it actually is. There is a Mrs. Ramsey who is symbolic, and another who is human. Both of the lighthouses, both of the Mrs. Ramseys, are "true." For there is the rational, absolute truth of Mr. Ramsey, and the intuitive, human truth of Mrs. Ramsey; both are necessary to the whole vision; both are a part of reality, which reconciles them as complements.

Mrs. Woolf seems to have conceived reconciliation to be a kind of creative tension, for it is only when the two conflicting truths are reconciled that Lily is able to complete her act of creation, her painting. And in *A Room of One's Own*, where Mrs. Woolf discusses the androgynous quality of the human mind, she states quite clearly: "Some collaboration has to take place in the mind between the woman and the man before the act of creation can be accomplished. Some marriage of opposites has to be consummated." [71] The idea of creative tension is merely touched upon, however; never in Mrs. Woolf is it as fully developed as in Eliot.

There is another, more important difference between Eliot's ideas and those of Virginia Woolf. Eliot believes that life has a divine pattern and an ultimate meaning, which one discovers upon union with the still point. The pattern is evolving, rather than final: "the pattern is new in every moment." [72] And the individual has his choice: simply to be moved in the movement, like a hollow man acted upon but not acting; to cut himself off and attempt to create an isolated pattern, which will end in spiritual destruction; or to move with and in "the dance," creating a pattern within the pattern.

The only pattern Mrs. Woolf acknowledges is that of the general flux and flow of life itself, the "eternal renewal, the incessant rise and fall and fall and rise again," which Bernard proclaims. Beyond that, for Mrs. Woolf, there is no divine pattern, no ultimate meaning; beyond that, whatever pattern or meaning life seems to have is that which one arbitrarily imposes *in defiance* of life's fluidity and chaos; and this pattern which the individual creates must, like Lily's vision, be perpetually remade.

For Eliot's divine pattern Mrs. Woolf substitutes impersonal reality, but one's relationship to it and one's choice is the same as in Eliot's case. One may let himself be completely absorbed by it and dissolve into nothingness, as Rhoda did; one may ignore it for an illusory, personal identity and suffer the spiritual isolation and deterioration of the people in *The Years;* or one may, like Bernard, submit oneself to it and, within it, develop that sense of personal reality without which no one can live.

In the final analysis, of course, the chief difference between the still point reached in Eliot's moment of ecstasy and the one reached in Mrs. Woolf's moment of reality lies in the religious significance of the former. Union with Eliot's still point is equivalent to union with God. The ecstasy one experiences upon reaching the still point is a religious ecstasy; and the peace, a religious peace.

Unsupported by orthodox religion and unable to believe in the existence of God, Mrs. Woolf felt an overwhelming need to be convinced of the solidity of things, an overwhelming desire to find some permanent, enduring quality in life with which one could identify himself. In "reality," her own concept of reality, she found an answer to her needs. The ecstasy one feels in Mrs. Woolf's moment of reality is a sense of triumph over the chaos, fluidity, and transitoriness of life; the peace one feels is the sense of security that comes from the reassurance of solidity and permanence and from the momentary union with the one indestructible quality in life—impersonal, total, reality.

NOTES

[1] *Granite and Rainbow*, pp. 16-17; passages following, pp. 12, 11.
[2] *The Common Reader, First and Second Series*, I, 81, 212.
[3] *Common Reader*, I, 212-213; passage following, p. 218.
[4] *A Room of One's Own*, pp. 191-192.
[5] *Mrs. Dalloway*, p. 11; *To the Lighthouse*, p. 96.
[6] See E. M. Forster, *Virginia Woolf*, p. 21.
[7] *A Room of One's Own*, p. 113.
[8] *Between the Acts*, p. 219.
[9] *The Waves*, p. 288; *The Years*, p. 369.
[10] *Mrs. Dalloway*, p. 231.

[11] In evaluating the character of Septimus, one would do well to remember such works as André Breton's *Nadja*, as well as Mrs. Woolf's mental disposition, for this was a time when men like Yeats indulged in séances, automatic writing, and cabalism, turning toward the unconscious in the hope that the irrational might by freeing man's imagination offer a salvation that reason had failed to provide.

[12] *The Waves*, pp. 114, 172.
[13] *The Waves*, p. 276; passage following, p. 277.
[14] *The Waves*, pp. 260, 105, 224.
[15] David Daiches, *Virginia Woolf*, p. 86.
[16] *The Waves*, p. 288.

[17] *The Waves*, p. 228; subsequent passage, p. 232. In the moment of reality, "when the walls of the mind become transparent," one merges with objective reality in a subject-object fusion similar to that which Coleridge experiences in the ecstatic moment.

[18] *The Waves*, pp. 204, 22, 43, 130; two subsequent passages, pp. 44, 43.
[19] *The Waves*, p. 139.
[20] *The Death of the Moth and Other Essays*, ed. Leonard Woolf, pp. 35-36.

[21] See the long passage on the "discrepancy between time on the clock and time in the mind" in *Orlando: A Biography*, pp. 98-99.

[22] *A Writer's Diary, Being Extracts from the Diary of Virginia Woolf*, ed. Leonard Woolf, p. 138.

[23] *Mrs. Dalloway*, p. 280; the following passage, which both Clarissa and Septimus keep quoting, is from a song in *Cymbeline*, IV: ii, the burial of Cloten.

[24] *Death of the Moth*, p. 33.
[25] *Diary*, pp. 217, 27-28; subsequent passage, pp. 175-176.
[26] *The Captain's Death Bed and Other Essays*, ed. Leonard Woolf, p. 165; passage following, p. 169.
[27] *The Voyage Out*, p. 185.
[28] *Lighthouse*, p. 147.
[29] *Orlando*, p. 55.

30 *The Waves*, p. 277; two passages following, p. 225.

31 *The Years*, p. 249.

32 *Mrs. Dalloway*, pp. 184-185.

33 *Lighthouse*, p. 126; passage following, pp. 240-241.

34 *Diary*, p. 351. Writing seems to have helped Mrs. Woolf gain a hold by externalizing the object, thus making it "real" to her, and establishing a connection with the externalized object, thus providing a link between the inner world and the outer, between subjective and objective reality.

35 Mrs. Woolf's emphasis upon and treatment of things-in-themselves led Bernard Blackstone, in *Virginia Woolf, A Commentary*, to classify Woolf as an "incomplete mystic" similar to the Chinese quietists, but there is also something of the Existentialist in her belief that objects alone are *complete* creations and have their identities given, fixed, whereas man must complete his own creation and establish his own identity.

36 *Lighthouse*, p. 169.

37 *The Waves*, pp. 249, 251.

38 *A Haunted House and Other Short Stories*, ed. Leonard Woolf, pp. 44-45. This passage explains the theme of a later short story, "Solid Objects" (also included in *A Haunted House*), which concerns a young man who becomes so absorbed in his collection of "solid objects"—oddly shaped bits of glass and stone—that he sacrifices a promising political career to his worship of solidity.

39 *Diary*, p. 85; subsequent passage, pp. 129-130.

40 Significantly, in a diary entry for 1926 (p. 97), one finds Mrs. Woolf describing the year as one marked by "moments of great intensity. Hardy's 'moments of vision.'"

41 See *Le Roman Psychologique de Virginia Woolf*, in which M. Florio Delattre discusses the similarities between Mrs. Woolf's moments and Bergson's concept of time.

42 *The Moment and Other Essays*, ed. Leonard Woolf, p. 213; two subsequent passages, pp. 3, 4.

43 See David Daiches, *The Novel and the Modern World*, and *Virginia Woolf*, for an analysis of the time-space shifts in *Mrs. Dalloway*.

44 *Mrs. Dalloway*, p. 47. It is interesting to note in this passage the intimations of a theory which Mrs. Woolf later expresses in *A Room of One's Own*, p. 181, where she accepts Coleridge's belief that the mind is androgynous and goes on to say: "It is fatal to be a man or woman pure and simple; one must be woman-manly or man-womanly."

45 *Mrs. Dalloway*, pp. 230, 232. Years later in *Roger Fry: A Biography*, p. 161, Mrs. Woolf concedes that in reality, "the origin of these moments of vision lies too deep for analysis."

46 *Death of the Moth*, pp. 201 ff.

47 The contradictions that Mrs. Woolf saw in time, death, and personal identity thus become two kinds of truth, the personal and the impersonal.

48 *Lighthouse*, pp. 10-11.

[49] For quotations in this paragraph, see *Lighthouse*, pp. 46, 65, 65-66, 98.

[50] *Lighthouse*, p. 277. Mrs. Woolf's concern for the two kinds of truth (i.e., two views of the same thing) is illustrated in two of her short stories (see *A Haunted House*). In "The New Dress," a young woman at a party feels dowdy and insecure in a dress which made her feel beautiful and self-confident when she first tried it on at the dressmaker's; she wonders which self is "true." And in "A Summing Up," Mrs. Latham ponders the contrast between the beautiful London of her vision and the ugly London of the streets and wonders which view is the "true" one. Virginia Woolf's answer would be that both "selves," both "views," are true, for there are two kinds of truth and nothing is simply one kind.

[51] *Lighthouse*, p. 236.

[52] *Lighthouse*, p. 287.

[53] *Lighthouse*, pp. 240, 270. The transitoriness of the moment, which but temporarily constitutes fixity in the midst of flux, is emphasized in the passage describing Mrs. Ramsey's departure from the dining room (*Lighthouse*, pp. 167-168): "With her foot on the threshold she waited a moment longer in a scene which was vanishing even as she looked, and then, as she moved and took Minta's arm and left the room, it changed, it shaped itself differently; it had become, she knew, giving one last look at it over her shoulder, already the past."

[54] *The Waves*, p. 278.

[55] *Lighthouse*, pp. 99-100.

[56] *Haunted House*, p. 110.

[57] *Lighthouse*, pp. 157-158.

[58] *The Waves*, p. 66.

[59] *Orlando*, p. 298; subsequent passages, pp. 320, 322.

[60] *Lighthouse*, p. 158.

[61] See *A Room of One's Own*, Chapter VI. One of the many themes of *To the Lighthouse* is the basic opposition of the sexes and their function as complements. The rational Mr. Ramsey, who has "an eye like an eagle" for the faraway and the extraordinary but is blind to ordinary things, is perfectly balanced by the intuitive, "short-sighted" Mrs. Ramsey. Each is sustained and completed by the other; Mrs. Ramsey herself describes their relationship and their support of each other as similar to the effect of two different notes which combine to produce a single harmony. See *Lighthouse*, p. 61.

[62] *Orlando*, pp. 327-328; subsequent passage, p. 313.

[63] *Orlando*, p. 329.

[64] *Diary*, p. 136.

[65] *The Waves*, p. 157.

[66] *The Years*, p. 87; subsequent passage, p. 391.

[67] *The Years*, pp. 427-428.

[68] *The Years*, p. 410.

[69] The failure of human communication is a theme in all of Mrs. Woolf's novels, but is particularly emphasized in *The Years*, which suggests three

reasons for that failure: the impossibility of adequate self-expression; the fear of being condemned or laughed at; and outside interruptions. Time and again one of the characters attempts to express something which he is unable to or afraid to communicate. Colonel Pargiter wants to discuss his extra-marital problems with his daughter, but is afraid to; when he attempts to discuss the matter with his sister-in-law, outside interruptions prevent him. At Kitty's party, Martin, struggling for something to say, no sooner finds his tongue than he is interrupted. At Delia's party, Peggy can find neither the right time nor the right words to express her vision. Meeting for the first time since childhood, Rose, Maggie, and Sally deplore the uselessness and futility of talk and admit to themselves that the attempted reunion is a failure. Mrs. Woolf's point is further emphasized by the number of people on the street who, failing to find satisfaction elsewhere, are caught talking to themselves.

⁷⁰ Life, says Mr. Ramsey, is a difficult affair requiring above all "courage, truth, and the power to endure." See *Lighthouse*, p. 11. The necessity of per-sonal integrity, which is implied in Mrs. Woolf's novels, is stated at length in *A Room of One's Own* and *Three Guineas*.

⁷¹ *A Room of One's Own*, p. 181.

⁷² T. S. Eliot, *Four Quartets*, p. 13.

6

The Sex Mysticism of D. H. Lawrence

Like many who protested the modern "Waste Land," D. H. Lawrence felt that by pursuing false values his age and his race had lost the meaning of life. He looked at the industrial, materialistic world he lived in and saw that it had somehow cut itself off, lost its connection with the past. "The new England blots out the old England. And the continuity is not organic, but mechanical." As a result, there was "a gap in the continuity of consciousness." [1] This gap, Lawrence believed, was due to the elevation of mind over body, and to a false individualism. In developing his mental consciousness, man had destroyed his "blood-consciousness" and become a mere half-being; and in the pursuit of individualism, he had lost the proper relationship to his fellow men and to the cosmos—a relationship that past races, in past ages, had known how to maintain. To cure the ills of modern man, Lawrence invented a religion of his own, one based upon the "blood wisdom" of the past and designed to elevate "blood-consciousness" to its rightful place, thus developing the "true" self, the whole man. [2]

Writing to Ernest Collings, January 17, 1913, Lawrence pronounced his faith and took the position he was to maintain throughout his life and writings:

208

My great religion is a belief in the blood, the flesh, as being wiser than the intellect. We can go wrong in our minds. But what our blood feels and believes and says, is always true. The intellect is only a bit and a bridle. What do I care about knowledge. All I want is to answer to my blood, direct, without fribbling intervention of mind, or moral, or what-not. I conceive a man's body as a kind of flame, like a candle flame, forever upright and yet flowing: and the intellect is just the light that is shed on to the things around. And I am not so much concerned with the things around—which is really mind—but with the mystery of the flame forever flowing, coming God knows how from out of practically nowhere, and being *itself*, whatever there is around it, that it lights up.[3]

From this simple beginning, Lawrence developed a highly complicated, sometimes contradictory, system of beliefs. But as confusing as Lawrence may be in minor instances, he is consistent in regard to major themes. His earliest novels, *The White Peacock* (1911), *The Trespasser* (1912), and *Sons and Lovers* (1913), contain in elementary form most of the themes that emerge full-blown in his later works; but the first clear exposition of his ideas is to be found in a series of essays written from 1915 to 1918. In the first of these, the "Crown" essays, Lawrence advances three fundamental beliefs: that the "law of polarity" is the basic law of the universe; that the achievement of one's whole being, one's absolute, transcendent self, involves the reconciliation of opposites; and that by physical union with the opposite sex (a reconciliation), the individual can achieve his absolute self and merge with "the dark almighty of the beginning."[4]

As his starting point, Lawrence takes the Lion and the Unicorn, who are fighting for the Crown. The two animals symbolize contending forces such as darkness and light, animality and spirituality, the unconscious and the conscious; and the Crown represents the state of timeless, absolute being that is achieved when the conflict is perfectly balanced. The Lion and the Unicorn are dependent upon one another for their existence. If either is destroyed, both are lost—and the Crown as well; for the Crown is absolute unity, which can be won only by the perfect balance of opposites. In *Women in Love*, this is the "oneness of struggle" that temporarily unites Birkin and Gerald during their wrestling bout, as it also unites Lawrence's various pairs of lovers. The balanced conflict that Lawrence describes is a creative tension; and the Crown is synonymous with the rainbow, "which leaps out of the breaking of light upon darkness, of darkness upon light, absolute beyond day or night; the rainbow, the iridescence which is darkness at once and light, the two-in-one; the crown that binds them both." [5] "But it is the fight of opposites which is holy. The fight of like things is evil." In *The Rainbow*, it is because Anna does not understand this that she is shocked to find Will "a dark opposite to her, that they were opposites, not complements."

The equilibrium symbolized by the Crown, or rainbow, is not a static condition. As Lawrence explains in another essay, it is really a matter of "relationship," one that is ever changing, for life is a process of becoming, of perpetual creation and destruction, "the two relative absolutes between the opposing infinities," which are light and darkness, or the beginning and the end. [6]

Man himself is founded on the two "infinities." He transcends them and is translated into absolute being when, for a brief moment, he achieves a perfectly balanced relationship; it is during that moment that his old self is destroyed and a new one created, for like the phoenix, Lawrence's favorite symbol, one's new self is created out of the destruction of the old. It is physical union with the opposite sex that enables man to experience the moment and achieve his new self, but neither the union nor the new self is lasting, for union must be followed by separation; and creation by destruction.

Love itself is simply a relationship, one that is in a constant state of flux and flow. "The recurrence of love and conflict" experienced by Anna and Will, and by Tom Brangwen in his relations with his wife and step-daughter, produces a gradual eddying forward. For Lawrence, love is a means, not an end—a kind of "traveling" toward a goal beyond love.

"The Reality of Peace," published in 1917, and "Love," published the following year, further explain Lawrence's concept of duality, and the kind of goal he seeks. Peace, writes Lawrence in the first essay, is "the state of fulfilling the deepest desire of the soul." [7] Man has two basic desires: the desire for creation, or life; and the desire for dissolution, or death; the desire for individuation, and the desire for union.

> Beyond these is pure being, where I am absolved from desire and made perfect. This is when I am like a rose, when I balance for a space in pure adjustment and pure understanding. The timeless quality of *being* is understanding; when I understand fully, flesh and bone, and mind and soul and spirit one rose of unison, then I *am*.

But man is incapable of *maintaining* the balance between his basic desires, so he must allow them to alternate, for both are essential to his development as a whole being; and, unlike the rose, man is born only partially created and must complete his own being. [8]

> I am not born fulfilled. . . . I am born uncreated. I am a mixed handful of life as I issue from the womb. Thenceforth I extricate myself into singleness, *the slow-developed singleness* of manhood. And then I set out to meet the other, the unknown of womanhood. [9] (italics mine)

This meeting, Lawrence explains in the second essay, must involve both spiritual love, which is outgoing—an expression of man's desire to unite with something outside himself—

and sensual love, which rises out of man's desire to complete his own isolate personality.[10]

> There must be two in one, always two in one—the sweet love of communion and the fierce, proud love of sensual fulfilment, both together in one love. And then we are like a rose. We surpass even love. . . .[11]

During a moment of perfect union, one achieves pure being and arrives "in the absolute." But the state of pure being cannot be maintained, for by the law of action and reaction what has been united must then fall asunder. "And, having united in a whole circle of unity, they can go no further in love. The motion of love, like a tide, is fulfilled in this instance; there must be an ebb." [12]

> There is a goal, but the goal is neither love nor death. It is a goal neither infinite nor eternal. It is the realm of calm delight, it is the other-kingdom of bliss. We are like a rose, which is a miracle of pure centrality, pure absolved equilibrium. Balanced in perfection in the midst of time and space, the rose is perfect in the realm of perfection, neither temporal nor spatial, but absolved by the quality of perfection, pure immanence of absolution.
>
> We are creatures of time and space. But we are like a rose; we accomplish perfection, we arrive in the absolute.

Love, when it is complete, leads one to a kind of still point—similar to Eliot's—in which one's absolute being is achieved; one's dualistic tendencies perfectly balanced, perfectly reconciled; and one's soul united with "the dark almighty of the beginning." When it is incomplete (either too spiritual or too sensual), love becomes a destructive force. *The White Peacock* studies a man caught between two women representing the mental and physical extremes of love; both contribute to his destruction. In *Sons and Lovers*, Paul suffers from the destructive effects of three women: his mother and

Miriam, who wish to possess him spiritually; and Clara, who wishes to possess him physically.

The Rainbow (published in 1915) contains Lawrence's first detailed treatment of love's positive effects. At the beginning of their marriage, Anna and Will succeed in reaching the still point, the "core of living eternity."

> Inside the room was a great steadiness, a core of living eternity. Only far outside, at the rim, went on the noise and the destruction. Here at the centre the great wheel was motionless, centred upon itself. Here was a poised, unflawed stillness that was beyond time, because it remained the same, inexhaustible, unchanging, unexhausted. . . .
>
> Then gradually they were passed away from the supreme centre . . . further and further out, towards the noise and the friction. But their hearts had burned and were tempered by the inner reality, they were unalterably glad.[13]

This is the intersection of the timeless with time, the "knowledge of Eternity in the flux of Time" that Ursula seeks; it is the timeless moment that Paul Morel experiences with Clara:

> It was as if he, and the stars, and the dark herbage, and Clara were licked up in an immense tongue of flame, which tore onwards and upwards. Everything rushed along in living beside him; everything was still, perfect in itself, along with him. This wonderful stillness in each thing in itself, while it was being borne along in a very ecstasy of living, seemed the highest point of bliss.[14]

Lawrence's moment of passion, like Eliot's moment of ecstasy, may enable one to reach the still point occasionally, but passion alone is not sufficient; it will not enable one to maintain contact.

Nor will "the timeless ecstasy" that Will experiences in the cathedral: "Here in the church, 'before' and 'after' were folded together, all was contained in oneness. Brangwen came to his consummation." But as Anna makes him realize, the church is an anachronism, an empty, meaningless form. "God burned no more in that bush. It was dead matter lying there. . . ." "Still he loved the church. As a symbol, he loved it. He tended it for what it tried to represent, rather than for that which it did represent."

And so Will continues to follow the old forms. "But in spirit, he was uncreated." [15]

Because theirs is an incomplete love, based on passion alone, Anna and Will fail to achieve a balanced relationship leading to that "beyond love," which is Lawrence's goal. Anna finds it impossible to give herself completely. "She was too much the center of her own universe," "a vain white peacock of a bride." "She believed in the omnipotence of the human mind." And Will, as Anna herself recognizes, "was unready for fulfilment. Something undeveloped in him limited him, there was a darkness in him which he *could* not unfold, which would never unfold in him." [16]

For the sake of his passion, Will relinquishes his soul to Anna; and Anna, unable to find completion in marriage, relinquishes her soul to her children. She sees something beyond, "a faint, gleaming horizon, a long way off, and a rainbow like an archway, a shadow-door with a faintly coloured coping above it." Intuitively, she senses the true goal, but she has neither the courage nor the strength of will to pursue it.

Ursula, like Anna, experiences a timeless moment that takes her to the "core of living eternity." As a preliminary, she and Skrebensky dance together under the moon. "She liked the dance: it eased her, put her into a sort of trance. But it was only a kind of waiting, of using up the time that intervened between her and her pure being." [17] Ursula accepts passion as a means of burning away one's outer shell and of reaching the hard kernel of pure being. But unlike her mother, she realizes that "passion is only part of love." It cannot bring happiness, for it cannot last. In the end, she frees herself from Skrebensky, and all the old, dead forms he stands for, to wait for the man who will come "out of Eternity," the man with whom she can achieve completion. In the rainbow she sees the promise of a new life, a new man—and, Lawrence implies, a new religion.

One may, as Eliot suggested, move negatively with the stream; this is the way of George, of Siegmund, of Paul, of Will—the male protagonists of Lawrence's first four novels. One may insist upon performing one's own isolated dance; this is the way of Lettie, of Helena, of Miriam, and of Anna— their women. Or one may move with and within the stream, creating one's dance within the dance; this is the way of Ursula and of Birkin in Lawrence's fifth novel, where Ursula finds the new man who seeks "something beyond love" and is capable of achieving it.

Women in Love (1920) has been called a book about marriage, but it might also be called a book about death, the two kinds of death: there is pure dissolution—resulting in Gerald's case from the complete immersion of self; in Gudrun's, from complete separation; and there is the death of the phoenix, the death that is a rebirth—it is this that Birkin and Ursula experience. The contrast runs throughout the book. In "Threshold," for example, while Mr. Crich lies dying, Birkin considers marriage, the death that leads to rebirth; and in "Death and Love," when the elder Crich dies, Gerald, who suddenly finds himself facing nothingness, goes in desperation to Gudrun's room, for what amounts to self-confirmation. Significantly, this chapter comes on the heels of one describing the ideal union of Ursula and Birkin.

The latter do not find the way easy, however. Ursula "was not at all sure that it was this mutual unison in separateness that she wanted." And Birkin, who insists upon the "separateness," resents Ursula's apparent desire to absorb him: "Why not leave the other being free, why try to absorb, or melt, or merge? One might abandon oneself utterly to the *moments*, but not to any other being." [18]

Despite his repeated insistence that man must acknowledge the basic duality of life and accept his own "limits," Lawrence himself found acceptance difficult, and particularly resented the limitations imposed by sex. All of his characters reflect this attitude, but none more so than Birkin, who is torn between resistance to, and desire for, further union; he would have preferred to be complete in himself.

> On the whole, he hated sex, it was such a limitation. It was sex that turned man into a broken half of a couple, the woman into the other broken half. And he wanted to be single in himself, the woman single in herself.

Though Birkin knows that one must first lose himself to find himself, he is afraid of submitting himself to another, afraid of the death he must undergo before rebirth is possible. It is the same fear that made Lydia hesitant to marry Tom, in *The Rainbow:* "A shiver, a sickness of new birth passed over her. . . . She wanted it, this new life from him, with him, yet she must defend herself against it, for it was a destruction." [19] It is the same fear that troubles Kate in *The Plumed Serpent.* She does not want to dissolve her personality in the impersonality of sex; nor does she want to admit the truth of Ramón's words: "Soul! No, you have no soul of your own. You have at best only half a soul. It takes a man and a woman together to make a soul." [20]

Lawrence's solution to the problem is not the submission of either sex to the other, but a "pure balance" of the two. In this way both may achieve completion, their individualities strengthened, not weakened; and both may attain the "crown" (one's soul, one's whole being). As Birkin explains to Ursula, what he wants is "a strange conjunction": "—not meeting and mingling;—you are quite right:—but an equilibrium, a pure balance of two single beings:—as the stars balance each other." [21]

To submit to another person's will is fatal. What one should submit to is something beyond either sex: "the great dark knowledge you can't have in your head—the dark involuntary being. It is death to one self—but it is the coming into being of another." To dominate or to allow oneself to be dominated is both sinful and fatal; so is the attempt to experience sensations *without* yielding oneself to "the dark involuntary being."

> between two particular people, any two people on earth, the range of pure sensational experience is limited. The climax of sensual reaction, once reached in any direction, is reached finally, there is no going on. There is only repetition possible, or the going apart of the two protagonists, or the subjugating of the one will to the other, or death.

This perfectly describes the love affair between Gerald and Gudrun, whose relationship typifies what Lawrence condemns as "the nervous, personal, disintegrative sort, the 'white' sex," in contrast to the "dark" sex, which he conceives as creative and impersonal (and one must remember that Lawrence associates darkness with mystery, with "otherness," with impersonality, and the unconscious).

Because they violate Lawrence's code of ethics, Gerald and Gudrun fail where Birkin and Ursula succeed. The pairs are direct contrasts. To Birkin, men and women are individuals with a soul, and it is the individual soul that counts. But to Gerald, human beings are mere instruments. Gerald is a will-driven "God of the machine." "What mattered was the pure instrumentality of the individual. As a man as of a knife: does it cut well? Nothing else mattered." [22] When Gerald assumes control of the family mines, the miners cease to be men and become parts of a machine, which Gerald operates

for the fulfilment of his own will and the subjugation of matter to his own ends.

> There it lay, inert matter, as it had always lain, since
> the beginning of time, subject to the will of men. The
> will of man was the determining factor. Man was the
> arch-god of earth. His mind was obedient to serve his
> will. Man's will was the absolute, the only absolute.
> And it was his will to subjugate Matter to his own
> ends. The subjugation was the point, the fight was the
> be-all, the fruits of victory were mere results. It was not
> for the sake of money that Gerald took over the mines.
> He did not care about money, fundamentally. He was
> neither ostentatious nor luxurious, neither did he care
> about social position, not finally. What he wanted was
> the pure fulfilment of his own will in the struggle with
> the natural conditions.

Once he succeeds in perfecting his machine, Gerald is lost,
for he has no more purpose in life. In desperation he turns to
Gudrun, hoping to regain his sense of being by subjugating
her.

But Gudrun is as strong-willed as he. Unlike her sister
Ursula, she will never yield mindlessly to her emotions. She
is unwilling to submit to "the dark involuntary being." She
wishes to be self-sufficient, to experience sensations with her
mind alone, without yielding anything of herself. Consequently, her love affair with Gerald becomes a battle to the
death.

Death comes in the Tyrolean Alps, where both couples
have gone for Christmas vacation. Having obtained all she
can from Gerald, Gudrun turns to Loerke, a gnome-like sculptor who offers "further subtleties of sensation." It is too much
for Gerald; infuriated by his degrading dependence on one
who has become indifferent to him, he attempts to kill her.
This signifies Gerald's spiritual death, which is followed by

his actual death from a fall in the Alps a short time later. Now free, Gudrun joins Loerke, an act that marks her last step along the path of self-destruction.

In *Psychoanalysis and the Unconscious* (published in 1921, a year after *Women in Love*), and its sequel, *Fantasia of the Unconscious* (1927), Lawrence clarifies many of the theories merely implied in his novels. Particularly important are his concepts of the conscious and the unconscious, and the limitations he imposes upon the mind and the will.

Psychoanalysis defines the conscious as "the spontaneous life-motive in every organism." And:

> By the unconscious we wish to indicate that essential unique nature of every individual creature, which is, by its very nature, unanalysable, undefinable, inconceivable. It cannot be conceived, it can only be experienced, in every single instance. And being inconceivable, we will call it the unconscious. As a matter of fact, *soul* would be a better word. But the word *soul* has been vitiated by the idealistic use, until nowadays it means only that which a man conceives himself to be. And that which a man conceives himself to be is something far different from his true unconscious. So we must relinquish the ideal word soul.[23]

"The true unconscious is the wellhead, the fountain of real motivity." Hence Lawrence calls it "the creative unconscious." But the mind (mental consciousness) "is not a creative reality." "It is a great dynamo of super-mechanical force." [24]

> True, we must all develop into mental consciousness. But mental-consciousness is not a goal; it is a cul-de-sac. It provides us only with endless *appliances* which we can use for the all-too-difficult business of coming to our spontaneous-creative fullness of being.[25]

Lawrence objects to idealism—"intellectualization" he sometimes calls it—because it represents the interference of mind in the passional sphere, the realm of the unconscious. "This motivizing of the passional sphere from the ideal is the final peril of human consciousness. It is the death of all spontaneous, creative life, and the substituting of the mechanical principle."

The mind is "the instrument of instruments"; and the will, "the faculty for self-determination," is its accomplice. When properly controlled, both contribute to the development of one's full being. But this development requires, first, the polarized balance of one's objective and subjective centers of consciousness and their conflicting tendencies toward separation and attachment. Second, since no man is complete in himself, full development requires the polarized union of a man and a woman, as well as a "polarized relation to the external universe." When the mind and the will interfere with this "circuit of polarized unison," they become forces of evil.

"For the end, the goal, is the perfecting of each single individuality, unique in itself—which cannot take place without a perfected harmony between the beloved, a harmony which depends on the at-least-clarified singleness of each being," [26] the "mutual unison in separateness" that Ursula at first rejects.

"Love is a thing to be learned, through centuries of patient effort. It is a difficult, complex maintenance of individual integrity throughout the incalculable processes of interhuman polarity." And this involves the two kinds of love discussed earlier.

A Soul cannot come into its own through that love alone which is unison. If it stresses the one mode, the sympathetic mode, beyond a central point, it breaks its own integrity, and corruption sets in. . . . On both planes of love, upper and lower, the two modes must act complementary to one another, the sympathetic and the separatist. It is the absolute failure to see this, that has torn the modern world into two halves, the one half warring for the voluntary, objective, separatist control, the other for the pure sympathetic.

Gerald and Gudrun are perfect examples of those who struggle for "separatist control"; both allow mind and will to become forces of evil. But of the two, Gudrun is the more sinful because, like Adam and Eve, she makes "a mental object" of sex, for it is *knowledge* of sex that is sinful; original sin is the act of making conscious that which belongs to the instinctual, non-mental sphere.[27]

In *The Trespasser* Lawrence recreates the Fall. The island and the fog, the mist which wraps about them, isolate the lovers in a world of their own, wherein Siegmund (who has never known happiness until this five-day holiday from his wife and children) sees himself as another Adam; and Helena, when the sun becomes too hot, thinks of herself and her lover as two cast forth from Eden, longing for shade. They are happy at first, but not for long, for Helena does not want Siegmund's passion. She wants idealized love, what Lawrence terms personal, *self*-conscious sex, as opposed to the impersonal, unself-conscious kind that Siegmund seeks. "It restored in him the full 'will to live.' But she felt it destroyed her." Siegmund's dawning self-realization, his gradually developing "singleness" leave Helena alone; and out of her sense of separation comes a sense of guilt, then of revulsion. In a terrible scene, during which she repulses him brutally, she transmits her self-consciousness to Siegmund—thus they repeat the Fall, and Siegmund, like the first Adam, feels naked and exposed:

> He went behind the small hill, and looked at the night. It was all exposed. He wanted to hide, to cover himself from the openness, and there was not even a bush under which he could find cover.[28]

In *Fantasia of the Unconscious*, Lawrence continues his attack upon the "ghastly white disease of self-conscious idealism" that kills the "true spontaneous self," and suggests that the white, northern races have gone too far in the development of mental consciousness; their salvation lies in an equivalent development of the "blood-consciousness" typified by the dark, southern races. To acquire "totality of consciousness" man must first seek the buried wisdom that the dark, southern races have inherited from the past. What Lawrence advocates is not a regression, not a return to the savages, but "a great curve in their direction, onwards." [29] This is the direction followed by the Brangwen men in *The Rainbow*. Theirs is the deep, instinctive wisdom of those who live close to the soil.

> It was enough for the men, that the earth heaved and opened its furrow to them, that the wind blew to dry the wet wheat, and set the young ears of corn wheeling freshly round about; it was enough that they helped the cow in labour, or ferreted the rats from under the barn, or broke the back of a rabbit with a sharp knock of the hand. So much warmth and generating and pain and death did they know in their blood, earth and sky and beast and green plants, so much exchange and interchange they had with these, that they lived full and surcharged, their senses full fed, their faces always turned to the heat of the blood, staring into the sun, dazed with looking towards the source of generation, unable to turn round. [30]

What Lawrence suggests is a direction merely; "blood-intimacy" alone is not enough, as the women of Marsh Farm realize. "On them too was the drowse of blood-intimacy, calves sucking and hens running together in droves, and young geese palpitating in the hand while the food was pushed down their throttle. But the women looked out from the heated, blind intercourse of farm-life, to the spoken world beyond." The women faced outwards, to a world in which men attempted to enlarge their "scope and range and freedom"; "whereas the Brangwen men faced inwards to the teeming life of creation, which poured unresolved into their veins."

The Brangwen wife can see that as her husband has power over the cattle, so the vicar has power over her husband; and pondering the matter, "she decided it was a question of knowledge." Hence, she is determined that her children shall be educated, "so that they too could live the supreme life on earth," and "learn the entry into the finer, more vivid circle of life." She is mistaken, Lawrence intimates, not in the goal, but in her way toward it.

The "refining influence" of women Lawrence hated, precisely because it tends to overemphasize mental consciousness at the expense of the "true spontaneous self." In *Fantasia* he writes:

> The business of the mind is first and foremost the pure joy of knowing . . . the pure joy of consciousness. The second business is to act as medium, as interpreter, as agent between the individual and his object. The mind should *not* act as a director or controller of the spontaneous centers.[31]

For "the final aim is not *to know*, but *to be*." "Yet we *must* know, if only in order to learn not to know. The supreme lesson of human consciousness is to learn how *not to know*. That is, how not to *interfere*." Especially in the passional sphere. "Sex is our deepest form of consciousness. It is utterly non-ideal, non-mental. It is pure blood-consciousness." And the true union of man and woman is mindless, unself-conscious.

"You want the paradisal unknowing," Ursula told Birkin. And it is also the "paradisal unknowing" that Lawrence seeks: a recovery of the mindless, undifferentiated state man experienced before the Fall, before consciousness of self made him aware of his isolation. But the recovery is only a temporary release from self in that unison which, Lawrence in-

sists, must be followed by separation; and the "unknowing"
is actually a *deeper* knowledge, because it is felt in one's being—one is a part of what he knows. As Tommy Dukes explains it, in *Lady Chatterley's Lover*:

> "while you *live* your life, you are in some way an organic
> whole with all life. But once you start the mental life
> you pluck the apple. You've severed the connection be-
> tween the apple and the tree: the organic connection.
> And if you've got nothing in your life *but* the mental
> life, then you yourself are a plucked apple . . . you've
> fallen off the tree." [32]

From man's lower, blood-consciousness which is sex-
consciousness) comes "the first and last knowledge of the
living soul." [33] But, according to *Fantasia*, his vision, purposiveness, and desire for power are derived from his upper,
mental consciousness. To achieve fullness of being, man must
balance the upper consciousness with the lower; purposiveness
with sex; the search for power with the search for love.

> Assert sex as the predominant fulfillment, and you get the
> collapse of living purpose in man. You get anarchy. As-
> sert *purposiveness* as the one supreme and pure activity of
> life, and you drift into barren sterility, like our business
> life of today, and our political life.

Though he is familiarly known as the "prophet of sex,"
Lawrence himself felt that Freudian theory went too far, in
that a sexual motive was "attributed to all human activity";
whereas, "the essentially religious or creative motive is the
first motive for all human activity." And for Tom Brangwen,
as for many of Lawrence's characters, sex itself is an expression
of "his desire to find in a woman the embodiment of all his
inarticulate, powerful religious impulses." [34]

At no time does Lawrence lose sight of his real goal, which
is the development of the soul, the whole being. If his writ-

ings seem to overemphasize the role of sex in this development, it is for two reasons: first, his belief that the sexual role is the one most abused, or most neglected, by modern man; and second, his belief that the sexual relationship is itself symbolic of the balance and unity he seeks.[35] Lawrence associates masculinity with light, with mental or upper consciousness, the desire for power, and the desire for separateness; femininity, on the other hand, he associates with darkness, with emotional or lower consciousness, the desire for love, and the desire for absorption. And these distinctions must be maintained, in order to preserve the necessary sense of "otherness"; it is wrong for either sex to adopt the other's traits. Man is the sun; and woman the moon, which balances the sun in a "polarized" relationship that confirms the organic unity of nature, and prefigures the reconciliation of opposites necessary for the development of man's unified self, "his tripartite being, the mother within him, the father within him, and the Holy Ghost, the self which he is supposed to consummate, and which mostly he doesn't," — [36] the self which he must develop out of the first two.

The task is not easy, as Ursula discovers when she passes from girlhood toward womanhood and feels "the cloud of self-responsibility" upon her.

For the woman, there is always the escape into motherhood—Lettie's way in *The White Peacock*. And man can always commit his soul to the care of women; this is the way of the Brangwen men. But the price of failure is the same for both sexes; whenever one depends upon another for the self-creation that is his own responsibility, the result is death of the self: spiritually, as it is for Will and Skrebensky; and sometimes literally, as it is for George, for Siegmund, and for Gerald.[37]

"The completion of the process of love," writes Lawrence in *Aaron's Rod*, "is the arrival at a state of simple, pure self-possession, for man and woman." [38] Jim Bricknell and Aaron mistakenly use love in an attempt to escape self; so does Paul

Morel, who would like "to melt out into the darkness and sway there, identified with the great Being." [39] One must have the courage to accept his singleness, his aloneness. As Alec says in "The Captain's Doll," "We must all be *able* to be alone, otherwise we are just victims." [40] Like Bricknell; or like Skrebensky, whose fear of aloneness, following Ursula's rejection, sends him scurrying into matrimony with the colonel's daughter, fourteen days later.

Lawrence agrees with Henry James that the victim invites the victimizer and is, therefore, equally responsible for the result. The miners are willing victims when Gerald reduces them to parts of an industrial machine; otherwise he could not do so. And Gerald might have pulled himself out of his frozen hollow by means of a great rope attached to iron stakes that the guides had driven into the snow-wall for just such a purpose. "It takes two people to make a murderer," Birkin had told Gerald earlier: "a murderer and a murderee"—the latter being "a man who in a profound if hidden lust desires to be murdered." [41]

Gerald commits the final act of his self-destruction when he attempts to kill Gudrun; yet when he sees the half-buried crucifix in his wild plunge through the snow afterwards, he associates himself with the martyred Jesus, who also died for love. They died because theirs is the wrong kind of love, Lawrence suggests later in *Aaron's Rod*, where Lilly tells Bricknell that his "love and sacrifice" attitude asks for betrayal. "A Jesus makes a Judas inevitable." This is the "Judas principle" that Lawrence returns to in *Kangaroo*, suggesting that Jesus, as master, should have prevented, not accepted, Judas's kiss. And in *The Plumed Serpent*, Ramón defends himself from his attackers, in contrast to Christ, who is presented as a willing victim.

"If I had kissed Judas with live love," says the resurrected Jesus in *The Man Who Died*, "perhaps he would never have kissed me with death." [42] "I lent myself to murder—"

The error, Lawrence explains in *Apocalypse* (1931), which contains the final statement of his beliefs, lies in a false love ideal. Jesus offered a love derived from humility, rather than the tenderness that comes from strength; moreover, he offered a dead love, one that is too spiritual. Reflecting on his mistakes, in *The Man Who Died*, Jesus says: "I would embrace multitudes, I who have never truly embraced even one."

What Lawrence wants is *true* resurrection of the *body*, a totality of being that cannot be achieved merely by seeking one's "isolate salvation," for "no man is or can be a pure individual." [43] "We and the cosmos are one. The cosmos is a vast living body, of which we are still parts"; therefore we must maintain an organic connection with the cosmos and with the other human beings who live in it. The trouble is, "we *cannot bear connection*. That is our malady. We *must* break away, and be isolate. We call that being free, being individual. Beyond a certain point, which we have reached, it is suicide."

The self-realization that Lawrence advocates is similar to Jung's "individuation" process. Man develops his own soul by becoming aware of the God within him. And "necessarily accompanying this more perfect being of myself is the more extended knowledge of that which is not myself." [44] For man is by nature fragmented; therefore, the very existence of his soul (his "wholeness") depends upon contacts and relationships:

> A man who has never had a vital relationship to any other human being doesn't really have a soul. . . . A soul is something that forms and fulfils itself in my contacts, my living touch with people I have loved or hated or truly known. I am born with the clue to my soul. The wholeness of my soul I must achieve. And by my soul I mean my wholeness.

The most vital of all relationships, the closest of all "touch" is that of sex. Therefore Lawrence seeks the regeneration of the world in terms of "sex," by which he means "the whole of the relationship between man and woman." The physical aspect is merely a part of sex, though its most vivid manifestation.

Lawrence recognizes an "eternal hostility" between mind and body; but believing that one's immortal self, one's "Holy Ghost" partakes of both,[45] he seeks a religion that will promote harmony between them, "instead of deliberately, as science and Socrates, Christianity and Buddha have all done, deliberately setting out to murder the one in order to exalt the other."[46] Man must know both if he is to achieve that "totality of consciousness" which is his when body and spirit, the self and the not-self are resolved into a oneness by the "Holy Ghost," which Lawrence conceives as the God within man, the flame of "Life Everlasting": "Out of the great world comes my strength and my reassurance. One could say 'God,' but the word 'God' is somehow tainted. But there *is* a flame or a Life Everlasting wreathing through the cosmos for ever and giving us our renewal, once we get in touch with it."[47]

The Holy Ghost itself is unknowable. "We can only know that from the unknown, profound desires enter in upon us, and that the fulfilling of these desires is the fulfilling of creation."[48] Fulfilling the sex desire is a fulfilling of creation. Through physical union one obtains his renewal; one gets in touch with the life flame; through physical union one reaches the still point and touches "the center of reality."[49] Physical union is "the turning pivot" of a man's life: "Upon this turns the whole rest of his life, from this emanates every motion he betrays."[50]

But, again, love is the means, not the goal, which is the development of one's "innate Holy Ghost"; and this, as Lilly explains in *Aaron's Rod*, requires a continual rebirth, a continual becoming, like the organic growth of a tree.

oint"

of mankind—which I call
brings to fruit your philo-
mbraces in the woman all
that one resultant, from
action.[60]

as temperamentally and
and Russell could long
ve directly, Lawrence at-
ough his writings. *The*
vision of the necessary
be accomplished only by
will promote the proper
en, between leaders and
to develop his soul to its

The Plumed Serpent) ex-
with political reform.
ust be achieved through
Serpent, Ramón makes it
a religious leader, not a
among men, and lords
asters of men we will
Ramón to make a move
: "I must stand in an-
d. —Politics must go
t will." Even President
ence between Ramón
rld with different eyes
ntry from poverty and
oul." [61]
God assumes different
has ceased to function
ute a living god for a
tasia, "Life is *always*

"You are your own Tree of Life, roots and limbs and trunk. Somewhere within the wholeness of the tree lies the very self, the quick: its own innate Holy Ghost. And this Holy Ghost puts forth new buds, and pushes past old limits, and shakes off a whole body of dying leaves. And the old limits hate being empassed, and the old leaves hate to fall. But they must, if the tree-soul says so——" [51]

It is not until Ursula is ready to break out of her old shell and put forth new buds that she sees the vision of the rainbow. Man must have the will and the courage to accept continual death and rebirth. As Birkin suggests in *Women in Love*, man must further creation, or cease to exist.

God can do without man. God could do without the ichthyosauri and the mastodon. These monsters failed creatively to develop, so God, the creative mystery, dispensed with them. In the same way the mystery could dispense with man, should he too fail creatively to change and develop. The eternal creative mystery could dispose of man, and replace him with a finer created being. Just as the horse has taken the place of the mastodon.

It was very consoling to Birkin, to think this. If humanity ran into a *cul de sac*, and expended itself, the timeless creative mystery would bring forth some other being, finer, more wonderful, some new more lovely race, to carry on the embodiment of creation. The game was never up.[52]

To maintain his place in the universe and achieve self-realization, man, like the phoenix, must be continually reborn. But not all men are capable of rebirth.[53] Hence, there must be leaders; there must be masters. There is no such thing as freedom "absolved from control." [54] The leader is a man whose control comes from within, but the average man is

dependent upon control from without; therefore, t[
must recognize his limitations, rid himself of false
and seek true ones, men who are greater in soul. C
can a man achieve the greatest possible developme
own soul, his own innate Holy Ghost.

Aaron's Rod (1922) is the story of a man's sear
leader, of Aaron's progress from an unwilling adi
his inadequacies to a recognition of the greater soul
Lilly and the necessity of *willing* submission to
"men must submit to the greater soul in a mar
guidance: and women must submit to the positive
in man, for their being." [55]

Once he has recognized his limitations, a man
his innate Holy Ghost to direct him to his true m
sin against the Holy Ghost to accept a false one. I
of the leader, on the other hand, to yield to h
Ghost, that he may discover a new vision for m
For "men live and see according to some gradual
and gradually withering vision." [56] By Lawrer
old vision was wearing thin and wanted replaci
needed was a new vision of God which would
society and create, once more, an organic con
vated by a body of living, community beliefs. '
need was Lawrence's hope when he joined fc
trand Russell during World War I. A letter to
Morrell, June 20, 1915, explains his purpose:

> We think to have a lecture hall in
> autumn, and give lectures: he on Ethics, I
> also to have meetings, to establish a littl
> around a *religious belief, which leads to*
> centre in the knowledge of the Infinite, o
> this centre each one of us must work to
> things of our own natures and of our c
> in accord with the Eternal God we kn

be within himself the whole
social passion—which is wha[
sophical writings. The man e
that is not himself, and from
that embrace, comes every nev

It was impossible that two men
ideologically opposed as Lawrenc
agree; but what they failed to achie
tempted to achieve indirectly, th
Plumed Serpent (1923) is Lawrence'
revolution of society, one that can
the establishment of a religion which
relationship between men and wom
followers, and thus enable each man
greatest possible extent.

Kangaroo (published, just prior to
pressed Lawrence's disillusionment
Whatever reforms are accomplished m
religion, not politics. In *The Plumed*
quite clear that his aim is to become
political boss: "We will be masters
among men. But lords of men, and n
not be." Again, when Cipriano urges
toward the presidency, the latter says
other world and act in another wor
their own way, and society must do as i
Montes recognizes the essential diffe
and himself: "Don Ramón sees the wo
from mine. . . . I want to save my cou
unenlightenment, he wants to save its
Like Lawrence, Ramón believes that
shapes; and, believing that Christianity
as a living religion, he wishes to substi
dead Christ. As Lawrence puts it in *Fa*

individual, and therefore never controlled by one law, one God." [62] Each country must have its own savior, and that a natural, not an artificial one: Thor and Wotan for the Teutonic world; Quetzalcoatl for the Mexican-Indian world. Christianity, Ramón tells the Bishop, is a religion of the spirit, beyond the reach of the Indians, who need a religion of the blood, one which will connect them with the universe. "And without a religion that will connect them with the universe, they will all perish. Only religion will serve; not socialism, nor education, nor anything." [63]

In assuming the mantle of Quetzalcoatl and bringing the return of the old gods, Ramón carefully limits his own role to that of a lesser deity serving as messenger of the supreme God, the "unfathomable life-mystery" that lies at the center of the universe. "If I call the mystery the Morning Star, surely it doesn't matter! A man's blood can't beat in the abstract."

Quetzalcoatl, "the Plumed Serpent," is an incarnation of the Morning Star, the lord of both ways come to replace Christ, who was Lord of but one way; for the new religion is designed to reconcile all opposites, to unite the mind and the body, the way of the spirit and the way of the blood.

As an abstract idea, the Morning Star, "Star between day and the dark," symbolizes the "unfathomable life-mystery," the "Unknown Mover" that produces all motion and reconciles all opposites in a "polarized," organic unity. As a concrete object,

> The Morning Star and the Evening Star shine together.
> For man is the Morning Star.
> And woman is the Star of Evening.

Ramón bases his religion upon the male-female relationship because he believes that "it takes a man and a woman together to make a soul. The soul is the Morning Star, emerging from the two." In a perfect union the man and the woman are "consummated into a spark of oneness"; [64] for a moment, they experience impersonal reality and become one with the great force of creation, the "Unknown Mover." Such is the true purpose, the true goal of sex. The Indian dance performed in the village plaza symbolizes that physical union which dissolves one's personal identity in the larger, impersonal reality and carries one to Lawrence's still point. The dance pattern is that of two separate wheels revolving in opposite directions, with the men forming the outer circle and the women, the inner one. "Men and women alike danced with faces lowered and expressionless, abstract, gone in the deep absorption of men into the greater manhood, women into the greater womanhood. It was sex, but the greater, not the lesser sex." [65] Having immersed themselves in the larger, impersonal reality of sex, the men and women join one another to form a single, great wheel, symbolizing their completed union.

Hating the mechanized quality of modern civilization, wishing to be delivered "from man's automatism" and to recover a sense of the mystery of life, Kate is drawn to the new religion and the men who promote it. But she has been dominated too long by will and intellect and developed too great a pride in her own individuality to yield herself completely to anything. Hence she resists Cipriano as she does Mexico itself, for both threaten her with a primitive force that would destroy her individuality and pull her down into the darkness; and she finds but little comfort in Ramón's words: "It may be you need to be drawn down, down, till you send roots into the deep places again. Then you can send up the sap and the leaves back to the sky, later."

Kate needs Cipriano if she would achieve self-realization. She must relinquish her lesser self before she can achieve a greater one and fulfill her own creation; she must be capable of the willing submission she has so despised in Teresa. As Teresa has tried to explain, it is not a question of subservience or domination, but simply the recognition that each is part of the other's soul.[66] Each yields in his own way to that which is both his opposite and his counterpart, and together they form a complete soul and achieve organic unity of being.

In accepting a mate, what one really submits to is the Holy Ghost, the God within himself and the God within the other; and one accepts the mate to whom his own innate Holy Ghost directs him. In accepting a leader, as Cipriano does Ramón, one follows the same principle. Thus, and only thus, can one develop his own soul and maintain "the light of the human adventure into consciousness, which is, essentially, the light of human God-knowledge." [67]

In his last novels, *Lady Chatterley's Lover* (twice revised), *The Escaped Cock* (later published as *The Man Who Died*), and *The Virgin and the Gipsy*, Lawrence drops all discussion of mass conversion and reform. Having apparently lost faith in the masses, he concentrates upon the relationships of individual men and women—the basis, from first to last, of all his writings and his theories. The final aim of every human being, the full achievement of himself, is to be accomplished by a "polarized" relationship with the opposite sex which enables him, in moments of consummation, to experience a "totality of consciousness," a oneness of being—"the Holy Ghost which is with us after our Pentecost, and which we may not deny." [68]

In the third edition of *Lady Chatterley's Lover* (originally to be entitled "Tenderness"), Lawrence attempts to describe the kind of physical relationship he advocates: a matter of "touch" and "tenderness" as natural as that of a deer nuzzling his doe; a response to the "otherness" of one's mate, and a meeting that increases one's awareness of the mystery of life.

If there is one characteristic of Lawrence's that stands out above all others, it is his sense of the mystery of creation, and his basic condemnation of modern civilization is that its mechanization destroys the simple wonder man once had when he lived close to the soil. This is the "ancient sense-consciousness" he speaks of in *Apocalypse*, the "sense-awareness" he would have us recover. This awareness he himself displays throughout his works, as in his description of the woods before Connie and Mellors' second meeting at the hut:

> The wood was silent, still and secret in the evening drizzle of rain, full of the mystery of eggs and half-open buds, half-unsheathed flowers. In the dimness of it all trees glistened naked and dark as if they had unclothed themselves, and the green things on earth seemed to hum with greenness. [69]

Every bush that hums with life is, like the one described in *The White Peacock*, a "sacred golden bush," for the God-flame is in everything; that is the mystery of creation.

"It is all very well to talk about a Supreme Being, an Anima Mundi, an Oversoul, an Infinite: but it is all just human invention. Come down to actuality. Where do you see Being?— In individual men and women. Where do you find an Anima?— In living individual creatures. Where do you look for a soul?— In a man, in an animal, in a tree or flower. And all the rest, about Supreme Beings and Anima Mundis and Oversouls, is just abstractions. . . . If we look for God, let us look in the bush where he sings. That is, in living creatures." [70]

One's soul, one's "totality of consciousness," is his awareness of the Holy Ghost, the God within each man, the flame of "Life Everlasting" which burns throughout the cosmos. And one maintains the growth of his soul by the periodic rebirth or renewal that he experiences during the moment when, by means of a physical union, he reaches the still point. In that moment all opposites are reconciled; one achieves impersonal reality; one is united with the life force, the "Unknown Mover," and undergoes the death and rebirth necessary for the further growth of his soul.

The still point Lawrence seeks is quite similar to Eliot's, despite the fact that Eliot's is defined in Christian terms,

whereas Lawrence's is not. The essential difference between
the two men lies in their approach. Eliot's begins with the
moment of ecstasy, which incidentally leads one to the still
point. Realizing that the ecstatic moment is neither frequent
nor enduring, he advocates a deliberate way of life that will
enable one to maintain contact with the still point. Lawrence
makes a similar beginning, the moment of passion, that leads
to a similar conclusion, a deliberate way of life; but Eliot
emphasizes the spiritual, Lawrence the sensual. Eliot seeks
purification *from* the passions, whereas Lawrence seeks purification *through* the passions, which are "necessary, forever
necessary, to burn out false shames and smelt out the heaviest
ore of the body into purity. With the fire of sheer sensuality." [71]

One is united with the *other* and becomes "whole" in love,
then by the "pure, fierce passion of sensuality" is "burned into
essentiality" and driven from the center outward into singleness. "It is a destructive fire, the profane love. But it is the
only fire that will purify us into singleness, fuse us from the
chaos into our own unique gem-like separateness of being." [72]

Though the ultimate goal is much the same, Eliot's approach is to develop one's mental consciousness and transcend
the body; physical love is to be transcended by spiritual love.
Lawrence would develop one's emotional consciousness and
sanctify the body; physical love and spiritual love are both to
be transcended by a complete love involving the whole being.
For Eliot the spirit *is* the soul. For Lawrence the spirit is but
half the soul; for that includes both spirit (or mind) and body.

What man wants, says Lawrence, is "his living wholeness
and his living unison," a matter of relationship which includes physical fulfillment while one is still in the flesh:

> For man, the vast marvel is to be alive. For man, as for
> flower, beast and bird, the supreme triumph is to be most
> vividly, most perfectly alive. Whatever the unborn and

the dead may know, they cannot know the beauty, the marvel of being alive in the flesh. The dead may look after the afterwards. But the magnificent here and now of life in the flesh is ours, and ours alone, and ours only for a time. We ought to dance with rapture that we should be alive and in the flesh, and part of the living, incarnate cosmos. I am part of the sun as my eye is part of me. That I am part of the earth my feet know perfectly, and my blood is part of the sea. My soul knows that I am part of the human race, my soul is an organic part of the great human soul, as my spirit is part of my nation. In my own self I am part of my family. There is nothing of me that is alone and absolute except my mind, and we shall find that the mind has no existence by itself, it is only the glitter of the sun on the surface of the waters.

So that my individualism is really an illusion. I am part of the great whole, and I can never escape. But I *can* deny my connections, break them, and become a fragment. Then I am wretched.

What we want is to destroy our false, inorganic connections, especially those related to money, and reestablish the living organic connections with the cosmos, the sun and earth, with mankind and nation and family. Start with the sun, and the rest will slowly, slowly happen.[73]

NOTES

[1] *Lady Chatterley's Lover*, pp. 209 and 212.
[2] Lawrence's "religion," like Yeats's system, is an eclectic one; for a study of the sources from which Lawrence drew his ideas, see William York Tindall's *D. H. Lawrence and Susan his Cow*.
[3] *The Letters of D. H. Lawrence*, ed. Aldous Huxley, p. 95.
[4] *Reflections on the Death of a Porcupine and Other Essays*, p. 24.
[5] *Reflections*, p. 16; passage following, p. 18.
[6] *Reflections*, pp. 135, 78.
[7] *Phoenix: The Posthumous Papers of D. H. Lawrence*, ed. Edward McDonald, p. 669; passage following, p. 680.

8 For a more detailed discussion of this point, see "Life," which was first published in 1918 and later included in *Phoenix*. Like Virginia Woolf, Lawrence felt that natural objects alone are 'finished' products, complete in themselves.

9 *Phoenix*, p. 694.

10 Throughout his writings Lawrence uses the term "spiritual" as synonymous with "mental"; and, as he explains in his essay on "New Mexico," he uses the term "sensual" to denote "an experience deep down in the senses, inexplicable and inscrutable." See *Phoenix*, p. 144.

11 *Sex, Literature, and Censorship: Essays*, ed. Harry T. Moore, p. 37. See T. S. Eliot's use of the rose in Part V of "Little Gidding"; see, also, Yeats's symbol of the rose, particularly in *The Shadowy Waters*.

12 *Sex, Literature, and Censorship*, p. 33; subsequent passage, p. 35.

13 *The Rainbow*, p. 135; passage following, p. 464.

14 *Sons and Lovers*, p. 427.

15 For this and preceding passages, see *Rainbow*, pp. 189-194.

16 *Rainbow*, p. 197; the three preceding quotations, pp. 89, 126, 162.

17 *Rainbow*, p. 301. Like Yeats, Lawrence was intensely interested in all forms of ritual—and particularly the dance—as a means of identifying oneself with the hidden forces of the universe and of attuning oneself to the rhythm of the cosmos; see *The Plumed Serpent*.

18 *Women in Love*, pp. 353-354; subsequent passage, p. 226.

19 *Rainbow*, p. 33.

20 *The Plumed Serpent*, p. 387.

21 *Women in Love*, pp. 167-168; subsequent passages, pp. 47 and 515.

22 *Women in Love*, p. 254; subsequent passage, p. 255.

23 *Psychoanalysis and the Unconscious*, pp. 41-42.

24 *Psychoanalysis*, pp. 26, 46, 121, 122. "Mind," as Lawrence uses the term, refers solely to mental consciousness.

25 *Psychoanalysis*, p. 126; subsequent passage, p. 31.

26 *Psychoanalysis*, p. 59; two subsequent passages, pp. 118, 105-106.

27 See *Psychoanalysis*, p. 23.

28 *The Trespasser*, p. 84.

29 *Studies in Classic American Literature*, p. 203. The gamekeeper or groom so often found in Lawrence's stories is Lawrence's version of the savage, whose merit lies in his protection of, and preference for natural life as opposed to mechanical life.

30 *Rainbow*, pp. 2-3; subsequent passages, see pp. 2-4.

31 *Fantasia of the Unconscious*, p. 190; subsequent passages, pp. 85, 98, 256.

32 *Lady Chatterley's Lover*, p. 75.

33 *Fantasia*, p. 256; subsequent passages, pp. 155, 34.

34 *Rainbow*, p. 13.

35 Realizing that men and women can never maintain a perfect relationship or achieve complete fulfillment, Lawrence advocates "blood-brotherhood" as supplementary to the sex relationship; see the chapter on "Blutbruderschaft," *Women in Love*, also Birkin's final discussion, p. 547.

[36] *Fantasia*, pp. 24-25.

[37] Though all three commit suicide, Siegmund's death alone is deliberately conceived; he accepts a solution that Paul Morel also considers, and rejects. Both Lawrence and Woolf would have agreed with Camus that "in a universe suddenly divested of illusions and lights," the "one truly philosophical problem" is suicide, and Siegmund's death seems to have served as a kind of vicarious suicide for Lawrence, as Septimus' death was for Mrs. Dalloway—and perhaps for Virginia Woolf herself.

[38] *Aaron's Rod*, p. 195.

[39] *Sons and Lovers*, p. 337.

[40] *The Captain's Doll*, p. 65.

[41] *Women in Love*, p. 36.

[42] *The Man Who Died*, p. 90; subsequent passages, pp. 91, 26.

[43] *Apocalypse*, p. 193; subsequent passages, pp. 45, 198.

[44] *Phoenix*, p. 433; subsequent passages, pp. 192, 194.

[45] See *Twilight in Italy*, pp. 80-82, where Lawrence discusses the "twofold" nature of the Infinite in relation to the Christian Trinity.

[46] *The First Lady Chatterley*, p. 192.

[47] *Phoenix*, p. 202.

[48] *Sex, Literature, and Censorship*, p. 39.

[49] *Rainbow*, p. 119.

[50] *Phoenix*, p. 444.

[51] *Aaron's Rod*, p. 344.

[52] *Women in Love*, p. 545. Lawrence's hope of a new race accounts for his interest in the Noah story and his symbolic use of the flood and the rainbow; see *The Rainbow* and *The Virgin and the Gipsy*.

[53] See Lawrence's treatment of this theme in *The Man Who Died*, first published in Paris, 1929, as *The Escaped Cock*.

[54] *Kangaroo*, p. 413.

[55] *Aaron's Rod*, p. 347.

[56] *Fantasia*, p. xiv.

[57] *Letters*, p. 243.

[58] *D. H. Lawrence's Letters to Bertrand Russell*, ed. Harry T. Moore, pp. 83, 53.

[59] *Assorted Articles*, p. 257.

[60] *Letters to Russell*, pp. 63, 36-37.

[61] *Plumed Serpent*, pp. 177, 190, 189.

[62] *Fantasia*, p. 187.

[63] *Plumed Serpent*, p. 261; three subsequent passages, pp. 271, 339, 387.

[64] *Reflections*, p. 90.

[65] *Plumed Serpent*, p. 128; subsequent passage, p. 76.

[66] See Virginia Woolf's theory of complementary souls as it is expressed in *Mrs. Dalloway* and *Orlando;* both Virginia Woolf and D. H. Lawrence believed that man's "self" is incomplete, but Lawrence believed that through his contacts with others—particularly those of the opposite sex—man can

ultimately achieve a complete self and establish his personal identity, whereas Mrs. Woolf maintained that such contacts merely establish one's *sense* of identity and that, in the final analysis, personal identity is an illusion, though a necessary illusion.

⁶⁷ *Assorted Articles*, p. 253.

⁶⁸ *Fantasia*, p. 191.

⁶⁹ *Lady Chatterley's Lover*, p. 171.

⁷⁰ *Phoenix*, p. 708.

⁷¹ *Lady Chatterley's Lover*, p. 312. Lawrence's notorious use of four-letter words is also intended "to burn out false shames."

⁷² *Phoenix*, p. 154.

⁷³ *Apocalypse*, pp. 222-224.

In Conclusion

In the preceding discussions, excluding that of Coleridge, I have attempted to show, first, the general attitude of despair which the modern authors share in regard to their age; then to point up the ideas that, resulting from that attitude, dominate the authors' writings and propel them in the direction Eliot took. Since Eliot's concept is my frame of reference, I have also attempted to indicate some of the basic similarities and differences between Eliot's ideas and those of the particular writer under discussion; there are, however, certain observations that one may make about the group as a whole—first of all, in regard to the four characteristic features of Eliot's concept.

In each of the writers one finds the concept of certain absolutes—complete reality, complete being, or unity of being, the complete vision, full consciousness—that involve a reconciliation of opposites, though with James it is more a matter of recognition than of reconciliation, and Virginia Woolf barely mentions the creative tension which Eliot, Coleridge, Yeats, and Lawrence consider a by-product of that reconciliation. The outside spiritual center that one finds in Yeats, in Lawrence, and is implied in Coleridge (who, like Eliot, approaches it in terms of Christian dogma), is entirely lacking in James and merely suggested by Mrs. Woolf. All, however, emphasize the timeless moment, "the trysting-place" of time and eternity, and the ideal state of enlightenment it provides. The ecstatic moment of Eliot and of Coleridge has its equivalent in Yeats's "moment of intensity," the "fiery moment"; in James's moment of experience; in Mrs. Woolf's moment of reality; and in Lawrence's moment of passion. And all advocate, with varying degrees of emphasis, a definite set of requirements or a conscious way of life as the only means of achieving the absolutes one seeks. For Eliot this means a lifetime of Christian effort, and Coleridge urges one to make himself "all permeable to a holier power," "God only to behold, and know, and feel,/ Till by exclusive consciousness of God/ All self-annihilated it shall make/ God its Identity: God all in all!/ We and our Father one!"; for Yeats it means finding one's anti-self, "the condition of arduous full life," and undergoing the antithetical cycles that lead to a "phaseless sphere"; for Lawrence it means acceptance of the mate one's innate Holy Ghost selects, and submission to the death-and-rebirth process required for the development of one's soul; for James it means the deliberate "practice of consciousness" and the application of the aesthetic ideal to all one does; and for Mrs. Woolf, the search for "reality," the whole vision, requiring "silence and solitude," "courage, truth, and the power to endure."

In all of the writers under discussion one finds an emphasis upon tradition and order; all imply a kind of super-consciousness that is acquired during moments of enlightenment; and four of them show a vital concern for self-integration. But by self-integration, Eliot means spiritual development in terms of orthodox Christianity, and his ultimate goal, complete union with the "still point," is to be achieved by a Christian way of life.

Yeats and Lawrence, on the other hand, define integration in terms of their private religions. For Yeats it means the soul's progress toward the "phaseless sphere," where one achieves "ultimate reality," a condition of absolute unity of being in which one is released from the conflicts and complexities of earthly life; to reach this sphere and be delivered from the material world, one's soul must pass through a series of antithetical phases or cycles.

In Eliot and Yeats the primary concern is for spiritual development. For Lawrence, however, the development of one's soul, one's whole being, involves both body and spirit. To achieve an organic unity of being and maintain the "organic" growth of his soul, one must establish a "polarized" relationship with the opposite sex; thus and only thus can one experience the ideal physical union that will lift him to the still point, where he will become one with the life force and undergo the death-and-rebirth process which his growth requires.

The condition of mindlessness that Lawrence believes one must submit to, from time to time, in the course of self-integration bears a marked similarity to the trance-like suspension of will and intellect that Yeats advocates in the process of obtaining the complete vision. Yeats wished to suspend both will and intellect to free the imagination, so that it, in turn, might free the personal unconscious, allow it to merge with the Great Memory (a kind of collective unconscious), and thus draw up both the complete vision and the images by which one might convey that vision. Similarly, Lawrence wished to suspend will and intellect to free the personal unconscious (the individual's "blood-consciousness"), so that during sexual union it might merge with a universal sex-consciousness (a kind of collective unconscious), and thus bring about the rebirth and the new vision required for the further development of one's self, or soul. In the process of self-integration, Lawrence's personal unconscious ("creative unconscious" he sometimes calls it) has a creative function similar to that which, in the process of artistic creation and the development of one's vision, is performed by Yeats's combined imagination and personal unconscious, and by Coleridge's secondary or poetic imagination.[1]

In considering their ultimate goals for the human being

and their attitudes toward self-development, one finds a metaphysical element in Eliot, Yeats, and Lawrence that is lacking in Henry James, who does not recognize any outside spiritual force to which man is subject. James's goal is full, personal consciousness, by which he means the extension of one's mental consciousness, in contrast to Lawrence's extension of emotional consciousness; for in James, even one's emotions are objectified, and emotional awareness becomes a mental quality. Ultimately, Lawrence seeks a "totality of consciousness," although he places greater emphasis upon its emotional aspects, which he believes to be the most neglected by modern man. His is the more comprehensive ideal. The concepts of self-development advanced by Eliot, Yeats, and Lawrence are also more comprehensive than the one advanced by James. Where the former seek unity of being, James seeks beauty of being; and where the former seek impersonal reality, James seeks personal reality.

For Virginia Woolf there is no final meaning or solution to life. The value of life is in the living of it and in one's moments of contact with "reality," which she considers the essence of objective life and subjective being. Like James and Lawrence, she is concerned with the problem of personal identity; and, like Lawrence, concludes that personal identity is an illusion, that individuals are not complete in themselves. She does not, however, advance a theory of self-development, as such. Her goal is to understand the meaning of reality, and perceive the whole vision. Mrs. Woolf believes that one's vision must be perpetually remade, just as Lawrence believes that one's soul must be continually remade; but unlike Lawrence, who desires a perpetual flux, a "creative chaos," Mrs. Woolf fears the continual flux and flow which necessitates the remaking of one's life and vision. Hers is an attempt to fix the moment, make it permanent, and thus to triumph over the chaos, the fluidity, and the transitoriness of life.

It is interesting to observe the way in which the six authors approach or define *reality*. Through nature, as perceived by the imagination, Coleridge identifies himself with the "Supreme Reality," which is God. For Eliot, also, the supreme reality is God; and personal reality is to be achieved by union with the still point (union with God); for Eliot believes that one is completely "real" only when he has become a part of a larger, impersonal reality.

Lawrence approaches reality through sexual union, advocating "the deep absorption of men into the greater manhood, women into the greater womanhood"—for he, too, believes that complete personal reality is attainable only by a submission to a larger, impersonal reality.

Yeats seeks "ultimate reality," a condition of absolute unity of being to be realized upon the soul's arrival in the "phaseless sphere." James attempts to develop personal reality through the extension of consciousness in moments of experience. And by means of similar moments, involving a similar extension, Virginia Woolf seeks contact with an abstract, total reality, which she considers the one permanent quality in life with which one may identify himself.

I suggest that the preoccupation with reality evidenced by the last five authors springs from a sense of insecurity caused by the present-day lack of a common body of beliefs; and that the search for some absolute value or spiritual center with which one may identify himself results from the overthrow of orthodox belief that is foreshadowed in Coleridge's impassioned defense of it. Lawrence has defined art as "a form of supremely delicate awareness and atonement—meaning at-oneness, the state of being at one with the object"—and insisted that his novels were written "from the depth of my religious experience." [2] Taken in its broadest interpretation, this is a statement that might be made of all the writers considered here, for each is seeking in his own way to renew the "bonds of union" which in his age seem broken. James, Yeats, Eliot, Mrs. Woolf, and Lawrence are each attempting an answer to or an escape from the spiritual isolation of the modern "Waste Land"; and their various manifestations of the still point concept are, therefore, as characteristic of our twentieth-century literature as the "Waste Land" theme itself.

NOTES

1 I am indebted to William York Tindall for drawing my attention to the similarity between Lawrence's concept of the unconscious and Coleridge's concept of the imagination; see Mr. Tindall's introduction to *The Later D. H. Lawrence*, p. vii.

2 *Assorted Articles*, p. 203; and *The Letters of D. H. Lawrence*, ed. Aldous Huxley, p. 192.

Bibliography

Adams, Hazard. *Blake and Yeats: The Contrary Vision*. Ithaca, 1955.

Anderson, Quentin. *The American Henry James*. New Brunswick, 1957.

Andreas, Osborn. *Henry James and the Expanding Horizon*. Seattle, 1948.

Anonymous. *On the Four Quartets of T. S. Eliot*, foreword by Ray Campbell. London, 1953.

Baker, James V. *The Sacred River: Coleridge's Theory of Imagination*, introduction by Richard Harter Fogle. Baton Rouge, 1957.

Barber, C. L. "T. S. Eliot After Strange Gods," *The Southern Review*, VI (Autumn, 1940), 387-416.

Beach, Joseph Warren. *The Method of Henry James*. New Haven, 1918.

Beer, John B. *Coleridge, the Visionary*. London, 1959.

Bennett, Joan. *Virginia Woolf: Her Art as a Novelist*. New York, 1945.

Blackstone, Bernard. *Virginia Woolf: A Commentary*. London, 1949.

Blavatsky, H. P. *The Secret Doctrine: The Synthesis of Science, Religion, and Philosophy*. 2 vols. in one. Los Angeles, 1925.

Blunden, Edmund, and Griggs, Earl Leslie, eds. *Coleridge: Studies by Several Hands on the Hundredth Anniversary of His Death*. London, 1934.

Boulger, James D. *Coleridge as Religious Thinker*. New Haven, 1961.

Bowden, Edwin T. *The Themes of Henry James: A System of Observation through the Visual Arts*. New Haven, 1956.

Brett, R. L. *Reason and Imagination: A Study of Form and Meaning in Four Poems*. New York, 1960.

Brewster, Dorothy, and Burrell, Angus. *Adventure or Experience, Four Essays on Certain Writers and Readers of Novels*. New York, 1930.

Cary, Elizabeth. *The Novels of Henry James*. New York, 1905.

Carter, Frederick. *D. H. Lawrence and the Body Mystical*. London, 1932.

Coleridge, E. H. "The Lake Poets in Somersetshire," *Transactions of the Royal Society of Literature of the United Kingdom*, 2d series, XX (1899), 105-131.

Coleridge, Samuel Taylor. *Anima Poetae: From the Unpublished Note-books of Samuel Taylor Coleridge*, ed. E. H. Coleridge. Boston, 1895.

——. *Biographia Epistolaris; Being the Biographical Supplement of Coleridge's Biographia Literaria*, ed. A. Turnbull. 2 vols. London, 1911.

——. *Biographia Literaria by S. T. Coleridge*, ed. with his aesthetical essays by John Shawcross. 2 vols. Oxford, 1907.

——. *Coleridge's Miscellaneous Criticism*, ed. T. M. Raysor. London, 1936.

——. *Coleridge's Shakespearean Criticism*, ed. T. M. Raysor. 2 vols. Cambridge, Mass., 1930.

——. *The Complete Poetical Works of Samuel Taylor Coleridge*. ed. E. H. Coleridge. 2 vols. Oxford, 1912.

——. *The Complete Works of Samuel Taylor Coleridge*, ed. William G. T. Shedd. 7 vols. New York, 1853.

——. *Letters of Samuel Taylor Coleridge*, ed. E. H. Coleridge, 2 vols. New York, 1895.

——. *Miscellanies, Aesthetic and Literary*, ed. T. Ashe. London, 1892.

Coleridge, Samuel Taylor. *The Notebooks of Samuel Taylor Coleridge*, ed. Kathleen Coburn. Vol. I, 2 parts: text and notes, 1794-1804. New York, 1957.

———. *The Philosophical Lectures, Hitherto Unpublished*, ed. Kathleen Coburn. London, 1950.

———. *The Table Talk and Omniana of Samuel Taylor Coleridge*, Oxford ed. London, 1917.

Crews, F. C. *The Tragedy of Manners: Moral Drama in the Later Novels of Henry James*. New Haven, 1957.

Daiches, David. *The Novel and the Modern World*. Chicago, 1939.

———. *Virginia Woolf*. Norfolk, Conn., 1942.

De Selincourt, Ernest. "Coleridge's *Dejection: An Ode*," in English Association's *Essays and Studies*, XXII (1936), 7-25.

Dobrée, Bonamy. *The Lamp and the Lute*. Oxford, 1929.

Drew, Elizabeth A. *The Modern Novel: Some Aspects of Contemporary Fiction*. New York, 1926.

———. *T. S. Eliot: The Design of His Poetry*. New York, 1949.

Dupee, F. W. *Henry James*. New York, 1951.

Dupee, F. W., ed. *The Question of Henry James: A Collection of Critical Essays*. New York, 1945.

Edel, L., and Laurence, D. *A Bibliography of Henry James*. London, 1957.

Eliot, T. S. *After Strange Gods: A Primer of Modern Heresy*. New York, 1934.

———. *The Cocktail Party*. New York, 1950.

———. *Collected Poems, 1909-1935*. New York, 1936. Copyright, 1936, by Harcourt, Brace and World, Inc.

———. *The Complete Poems and Plays*. New York, 1952.

———. *The Confidential Clerk*. New York, 1954.

———. "The Development of Leibniz's Monadism," *The Monist*, XXVI (October, 1916), 534-556.

———. *The Elder Statesman*. New York, 1959.

———. *Essays Ancient and Modern*. London, 1936.

Eliot, T. S. *The Family Reunion*. New York, 1939. Copyright, 1939, by T. S. Eliot. Reprinted by permission of Harcourt, Brace and World, Inc.

——. *For Lancelot Andrewes: Essays on Style and Order*. New York, 1929.

——. *Four Quartets*. New York, 1943. Copyright, 1943, by T. S. Eliot. Reprinted by permission of Harcourt, Brace and World, Inc.

——. *The Idea of a Christian Society*. New York, 1940.

——. "Leibniz's Monads and Bradley's Finite Centers," *The Monist*, XXVI (October, 1916), 566-576.

——. "Literature and the Modern World," *American Prefaces*, I (November, 1935), 19-22.

——. *Murder in the Cathedral*. New York, 1935. Copyright, 1935, by Harcourt, Brace and World, Inc.

——. *Notes Towards the Definition of Culture*. New York, 1949.

——. *On Poetry and Poets*. New York, 1957.

——. "Poetry and Propaganda," *The Bookman*, LXX (February, 1930), 595-602.

——. *The Rock: A Pageant Play*. London, 1934.

——. *Selected Essays*, New Edition. New York, 1950.

——. " 'Ulysses,' Order, and Myth," *The Dial*, LXXV (November, 1923), 480-483.

——. *The Use of Poetry and the Use of Criticism*. Cambridge, Mass., 1933.

Ellmann, Richard. *The Identity of Yeats*. New York, 1954.

——. *Yeats: The Man and the Masks*. New York, 1948.

Fogle, R. H. "The Dejection of Coleridge's Ode," *ELH*, XVII (1950), 71-77.

Forster, E. M. *Virginia Woolf*. New York, 1942.

Foster, Genevieve W. "The Archetypal Imagery of T. S. Eliot," *PMLA*, LX (1945), 567-585.

Freeman, Mary. *D. H. Lawrence: A Basic Study of His Ideas*. Gainesville, 1955.

Gallup, Donald. *T. S. Eliot: A Bibliography*, including con-

tributions to periodicals and foreign translations. New
York, 1953.

Gibbon, Monk. *The Masterpiece and the Man.* New York, 1959.

Gwynn, Stephen, ed. *Scattering Branches: Tributes to the Memory
of W. B. Yeats.* New York, 1940.

Haney, J. L. *A Bibliography of Samuel Taylor Coleridge.* Philadelphia, 1903.

Hoare, Dorothy M. *Some Studies in the Modern Novel.* Litch-
field, Conn., 1940.

Holder-Barell, Alexander. *The Development of Imagery and Its
Functional Significance in Henry James's Novels.* Bern, 1959.

Holtby, Winifred. *Virginia Woolf.* London, 1932.

Hone, Joseph. *W. B. Yeats: 1865-1939.* New York, 1943.

Hough, Graham. *The Dark Sun: A Study of D. H. Lawrence.*
New York, 1957.

James, Henry. *The Ambassadors,* introductions by Martin S.
Sampson and John C. Gerber. New York, 1948.

———. *The American,* introduction by Joseph Warren Beach.
New York, 1950.

———. *The American Novels and Stories of Henry James,* ed.
F. O. Matthiessen. New York, 1947.

———. *The American Scene.* New York, 1907.

———. *The Art of Fiction and Other Essays,* ed. Morris Roberts.
New York, 1948.

———. *The Art of the Novel: Critical Prefaces by Henry James,* ed.
R. P. Blackmur. New York, 1937.

———. *The Aspern Papers; The Europeans,* introduction by
Joseph Bottkol. Norfolk, Conn., 1950.

———. *The Awkward Age.* London, 1899.

———. *The Bostonians.* New York, 1945.

———. *The Complete Plays of Henry James,* ed. Leon Edel. New
York, 1949.

———. *Daisy Miller.* Vol. XVIII of *The Novels and Tales of
Henry James.* 26 vols. New York, 1907-1917.

———. *English Hours.* Boston, 1905.

James, Henry. *Essays in London and Elsewhere*. New York, 1893.

——. *French Poets and Novelists*. London, 1904.

——. *The Golden Bowl*, introduction by R. P. Blackmur. 2 vols. in one. New York, Grove Press, 1952. Copyright, 1904, by Charles Scribner's Sons.

——. *Hawthorne*. New York, 1880.

——. *Henry James: Selected Short Stories*, ed. Quentin Anderson. New York, 1950.

——. *An International Episode*. New York, 1902.

——. "Is There a Life After Death?" in *In After Days: Thoughts on the Future Life*, contributions by W. D. Howells and others. New York, 1910.

——. *The Letters of Henry James*, selected and ed. Percy Lubbock. 2 vols. New York, 1920.

——. *Letters to A. C. Benson and Auguste Monod*, ed. E. F. Benson. London, 1930.

——. *Master Eustace*, short story collection ed. Albert Mordell. New York, 1920.

——. *The Notebooks of Henry James*, ed. F. O. Matthiessen and Kenneth Murdock. New York, 1947.

——. *Notes and Reviews*, ed. Pierre de Chaignon la Rose. Cambridge, Mass., 1921.

——. *Notes of a Son and Brother*. New York, 1914.

——. *Notes on Novelists, with Some Other Notes*. New York, 1914.

——. *The Portrait of a Lady*. 2 vols. in one. New York: Modern Library [1936].

——. *Portraits of Places*. New York, 1948.

——. *The Princess Casamassima*, introduction by Lionel Trilling. New York, 1948.

——. *The Question of Our Speech; The Lesson of Balzac*. Boston, 1905.

——. *Roderick Hudson*. Vol. I of *The Novels and Tales of Henry James*. 26 vols. New York, 1907-1917.

James, Henry. *The Sacred Fount*. New York, 1901.

———. *The Sense of the Past*. Vol. XXVI of *The Novels and Tales of Henry James*. 26 vols. New York, 1907-1917.

———. *A Small Boy and Others*. New York, 1913.

———. *The Spoils of Poynton*. Norfolk, Conn., 1943.

———. *Stories of Writers and Artists*, ed. F. O. Matthiessen. New York, 1944.

———. *The Tragic Muse*. London, 1948.

———. *What Maisie Knew*. Vol. XI of *The Novels and Tales of Henry James*. 26 vols. New York, 1907-1917.

———. *The Wings of the Dove*. New York, 1902.

Jeffares, A. Norman. "The Byzantine Poems of W. B. Yeats," *The Review of English Studies*, XXII (January, 1946), 44-52.

———. " 'Gyres' in the Poetry of W. B. Yeats," *English Studies*, XXVII (June, 1946), 65-74.

———. *W. B. Yeats, Man and Poet*. New Haven, 1949.

Kenmare, Dallas. *Fire-Bird: A Study of D. H. Lawrence*. New York, 1952.

Kennedy, V. W., and Barton, M. N. *Samuel Taylor Coleridge: A Selected Bibliography*. . . . Baltimore, 1935.

Kenner, Hugh. *The Invisible Poet: T. S. Eliot*. New York, 1959.

Kermode, Frank. *Romantic Image*. New York, 1957.

Kirkpatrick, B. J. *A Bibliography of Virginia Woolf*. London, 1957.

Krutch, Joseph Wood. *The Modern Temper: A Study and a Confession*. New York, 1933.

Lawrence, D. H. *Aaron's Rod*. New York, 1922.

———. *Apocalypse*, introduction by Richard Aldington. New York, 1932.

———. *Assorted Articles*. New York, 1930. Reprinted in *The Later D. H. Lawrence*, ed. William York Tindall. Copyright, 1952, by Alfred A. Knopf, Inc.

———. *The Captain's Doll*. New York, 1930.

———. *The Collected Letters of D. H. Lawrence*, ed. Harry T. Moore. New York, 1962.

———. *David: A Play*. New York, 1926.

Lawrence, D. H. *The Collected Poems of D. H. Lawrence.* 2 vols. New York, 1929.

———. *D. H. Lawrence's Letters to Bertrand Russell*, ed. Harry T. Moore. New York, 1948.

———. *D. H. Lawrence: Selected Poems*, introduction by Kenneth Rexroth. New York, 1947.

———. *England, My England, and Other Stories.* New York, 1922.

———. *Etruscan Places.* New York, 1933.

———. *Fantasia of the Unconscious.* New York, 1930.

———. *The First Lady Chatterley.* New York, 1944.

———. *Kangaroo.* New York, 1923.

———. *Lady Chatterley's Lover*, introduction by Mark Schorer, letter from Archibald MacLeish. New York, 1959.

———. *The Later D. H. Lawrence: The Best Novels, Stories, Essays, 1925-1930*, ed. William York Tindall. New York, 1952.

———. *The Letters of D. H. Lawrence*, ed. Aldous Huxley. New York, 1932.

———. *The Lost Girl.* New York, 1921.

———. *The Man Who Died.* New York, 1931.

———. *Mornings in Mexico.* New York, 1927.

———. *Movements in European History.* London, 1925.

———. *Phoenix: The Posthumous Papers of D. H. Lawrence*, ed. Edward McDonald. New York, 1936.

———. *The Plumed Serpent (Quetzalcoatl)*, introduction by William York Tindall. New York, 1951.

———. *Psychoanalysis and the Unconscious.* London, William Heinemann, Ltd., acknowledgments to Lawrence Pollinger, Ltd., and the estate of the late Mrs. Frieda Lawrence. Copyright 1921 by Thomas Seltzer, Inc., 1949 by Frieda Lawrence; reprinted by permission of The Viking Press, Inc. Martin Secker and Warburg, Ltd., edition (New Adelphi Library), 1931, cited in text.

———. *The Rainbow.* New York: Modern Library [1927]. Copyright 1915 by D. H. Lawrence, 1943 by Frieda Lawrence. Reprinted by permission of The Viking Press, Inc.

Lawrence D. H. *Reflections on the Death of a Porcupine and Other Essays*. Philadelphia, 1925.

———. *Sex, Literature, and Censorship: Essays*, ed. Harry T. Moore. New York, 1953.

———. *Sons and Lovers*, introduction by John Macy. New York: Modern Library [1922]. Reprinted by permission of The Viking Press, Inc. All rights reserved.

———. *Studies in Classic American Literature*. New York, 1923.

———. *The Trespasser*, introduction by Richard Aldington. London, 1950.

———. *Twilight in Italy*, introduction by Richard Aldington. London, 1954.

———. *The Virgin and the Gipsy*. New York, 1930.

———. *The White Peacock*, introduction by Richard Aldington. London, 1950.

———. *The Widowing of Mrs. Holroyd: A Drama in Three Acts*. New York, 1914.

———. *Women in Love*. New York, Modern Library, [1950]. Copyright 1920, 1922 by D. H. Lawrence, 1948, 1950 by Frieda Lawrence. Reprinted by permission of The Viking Press, Inc.

Leavis, F. R. *D. H. Lawrence: Novelist*. New York, 1956.

———. *New Bearings in English Poetry*. New ed. New York, 1950.

Lubbock, Percy. *The Craft of Fiction*. New York, 1929.

Lucy, Seán. *T. S. Eliot and the Idea of Tradition*. New York, 1961.

McCarthy, Harold T. *Henry James: The Creative Process*. New York, 1958.

McDonald, Edward D. *A Bibliography of the Writings of D. H. Lawrence*, foreword by D. H. Lawrence. Philadelphia, 1925.

———. *The Writings of D. H. Lawrence, 1925-1930: A Bibliographical Supplement*. Philadelphia, 1931.

McKenzie, Gordon. *Organic Unity in Coleridge*. Berkeley, 1939.

Marks, Robert. *James's Later Novels, an Interpretation*. New York, 1960.

Martz, Louis L. "The Wheel and the Point: Aspects of Imagery and Theme, in Eliot's Later Poetry," *The Sewanee Review*, LV (Winter, 1947), 126-147.

Matthiessen, F. O. *The Achievement of T. S. Eliot.* 2d ed. revised. London, 1947.

———. *Henry James: The Major Phase.* New York, 1944.

Menon, V. K. N. *The Development of William Butler Yeats.* Chester Springs, 1961.

Moore, Harry T., and Hoffman, Frederick J., eds. *The Achievement of D. H. Lawrence,* collected criticisms. Norman, 1953.

Moore, Harry T., ed. *A D. H. Lawrence Miscellany.* Carbondale, 1959.

———. *The Intelligent Heart: The Story of D. H. Lawrence.* New York, 1954.

———. *The Life and Works of D. H. Lawrence.* New York, 1951.

Moore, Virginia. *The Unicorn: William Butler Yeats' Search for Reality.* New York, 1954.

Muirhead, John H. *Coleridge as Philosopher.* London, 1930.

Nehls, Edward, ed. *D. H. Lawrence: A Composite Biography.* 3 vols. Madison, 1957-1959.

Panicker, G. T. *The Whole of Feeling: A Study of the Place of Emotion and Feeling in the Poetic Theory of T. S. Eliot.* Washington, D.C., 1959.

Peckham, Morse. "Toward a Theory of Romanticism," *PMLA*, Vol. LXVI (March, 1951), 5-23.

Phillips, Le Roy. *A Bibliography of the Writings of Henry James,* 2d ed. revised. New York, 1930.

Pippet, Aileen. *The Moth and the Star: A Biography of Virginia Woolf.* Boston, 1955.

Richards, I. A. *Coleridge on Imagination.* New York, 1950.

Roberts, Morris. *Henry James's Criticism.* Cambridge, Mass., 1929.

Rudd, Margaret. *Divided Image: A Study of William Blake and W. B. Yeats.* London, 1953.

Sherman, Stuart P. "The Aesthetic Idealism of Henry James," *On Contemporary Literature*. New York, 1917.

Smith, Grover, Jr. *T. S. Eliot's Poetry and Plays: A Study in Sources and Meaning*. Chicago, 1956.

Snyder, Alice D. *The Critical Principle of the Reconciliation of Opposites as Employed by Coleridge*. Ann Arbor, 1918.

———. "A Note on Coleridge's Shakespeare Criticism," *MLN*, XXXVIII (January, 1923), 23-31.

Spender, Stephen. *The Creative Element: A Study of Vision, Despair and Orthodoxy Among Some Modern Writers*. New York, 1954.

———. *The Destructive Element*. London, 1938.

Spilka, Mark. *The Love Ethic of D. H. Lawrence*. Bloomington, 1957.

Stallman, R. W., ed. *Critiques and Essays in Criticism, 1920-1948*. New York, 1949.

Stevenson, Elizabeth. *The Crooked Corridor: A Study of Henry James*. New York, 1949.

Stock, A. G. *W. B. Yeats: His Poetry and Thought*. Cambridge (England), 1961.

Suther, Marshall E. *The Dark Night of Samuel Taylor Coleridge*. New York, 1960.

Symons, A. J. A. *A Bibliography of the First Editions of Books by William Butler Yeats*. London, 1924.

Tindall, William York. *D. H. Lawrence and Susan His Cow*. New York, 1939.

Tiverton, Father William. *D. H. Lawrence and Human Existence*, foreword by T. S. Eliot. New York, 1951.

Unger, Leonard. "T. S. Eliot's Rose Garden: A Persistent Theme," *The Southern Review*, VII (Spring, 1942), 667-689.

———, ed. *T. S. Eliot: A Selected Critique*. New York, 1948.

Vivas, Eliseo. *D. H. Lawrence: The Failure and the Triumph of Art*. Evanston, 1960.

Wade, Allan. *A Bibliography of the Writings of W. B. Yeats*, 2d ed. rev. London, 1958.

Waggoner, Hyatt, H. *The Heel of Elohim: Science and Values in Modern American Poetry.* Norman, 1950.

Wegelin, Christof. *The Image of Europe in Henry James.* Dallas, 1958.

White, W. D. *D. H. Lawrence: A Checklist, 1931-1950.* Detroit, 1950.

Wilson, Edmund. *Axel's Castle: A Study in the Imaginative Literature of 1870-1930.* New York, 1931.

Wilson, F. A. C. *C. W. B. Yeats and Tradition.* New York, 1959.

————. *Yeats's Iconography.* New York, 1960.

Winters, Yvor. *The Poetry of W. B. Yeats.* Denver, 1960.

Wise, Thomas J. *A Bibliography of the Writings in Prose and Verse of Samuel Taylor Coleridge.* London, 1913.

Woolf, Virginia. *Between the Acts.* New York, 1941.

————. *The Captain's Death Bed and Other Essays,* ed. Leonard Woolf. New York, 1950.

————. *The Common Reader.* New York, 1925.

————. *The Common Reader, First and Second Series.* 2 vols. in one. New York, 1948.

————. *The Death of the Moth and Other Essays,* ed. Leonard Woolf. New York, 1942.

————. *Flush: A Biography.* New York, 1933.

————. *Granite and Rainbow,* ed. Leonard Woolf. New York, 1958.

————. *A Haunted House and Other Short Stories,* ed. Leonard Woolf. New York, 1944.

————. Introductory letter to *Life as We Have Known It,* ed. M. L. Davies. London, 1931.

————. *Jacob's Room.* New York, 1923.

————, and Strachey, Lytton. *Letters,* ed. Leonard Woolf and James Strachey. New York, 1956.

————. *Mrs. Dalloway.* New York, 1925.

————. *The Moment and Other Essays,* ed. Leonard Woolf. New York, 1948.

Woolf, Virginia. *Monday or Tuesday*. London, 1921.

———. *Night and Day*. London, 1919.

———. *Orlando: A Biography*. New York, 1928.

———. *Roger Fry: A Biography*. New York, 1940.

———. *A Room of One's Own*. New York, 1929.

———. *Three Guineas*. New York, 1938.

———. *To the Lighthouse*, introduction by Terence Holliday. New York: Modern Library [1937]. Copyright, 1927, by Harcourt, Brace and World, Inc.; renewed, 1955, by Leonard Woolf.

———. *The Voyage Out*. New York, 1920.

———. *The Waves*. New York, 1931.

———. *A Writer's Diary, Being Extracts from the Diary of Virginia Woolf*, ed. Leonard Woolf. New York, 1954.

———. *The Years*. New York, 1937.

Wright, George T. *The Poet in the Poem: The Personae of Eliot, Yeats, and Pound*. Berkeley, 1960.

Yeats, William Butler. *Autobiographies: Reveries over Childhood and Youth, and The Trembling of the Veil*. New York, 1927.

———. *The Autobiography of William Butler Yeats, Consisting of Reveries over Childhood and Youth, The Trembling of the Veil, and Dramatis Personae*. New York, 1938.

———. *Collected Plays*. London, 1934.

———. *The Collected Poems of W. B. Yeats*, definitive ed. with author's final revisions. New York, 1957.

———. *The Cutting of an Agate*. New York, 1912.

———. *Early Poems and Stories*. London, 1925.

———. *Essays, 1931-1936*. [Dublin]: Cuala Press, 1937.

———. *The Herne's Egg and Other Plays*. New York, 1938.

———. *Ideas of Good and Evil*. New York, 1903.

———. *Last Poems and Plays*. London, 1940.

———. *The Letters of W. B. Yeats*, ed. Allan Wade. London, 1954.

———. *Letters on Poetry from W. B. Yeats to Dorothy Wellesley*, ed. Dorothy Wellesley. London, 1940.

Yeats, William Butler. *Letters to the New Island,* ed. Horace Reynolds. Cambridge, Mass., 1934.

————, ed. *The Oxford Book of Modern Verse, 1892-1935.* New York, 1936.

————. *Per Amica Silentia Lunae.* London, 1918.

————. *Plays and Controversies.* London, 1923.

————. *Responsibilities and Other Poems.* New York, 1916.

————, and Swami, Shree Purohit, trans. *The Ten Principal Upanishads.* New York, 1937.

————. *A Vision.* London, 1925.

————. *A Vision,* 2d ed. revised. London, 1937.

————. *Wheels and Butterflies.* New York, 1935.

————, and Ellis, E. J., eds. *The Works of William Blake, Poetic, Symbolic, and Critical.* 3 vols. London, 1893.

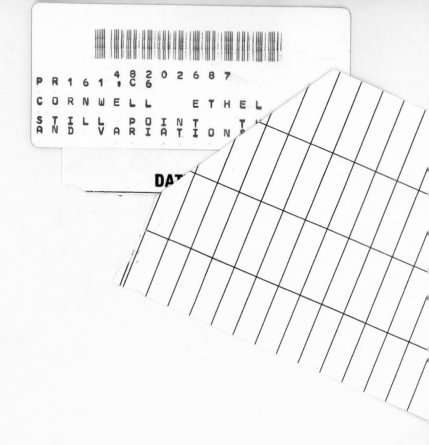